Paul Ricoeur's Hermeneutics and the Discourse of Mark 13

Studies in the Thought of Paul Ricoeur

Series Editors
Greg S. Johnson, Pacific Lutheran University/Oxford University (ELAC), and Dan R. Stiver, Hardin-Simmons University

Studies in the Thought of Paul Ricoeur, a series in conjunction with the Society for Ricoeur Studies, aims to generate research on Ricoeur, about whom interest is rapidly growing both nationally (United States and Canada) and internationally. Broadly construed, the series has three interrelated themes. First, we develop the historical connections to and in Ricoeur's thought. Second, we extend Ricoeur's dialogue with contemporary thinkers representing a variety of disciplines. Third, we utilize Ricoeur to address future prospects in philosophy and other fields that respond to emerging issues of importance. The series approaches these themes from the belief that Ricoeur's thought is not just suited to theoretical exchanges, but can and does matter for how we actually engage in the many dimensions that constitute lived existence.

Titles in the Series

Paul Ricoeur's Hermeneutics and the Discourse of Mark 13

Appropriating the Apocalyptic

Peter C. de Vries

LEXINGTON BOOKS
Lanham • Boulder • New York • London

Published by Lexington Books
An imprint of The Rowman & Littlefield Publishing Group, Inc.
4501 Forbes Boulevard, Suite 200, Lanham, Maryland 20706
www.rowman.com

Unit A, Whitacre Mews, 26-34 Stannary Street, London SE11 4AB

British Library Cataloguing in Publication Information Available

Library of Congress Cataloging-in-Publication Data
Name: Vries, P. de, 1956- author.
Title: Paul Ricoeur's hermeneutics and the discourse of Mark 13 : appropriating the
    apocalyptic / Peter C. de Vries.
Description: Lanham : Lexington Books, 2016. | Series: Studies in the thought of
    Paul Ricoeur | Includes bibliographical references and index.
Identifiers: LCCN 2016043866 (print) | LCCN 2016045067 (ebook) |
    ISBN 9781498512282 (cloth : alk. paper) | ISBN 9781498512299 (Electronic)
Subjects: LCSH: Bible. Mark, XIII—Criticism, interpretation, etc. |
    Eschatology—Biblical teaching. | Apocalyptic literature—History and criticism. |
    Ricoeur, Paul. | Hermeneutics.
Classification: LCC BS2585.52 .V75 2016 (print) | LCC BS2585.52 (ebook) |
    DDC 226.3/06—dc23
LC record available at https://lccn.loc.gov/2016043866

∞ ™ The paper used in this publication meets the minimum requirements of American
National Standard for Information Sciences—Permanence of Paper for Printed Library
Materials, ANSI/NISO Z39.48-1992.

Printed in the United States of America

Contents

Preface

The English language suffers from the lack of a third person personal pronoun that is gender neutral. The "he/she" construct is stylistically awkward, as are attempts to avoid the use of pronouns altogether. In this project, therefore, I refer to generic authors with male pronouns and to generic readers with female pronouns. I do so not to imply that only men write texts and that only women read them, but to provide a balance in gender reference. This strategy also cues the reader about the one to whom I refer if it may otherwise be confusing. This deficiency of English also affects references to God. Christianity does not typically consider God to be male ("he"), female ("she"), or impersonal ("it"). Again, I find it stylistically awkward to disavow the use of any pronoun to refer to God. While I limit its use as much as possible, I use the male pronoun traditionally associated with God. I note the inadequacy of this practice, however, and consider it to be the least objectionable of the options available to me.

I am grateful to a number of people who have made this project possible. I appreciate the expertise in Biblical apocalyptic literature that Dale Allison provided, the guidance in Ricoeur studies that George Taylor offered, and the high standard for philosophical argumentation that Tony Edwards contributed. I am also grateful for the prayerful support and encouragement I received from Old Union Presbyterian Church of Mars, Pennsylvania as their pastor undertook this project. David Huegal and Allan Reed persistently prayed for guidance and strength during the writing process, and I appreciate their regular inquiries into my progress. I have been inspired by the prestigious academic career of my grandfather, Egbert de Vries, and by the faith and courage of my nephew Alec Hillegass during his battle with osteosarcoma. I trust that they are both included in the elect who have been gathered from the ends of the earth (Mark 13:27).

Finally, and most importantly of all, I want to express my gratitude and devotion to my wife and best friend, Rebecca. She encouraged me when I was discouraged, she probed me when I was confused, and she believed in me when I did not. She is the greatest blessing that God has brought into my life, and I dedicate this project to the love we share.

Chapter 1

The Resolution of a Hermeneutical Problem

This project shows how Paul Ricoeur's hermeneutics enables appropriation of Mark 13 in a new way. The meaning of the text that was apparent when it was written is appropriated by today's reader only as a false description of the world, because it predicts that certain events will happen in the near future which did not. I use Ricoeur's hermeneutics to argue that Mark 13 is able to present meaning that was latent when it was written but that is now apparent, and this meaning allows this reader to appropriate the text in a new way that is not false. To do so, I define appropriation and demonstrate how Ricoeur's hermeneutics makes appropriation of this text possible in a different way. To my knowledge, this is the first extended study of apocalyptic literature informed by Ricoeur's hermeneutic approach.

Both Biblical scholars and Ricoeur researchers will benefit from bringing together this methodology and this field of inquiry. First, Biblical scholars will find an approach other than the traditional historical-critical method that provides rigorous analysis of the text. Ricoeur offers insight for the study of non-literal or figurative texts, of which apocalyptic is certainly a type, with a clear definition of metaphor that is frequently lacking in such studies. This insight makes it possible to discern meanings inherent to these texts that provide recognition of truth. His description of limit experience, a textual referent at the boundaries of human world-conception, is particularly apt for a genre that deals primarily with the description of the in-breaking and influence of spiritual forces upon human existence. Second, Ricoeur scholars will appreciate the application of his thought to a Biblical genre particularly suited to his consideration of metaphorical meaning and truth, as the literal or conventional meaning appears to be absurd or false. Apocalyptic texts' portrayal of future events in a manner similar to historical narrative offers evocative avenues of exploring Ricoeur's narrative analysis. By presenting

1

the reader with a world at limits, and beyond, of human experience, apocalyptic provides the reader with a novel partner for the work of self-recognition.

Hermeneutics, as Ricoeur describes it, is the process by which a reader
reaches the goal of appropriation, or critical understanding.[1] It is necessary
when the text's description of the world is different from that of the reader,
even if the reader and text come from the same cultural and linguistic milieu.
The greater the difference between the conceptual frameworks within which
the text and the reader operate, the more difficult the hermeneutical task
becomes. As a heuristic, we may refer to this difference between text and
reader as a "gap" or "distance" between the two. Understanding cannot occur
until this gap is narrowed sufficiently for the text to become comprehensible.
The text's presentation of the world and its milieu does not become identical
with those of the reader, but there are sufficient commonalities between the
two for the reader to interact with the text.[2]

Appropriation occurs when the text's configuration of the world changes
the reader by confirming, clarifying, challenging, or reorienting at least some
of her conceptions of the world. If the reader is open to the message of the
text, her reading of it enhances her understanding of the world, even if she
ultimately rejects the world-description of the text.[3] As described by Ricoeur,
a reader's appropriation of a text involves two issues. First, the reader does
not require the text to conform to her world-understanding in order to consider the appeal of its description. The text creates a new conceptualization
of the world with which the reader engages. The reader does not place herself
in the role of adjudicator of the text, but recognizes the possibility that the
text has the potential to challenge and change her prior concepts.[4] Second, the
reader moves from an initial naïve first understanding of the text by engaging
in critical analysis to correct or change the reader's initial understanding of
it (what Ricoeur calls "explanation"), in order to reach an informed understanding of the text, which Ricoeur calls appropriation or a "second naiveté."
Through explanation, the reader comprehends more fully what the text presents through linguistic and historical inquiry.[5] Stiver explains that the reader's
movement to this "post-critical" understanding of the text is the definitive
step by which she appropriates it as an element of her world-understanding.
But it is only possible after the critical, or explanatory, move.[6]

The text's description of the world may take two forms. First, a text may
describe the world as it is. Ricoeur identifies this sort of description as
adequation, or a configuration of the world that conforms to historical conditions or prevalent conceptual norms. Second, a text may describe the world
as it may be or as it could be. This sort of description is manifestation: the
disclosure of ways to understand the world that were not previously available
either because they are new or because previous conceptual frameworks did

not make these understandings available. As manifestation, a text changes the world by configuring it in a new way or by creating a new reality, even if the completion of that new configuration or reality lies in the future.[7] Mark 13 is a hybrid of adequation and manifestation because it claims to predict future events. As adequation, the text is open for verification or refutation depending upon the occurrence of the predicted events. As manifestation, Mark 13 does not describe past or present historical events, but offers a promise of events that will occur in the future. The promise of these future historical events creates a new understanding of the present, and the text invites the reader to participate in the fulfillment of that promise. Analysis of this text must therefore incorporate consideration of both forms of world-description.

The meaning of Mark 13 which was apparent when it was written was that certain events would happen in the near future. The hermeneutic problem for today's reader is that she knows these events did not occur. If this is the only meaning available for the reader, she is only able to appropriate Mark 13 as a false prediction of imminent historical events. Based on Ricoeur's work, I argue that Mark 13 presents other meanings in addition to the world referent that was apparent when it was written, and that these other meanings provide an additional way for today's reader to appropriate this text. Mark 13 offers meaning which was originally concealed but is apparent in today's circumstances. Ricoeur demonstrates that the meaning of the text is not limited to its original meaning, and so this now-apparent meaning is a meaning of the text itself.[8] Although the text was originally understood only literally, it is able today to present metaphoric meaning as well. The reader who appropriates this text does not need to agree with this meaning, but she changes through her encounter with it. In presenting this argument, I identify the premises which must be supported for the argument to succeed. Chapters 2 through 6 present and evaluate elements of Ricoeur's work that provide this support. The concluding chapter describes how a reader today is able to appropriate this text.

THE HERMENEUTICAL PROBLEM OF MARK 13

Mark 13 offers particular hermeneutic challenges. It begins with an account of Jesus' prediction of the temple's destruction, which prompts inquiry by four of his disciples. Jesus' answer to this inquiry is termed the Olivet Discourse because of its setting on the Mount of Olives. This apocalyptic speech[9] describes catastrophic and fantastic events in the future. Some of Jesus' predictions that Mark reports were fulfilled, and others were not. Specifically, Mark 13 predicts a cosmic upheaval (vv. 24–25), the appearance of a spiritual being named the Son of Man (v. 26), and the ingathering of "the elect," or God's chosen people from the far corners of the world (v. 27). Mark asserts that all of these events, together with others (described in vv. 5–23), will take place before the passing of Jesus' generation, or within a few decades at most. The primary hermeneutic problem for today's reader, who is removed by two millennia from the context of the text's production, is the fact that these events did not take place when predicted.[10] Commentators such as Russell suggest that in Mark's account of Jesus' response to the disciples' question about the destruction of the temple, the document does not provide any indication that Jesus moves from one topic (the temple's doom) to another (the world's end). Russell argues instead that the discourse provides a unified and continuous prediction: judgment of the present evil generation will consist of the destruction of the temple and its attendant tribulations at the hands of the Son of Man, who will vindicate the faithful. Russell notes the disparity of apocalyptic expectation between first century Christians (the original readers of the text) and readers today. The pervasive presence of parousia predictions in other texts at the time of Mark's writing is evidence that the original readers expected the parousia to take place in the near future, but Russell claims that modern readers do not share this conviction.[11]

This project challenges the second premise of the following logical argument that describes the hermeneutical problem of Mark 13:

1. A reader is able to appropriate Mark 13 as a true text. (Thesis to prove)
2. Mark 13 predicts a cosmic upheaval, the universal perception of the Son of Man, and the ingathering of the elect before the end of the first century. (Premise to support)
3. If such an upheaval and perception had occurred, evidence of it would be available. (Presumed)
4. No evidence of this upheaval and perception exists. (Presumed)
5. Therefore the upheaval and perception did not occur. (From 3 and 4)
6. Mark 13 predicts events which did not happen as predicted in the text. (From 2 and 5)
7. A text which predicts events which did not happen as predicted is not true. (Presumed)
8. Mark 13 is not true. (From 6 and 7)
9. A reader is not able to appropriate Mark 13 as a true text. (From 7 and 8).
10. A reader is able to appropriate Mark 13 as a true text. (Premise contradicted by 9)

Based on this logical argument, the text's inaccurate prediction of future events renders it false. The original readers were not able to recognize that the text is false, but today's reader can.

PREVIOUS ATTEMPTS TO RESOLVE THE PROBLEM

This project focuses on the text of Mark 13 as the modern reader encounters it, not with whatever Jesus may or may not have said or intended, nor with how early Christians understood or altered whatever Jesus may have said. As Ricoeur points out, the purpose for critical analysis is not simply to ascertain the circumstances of a text's production, but to encounter the world that it presents. Scholarly investigation of the authenticity of Mark 13 as a genuine Jesus saying appears to come from two motivations. First, one may assume that if the Olivet discourse configures a speech that Jesus actually gave, its claim upon the reader is more compelling. If so, the text itself can no longer speak to us because its voice has been silenced by the idol of authenticity. A significant element of the explanatory aspect of Ricoeur's hermeneutics is suspicion: to shatter idols so that the symbols themselves can speak. Second, these investigations may arise from a desire to identify the historical Jesus. While this may be a laudable endeavor, the purpose for this project is not to understand Jesus, or how the early church may have amended or invented sayings. It is to understand the text that we have.

Commentators have recognized and sought to address Mark 13's failed prediction that the parousia would occur within a generation. I classify these efforts into two categories: those who argue that the Olivet discourse is to be taken literally, and those who argue that it is figurative. This section briefly surveys the two categories of interpretive approaches commonly used for Mark 13 and explains how each fails to describe how today's reader is able to appropriate it as a true text.

Theories for Literal Meaning of Mark 13

Russell, who takes a literal approach to the text, rejects interpretive strategies which are based on the assumption that the text is to be approached as an ambiguous and mysterious oracle, like those provided in Delphi. Instead, he argues that Jesus wanted his disciples to understand what he said, and that they would not recognize his answer to their question as a mixture of prophecies. Relying on Matthew's version of the discourse (24:3ff), Russell explains that the disciples' question about the συντελείας τοῦ αἰῶνος was about the end of the age of Jewish "dispensation," and not about the collapse of the physical world.[12] However, Russell contradicts his own straightforward approach by treating the text in the same mysterious oracular manner that he rejects; he argues that the text deals with "dispensation" rather than what it appears to address: the end of the world.

Alternately, Bolt argues that the predictions of Mark 13 were fulfilled literally in the passion and resurrection of Jesus. Bolt asserts that the four time references of v. 35 find fulfillment in the passion narrative: the last supper occurred in the evening (14:17), Jesus was arrested in the middle of the night, Peter denied him at the cockcrow (14:72), and the empty tomb was discovered at dawn (16:2). He argues that the events surrounding Jesus' arrest and trial fulfilled the prediction of distress, and that the rejection and abuse of the Messiah by Israel's leaders in the city of Jerusalem is the abomination. The young man at the empty tomb fulfilled the prediction that the Son of Man appeared as the resurrected Christ. That is, the resurrection is the "coming" of the Son of Man, who has received authority from heaven. Jesus' command to go to Galilee demonstrates the beginning of God's chosen people gathering together. In this way, according to Bolt, each of the predictions of the Olivet discourse were fulfilled literally very soon after they were made.[13]

Augmenting Bolt's argument with contributions from scholars such as Robinson,[14] one may present a literal interpretation of Mark 13 by which "all these things" took place in Jesus' crucifixion and resurrection and in the experiences of early Christians immediately following those events. As Chapter 3 indicates, the events of vv. 5–23 are relatively easy to reconcile with events that the early Christians faced: deceptive teachers, warfare, earthquakes and famine, and persecution as an opportunity for testimony to faith. As pp. 71–74 demonstrates, the abomination of desolation described in v. 14 refers to the contemptible temple leaders whom Jesus had criticized. The fulfillment of vv. 24–27's predictions of celestial chaos, the coming of the Son of Man, and the ingathering of the elect can be found or inferred in Mark's description of Jesus' crucifixion and resurrection.[15]

The explanation that the predictions were fulfilled through Jesus' crucifixion and resurrection can be considered at best to be a provisional fulfillment of the predictions, or a hint of what the actual fulfillment will be. Even if we assume that the events which Mark reports to have surrounded Jesus' death and resurrection are historical, they do not rise to the level of a full and literal completion of the discourse's predictions. For example, a temporary episode of darkness does not fulfill vv. 24–25's description of the collapse of the stars and the darkening of the sun and moon.

Theories for Figurative Meaning of Mark 13

Commentators on the Olivet discourse, particularly those of the modern critical era, offer a wide variety of approaches for the figurative fulfillment of Mark 13's predictions, which includes all non-literal understandings of Mark 13's predictions. The primary focus for these explanations is vv. 24–27. I address the large number of these theories in three broad categories, even though there is considerable variation within each. First, some interpreters understand the discourse to refer to the destruction of old world patterns and the emergence of something new. The second broad category of interpreters claim that the predictions have been fulfilled provisionally, with complete fulfillment to come in the future. A third set of interpreters argue that the discourse describes an individual transformation which relates to spiritual or existential experience rather than historical events.[16] However, none of these explanations take into account the documented evidence that early Christians continued to expect their fulfillment.[17]

A New World Pattern

Robinson and Wright offer two influential theories that the Olivet discourse's predictions were fulfilled figuratively through the creation of a new world pattern; the kingdom of God has arrived. Robinson asserts that no future parousia is necessary to fulfill eschatological expectation because it was fulfilled by Jesus' entrance into Jerusalem and his condemnation of the temple practices.[18] His argument states that Jesus' resurrection from the dead and ascension into heaven are a single event that demonstrates Jesus' vindication and glorification, fulfilling predictions of the inauguration of his rule within the generational period that Mark 13 describes.[19] Therefore, no future parousia is necessary. Robinson claims that the promised kingdom of God is a present reality; "that beyond which nothing can happen has already happened."[20] He also advocates for an "inaugurated eschatology," claiming that Christ's vindication and rule have already begun as the final defining event of history which continues to develop and unfold.[21]

Robinson considers New Testament texts such as Mark 13 to be mythological or poetic descriptions of spiritual situations using historical terms.[22] He argues that these texts ought therefore not to be interpreted as a comprehensive time-line of future events, but as convictions about the nature of God expressed in mythological terms.[23] Robinson's interpretation fails to capture the force of the text's prediction of the parousia. He argues that early Christians replaced the original figurative meaning of the text with hope for future fantastic events.[24] But as I demonstrate in Chapter 3, only a literal meaning of the text was accepted at the time it was written, because that was the approach used for reading such texts at the time.

Wright's seminal explanation for a figurative meaning of the Olivet discourse claims that the early Christians had no concept of a cosmic upheaval or of the descent of a heavenly being to the earth, since these were not features of Second Temple Jewish thought. Therefore, he asserts that Mark 13 deals solely with the physical destruction of the temple, the attendant socio-political upheaval, and the theological implications of this event.[25] To further his argument for a figurative meaning of the text, Wright discounts understandings of vv. 24–27 as a description of a spiritual being descending upon the earth while the heavenly lights fail as "crass literalism, in view of the many prophetic passages in which this language denotes socio-political and military catastrophe. . . . This is simply the way regular Jewish imagery is able to refer to major socio-political events and bring out their full significance."[26]

Wright's thesis rests upon the premise that socio-historical forces, spiritual beings, and celestial bodies are distinct from each other. However, this premise is false because Second Temple Judaism saw an integral connection among these entities, which I explain on p. 74. Therefore, Wright's understanding of the collapse of the celestial bodies as mere "imagery" is erroneous. It does not take into account the fact that for that culture, the collapse of the celestial bodies must be a literal event in order for God's enemies to be defeated.

Because Wright is a prominent representative of scholars who argue for a figurative interpretation of Mark 13, it is helpful to note additional flaws in his presentation that other scholars have identified. First, as Eddy explains, Wright improperly characterizes Jesus' apocalyptic statements as metaphor. Even if one concedes Wright's contention that no first-century Jews expected the physical world to be obliterated, that does not prohibit a literal reading of other elements of Jesus' predictions in the text; Eddy cites the parousia as a salient example of this. You can believe in the literal return of Jesus even if you do not believe that the world will come to an end. Eddy further challenges Wright's assertion that our only two interpretive choices for the Olivet discourse are the destruction of the world or dramatic historical events. He asks, "Why not a 'non-natural' in-breaking of God, a divine intervention of such *cosmic* qualities and proportions that—although the cosmos itself would remain—to call it purely 'historical' in Wright's sense would be woefully inadequate?"[27]

Second, despite Wright's claim that his thesis "possesses the strengths required for any scientific hypothesis," such as inclusion of data, simplicity, and explanation of previously unexplainable data,[28] it is not falsifiable. In response to Wright's assertion that Mark 13:24–27 is to be read metaphorically, Allison asks how the passage would be different if it was meant literally.[29] Overlooking numerous flaws in Wright's attempt to be scientific, what is most notable is that he does not provide a scientific hypothesis stated such that it can be proven false. Furthermore, under scientific examination just one exception proves a hypothesis false. In this case, Wright's hypothesis is false because Second Temple Jews believed descriptions of cosmic collapse to be predictions of literal events, as Allison demonstrates.[30]

Third, Allison points out a logical inconsistency in Wright's argumentation. On the one hand, Wright asserts (and Allison agrees) that Second Temple Jewish discussions of the temple and of the land of Israel were intended literally. On the other hand, Wright considers descriptions of the coming of the Son of Man in Mark 13 to be figurative expressions of God's redemptive work. As Allison asserts, the close association of these themes demands that they be considered in similar fashion. If predictions about the temple and land in Mark are literal, then the prediction is for a literal return from exile, a physically rebuilt temple, and a visible descent of the Son of Man from the sky. Because these events did not take place, Wright is unable to claim that they were fulfilled literally. Noting this, Allison suggests that Wright offers his figurative interpretation as an apologetic for Jesus' prediction which failed on a literal level.[31]

Partial Fulfillment

A second set of commentators explains that the Olivet discourse can be understood figuratively as a prediction which has been partially fulfilled, and whose complete fulfillment is pending. Cranfield, for example, claims that the predictions of the Olivet discourse were fulfilled by the events of the Jewish War, "but it was not a fulfillment without remainder." They are merely the first instance of events that will continue to occur until the "the last supreme concentration of the rebelliousness of the devil before the End." In this sense, the predictions of the discourse relate to the "past, present, and future."[32] Cranfield's thesis rests upon the ambiguous use of the term "fulfill." One cannot speak of the fulfillment of predictions in the past and claim that they have not been fully fulfilled, and will be fulfilled in the future. Cranfield speaks of contingent temporal fulfillment in the past as though it is the same as the absolute fulfillment of the Olivet discourse's predictions.

Caird also purports that Mark 13's predictions have been partially fulfilled. Through his figurative approach, he asserts that the discourse operates similarly to Old Testament prophecy which viewed the future "with bifocal vision"; near-future historical events are described in terms of the end-of-world Day of the Lord.[33] Reading the discourse from the perspective of inaugurated eschatology, Caird proposes that when Mark 13 predicts the destruction of Jerusalem, it instructs believers to "see in it the coming of the Son of Man." He seeks to resolve the apparent contradiction of vv. 30 and 32 by proposing that Jesus speaks of two different events. Caird claims that the text states that the kingdom will begin within a generation, but only the Father knows when "its full, final, literal reality" will come.[34] However, his claim that end-of-world language can only be used to guide readers to understand historical events in a particular way makes it impossible to speak of an actual eschaton. There can be no "full, final, literal reality" for only the Father to know.

Adams, Theophilos, Beasley-Murray, and Dunn each claim that the discourse brings together related predictions, but that the author did not expect all of them to take place before the passing of the generation. As Adams

put it, the predicted events of the discourse are related conceptually but
not temporally. Mark combines a number of prophecies because they deal
with the same topic, not because they will be fulfilled at the same time.[35]
Theophilos proposes a "two-stage process" of fulfillment, in which the parousia for the Jews and for the Gentiles come at different times.[36] Recasting
the old "mountain-peak" theory, Beasley-Murray appeals to examples from
the physical sciences to explain why that which is said to be temporally
near may be farther away than it appears. Beasley-Murray's thesis, however,
requires us to discern a symbolic understanding for the "generation" which
will not pass away before the awaited event. In response to charges that the
discourse's prediction of the parousia is invalidated by the fact that it did not
come as quickly as he said, Beasley-Murray answers that the coming of the
new age had already begun through Jesus' ministry, death, and resurrection.
That which is already "powerfully present" can be expected to reach fulfillment. To support his contention, Beasley-Murray explains that Mark 13:32
should be understood as an indication that Jesus' prediction was "hope," not
"dogma." The time for the eschaton will come, but it will not be determined
"by the accidents of history."[37] Dunn argues for an understanding of eschatology that is more nuanced than a simple expectation of a singular historical
event (or single complex of events) which result in the dissolution of the
physical world. The discourse's unfulfilled predictions ought to be understood in light of "prophetic hope." Dunn points to examples of partially filled
prophecies which inspire new prophecies, and suggests this as a way to read
Mark 13. That is, incompletely fulfilled prophecies do not indicate a false
or a mistaken prophet. Hope is not nullified; it "looks beyond the known of
the present and past into the unknown of the future." Dunn asserts that when
prophecy is understood this way, events of the past and present provide a
template for the future.[38]

Each of these theories of partial fulfillment, however, requires the reader
to come to terms with a halfway completed prediction. As I explain in
Chapter 3, Mark 13 predicts that all of the events will take place within a certain time. If it is wrong about some of these events, the fact that it was correct
about others does not eliminate the error.

Personal or Spiritual Transformation

A third category of commentators who offer theories of figurative fulfillment
assert that Mark 13 does not predict historical events but describes personal,
moral, or spiritual transformation. For these interpreters, the Olivet discourse
presents hope and challenge for the possibilities of human existence.

While von Dobschütz accepts the notion that early Christians expected
a historical parousia, he argues that it was of minor importance to them.

He distinguishes between two types of eschatological beliefs: a personal "moral" transformation and an external "physical" one. He explains that early Christians understood themselves as having already experienced the individual, spiritual change. The historical, cosmic transition from the old world order to the new kingdom of God was yet to come. But as von Dobschütz explains, the early Christians were so enthusiastic about the personal transformation that they paid little attention to the physical one. He argues that eschatological expectation was merely one of several factors used by the early church for moral exhortation. The historical parousia was less significant for them than the personal experience of Christ's presence. While early Christians expected a physical return of Christ, it was not a central element of their faith. When it failed to occur, apocalyptic expectation faded but "Christianity did not change in its essence."[39] Even though the emphasis on the parousia in early Christian documents[40] suggests that it was important for them, von Dobschütz claims that early Christians were not concerned about a physical parousia. But he offers no evidence to support this claim.

Bultmann disagrees with von Dobschütz and others who claim that the early Christians rejected or trivialized the notion of a historical parousia; he asserts that it was significant for the original readers. He considers the concept no longer to be compelling for modern readers, but suggests that its underlying message continues to be relevant. For Bultmann, eschatology is based on the presumption that the world is finite; predictions of the approaching dissolution of the world present a crisis of finitude. But eschatology also directs its readers and listeners to the transcendence of God beyond or outside of the limited world of human existence.[41] For Bultmann, that which is expected is experienced through a self-understanding mediated by an individual's encounter with the gospel. There is no future historical event to be anticipated, but a personal transformation to be experienced.[42] As he expresses elsewhere, "The judgment of the world is not a cosmic event that is still to happen but is the fact that Jesus has . . . issued the call to faith."[43]

Bultmann does not deal with Mark 13 per se but develops a message of his own and seeks to conform the text to it. That is, he privileges his philosophical commitments and cosmological preconceptions over the text. The text becomes a cipher for him to present his own message, instead of an "other" to encounter. Bultmann's approach therefore does not qualify as appropriation because he requires that the text conform to his prior concepts, instead of considering how it may change those concepts.

Dodd, as a third example of a commentator who describes eschatology as personal and spiritual transformation, considers the Olivet discourse to be a description of the impending Roman attack as a demonstration of God's

punishment upon Israel. But he claims that the historical event was only inci-
dental because "the political fortunes of Judea had little relevance" for Mark's
readers. For Dodd, historical events such as the fall of Jerusalem are significant
only as they serve as a canvas upon which eschatological concepts can be
presented.[44] He presents his thesis of "realized eschatology" by writing, "At a
particular point in time and space, the eternal entered decisively into history.
An historic crisis occurred by which the whole world of man's spiritual experience is controlled. To that moment in history our faith always looks back. The
Gospel is not a statement of general truths of religion, but an interpretation of
that which once happened."[45] Dodd claims that the message of the New Testament is not that the hoped-for kingdom of God is about to be revealed, but that
it has actually and already come. Fulfillment of eschatological hope is not a
"fantasy" of the future, because it has already happened through the ministry
of Jesus.[46]

According to Dodd, Jesus offers no promise in the gospels for a historical
state of blessing that will exist in time and space such as a restored kingdom of David. There is no political, military, or social agenda. The only
hope Jesus offers is for "the glories of a world beyond this."[47] As Dodd puts
it, "There is no *coup d'état*, no summoning of legions of angels. There is
only a Galilean Carpenter preaching in the streets and healing the sick."[48]
He explains that the kingdom of God as it appears in the gospels expresses
both the present rule of God to which the individual is challenged to submit
and the future time when God's reign will be accepted universally. The latter,
for Dodd, is the eschatological hope: "eschatological" in this sense meaning ultimate or climactic. This final beatific state will be realized in "God's
sovereign power becoming manifestly effective in the world of human
experience."[49]

Dodd's initial assumptions are so similar to his conclusion that his inquiry
appears to be controlled by those assumptions and not by the text itself.
For example, in his interpretation of the "parables of growth,"[50] Dodd asserts
that they emphasize the already-present nature of the kingdom of God,[51] when
the parables actually focus on how the kingdom comes into being.

Each of these categories of theories for figurative meaning of the Olivet
discourse ("A New World Pattern," "Partial Fulfillment," and "Personal or
Spiritual Transformation") fail to function as appropriation. Appropriation
requires that the reader does not privilege her perspective over that of the text,
and that she engage in "explanation," or critical analysis of the text. These
interpretations force the text to conform to the reader's prior conceptualizations. And as I explain in Chapter 3, figurative interpretations predicated on
first century Christians not anticipating a historical parousia such as vv. 24–27
describe are not supported by historical evidence.

OUTLINE OF A RICOEUR-ORIENTED RESOLUTION

As the previous section demonstrates, current scholarship is unable to present a means by which Mark 13 can be read today as a true text. For those who claim that the Olivet discourse is a prediction of historical events, the failure of these events to occur demonstrates that the predictions are false. Alternative arguments that the text is to be read figuratively collapse as well, for four reasons. First, some theorists claim that Jesus' ministry, crucifixion, and resurrection established a new world pattern that fulfills the text's predictions. However, these purported events fall short of fulfilling the text's prediction of spectacular events. Second, theories claiming that the predictions have been partially fulfilled fail to account for the unfulfilled features of the predictions. Third, theories of personal or spiritual transformation impose modern cosmological conceptions upon the text, such as disbelief in miracles. Fourth and most importantly, historical evidence does not support the contention that the text was originally understood non-literally.

Using Ricoeur's hermeneutics, I define and evaluate a proposal by which the unfulfilled predictions of Mark 13 can be reconciled with the modern reader's perspective of the world such that she is able to appropriate the text. The following logical argument outlines my project to appropriate meaning from Mark 13 today.

1. A modern reader is able to appropriate Mark 13 in a new way. (Thesis to prove)
2. The meaning for Mark 13 that was apparent when it was written is a literal prediction that certain events will happen relatively soon. (Premise to support)
3. Some of the events predicted in Mark 13 did not happen within the predicted time frame. (Premise to support)
4. The meaning of Mark 13 that was apparent when it was written is recognized today not to be true; it is now apparent that some aspects of its literal prediction were not fulfilled. (From 2 and 3)
5. A modern reader is only able to appropriate the meaning of Mark 13 that was apparent when it was written as a false description of the world (From 4).
6. For a modern reader to be able to appropriate meaning from Mark 13 in a new way, meaning must be apparent today which is other than or in addition to the meaning that was apparent when Mark 13 was written. (From 5)
7. The meaning of a text is not limited to the meaning that was apparent when it was written. (Premise to support)

8. Metaphor presents meaning different from and in addition to literal meaning. (Premise to support)
9. This metaphorical truth is able to be true. (Premise to support)
10. As it is read today, Mark 13 is a metaphorical text. (Premise to support)
11. Mark 13 presents meaning today that is different from and in addition to the literal meaning that was apparent when it was written. (From 8 and 10)
12. The metaphorical, non-literal meaning of Mark 13 can be true. (From 9 and 10)
13. Mark 13 as metaphor is able to present meaning today that is true. (From 11 and 12)
14. A true description of the world is different from a false one. (Presumed)
15. A reader's appropriation of Mark 13's meaning as metaphor is different from her appropriation of the meaning that was apparent when it was written. (From 5, 13, and 14)
16. A reader is able to appropriate Mark 13 in a new way. (From 15)

This argument serves as the framework of this project. A Ricoeur-based resolution of the hermeneutical problem of Mark 13 depends upon the success of each of the argument's premises. The remainder of this section explains the premises and what is necessary to support them. Chapters 2 through 6 provide this support, and the concluding chapter describes how today's reader is able to appropriate the text.

1. The Possibility for New Appropriation

The argument's opening premise, "A modern reader is able to appropriate Mark 13 in a new way," states this project's thesis as explained at the beginning of this chapter. Previous interpretations either fail to function as appropriation, or they only allow for the text to be appropriated as a false one. Chapter 2 defines appropriation and discusses the issues of appropriating Mark 13 in particular.

2. Mark 13's Literal Predictions When Written

Chapter 3 supports the premise that when Mark 13 was written, its apparent meaning was that certain events would take place relatively soon:

A. The Jerusalem temple will be destroyed (v. 2).
B. The Christian community will experience deception (vv. 5b-6, 21–23).
C. Calamities will strike the world (vv. 7–8, 17–20).
D. Christians will be persecuted (vv. 9, 11–13).

E. The Christian gospel will be preached to all peoples (v. 10).
F. A profoundly (and perhaps uniquely) evil figure will emerge (vv. 14–16).
G. The cosmos will be disrupted (vv. 24–25).
H. A spiritual being will be perceived universally (v. 26).
I. God's people will be gathered (v. 27).

The discourse predicts that these events will take place during the lifetime of the generation alive when Jesus is purported to have made the predictions (v. 30). Although v. 32 states that the exact time when the events will take place is unknowable, the passing of nearly two millennia makes it clear that the generation alive during the first century has "passed away." If the events were to take place within the text's predicted time, they would have happened long ago: by the end of the first century at the very latest.

3. Events Did Not Occur When Predicted

The third premise states, "Some of the events predicted in Mark 13 did not happen within the predicted time frame." As Chapter 3 explains, Mark 13 predicts nine events, which can be divided into two sets: those that did not take place when predicted, and those that did.

The first set of events predicted by the discourse are those which did not take place within the predicted time, or even after that time. The text's original readers would not have known if the predictions were true, because it was still possible for them to be fulfilled. But today's reader is able to recognize the failure of the predictions. Three of the predicted events belong to this set. No record of the occurrence of events G, H, and I exists and they are events of such a dramatic nature that it is reasonable to assume that if they had occurred, we would have evidence of them. Therefore, it is reasonable to assume that they have not taken place. In their treatment of Matthew's parallel to Mark 13, Allison and Davies assert that these unfulfilled predictions are too significant for them to be considered to have been fulfilled by the events in the mid-first century.[52] Therefore the predictions of events G, H, and I are false.

The second set of predicted events includes six that today's reader is able to accept as having occurred within the text's predicted timeline. As descriptions of historical events the predictions are true. I argue that this second set of events includes A, B, C, D, E, and F. The occurrence of A, B, and D is evident in the historical record. The wars and natural disasters of the first century fulfilled C's prediction of calamities. The spread of Christianity through most of the Mediterranean basin and Near East fulfilled E's prediction that the gospel will reach "all nations," as dissemination occurred to all those nations known to the author and original readers. And as F predicts, the abomination of desolation was present in the expected time. Scholars have proposed many candidates for the abomination, such as Pilate's standards,[53] Judas,[54] Caligula's proposed desecration,[55] Eleazar's band of fighters,[56] the Roman presence in the temple at its destruction,[57] and Titus' acclamation.[58] In contrast, I argue that the abomination is the high priest and the temple cultus which he represents.

4. Originally Apparent Meaning Is Recognized Today Not to Be True

The fourth premise, "The meaning of Mark 13 that was apparent when it was written is recognized today not to be true; it is now apparent that some aspects of its literal prediction were not fulfilled," follows from the second and third premises. As premise 2 states, the meaning of Mark 13 that was apparent when written is a prediction that events G, H, and I (along with other events) will take place by the end of the first century at the latest. As premise 3 states, these three events did not take place. It follows that the predictions are false. Therefore, the meaning apparent when the text was written is not true.

5. Appropriable Today Only as a False Text

The original readers of Mark 13 could appropriate it as a true text (i.e. consider it to be an accurate world description), because the generational deadline for the predicted events had not yet taken place. But as the fourth premise states, this is no longer the case for today's reader. The meaning of Mark 13 that was apparent when written is recognized today as not true. Therefore, if the only meaning of Mark 13 that is available is the meaning that was apparent when it was written, the text is false. It predicts things that did not happen.

6. Appropriation Is Possible for Meaning Other Than That Apparent When Written

Premise 5 eliminates the permissibility of appropriating the literal meaning of Mark 13 as true. But if other meaning is available, then a reader may be able to appropriate Mark 13 as a true text.

7. Textual Meaning Not Limited to Meaning When Written

The seventh premise of this argument claims that a text's meaning is not limited to the meaning that was apparent when the text was written. A text makes multiple truth claims, including those which were not recognizable at the time that the text was written. These meanings are inherent to the structure of the text itself. Latent meaning exists within the linguistic constructs of a text in addition to those meanings which are foregrounded by the conditions present when it was written. The latent meanings become evident when the conditions in which a text is read are different from the conditions in which it is written. This claim is supported by example. For instance, Sophocles' play *Oedipus Rex* has latent possibilities for describing an individual's emotional relationship with his parents. However, this meaning was not recognized until the conditions under which Freud read it. Saying that a text has latent meaning is different from saying that different people find different meanings in a text depending upon their reading context. The meaning comes not from what the reader brings to the text, but from what the text brings as a subject to the reader. Chapter 4 supports this assertion.

I present Ricoeur's argument for a text's independence, or autonomy, from its author and from the circumstances of its production. This autonomy exists because a text, as written discourse, differs from speech, as oral discourse, in several significant ways. First, its relatively permanent nature makes it available to anyone with the linguistic competence to read the text. Second, in textual discourse dialogue between the discourse-maker and the discourse-receiver is not possible because of the temporal, spatial, or cultural gap between them. Third, the referent of the discourse is no longer ostensive or situationally-oriented.

To support Ricoeur's concept of textual autonomy, I address two other theories about how texts present meaning: authorial intention, as championed primarily by Hirsch, and reader response, as advocated by Fish. In responding to these challenges to Ricoeur's approach, I assert that textual meaning is not determined by the author's purpose for writing (authorial intention), and that the text affects and changes the reader and her linguistic community, even while her preconceptions and conventions are a necessary element of the reading process (reader response). This argument demonstrates that Mark 13 is able to mean something other than and in addition to the meaning that was apparent to its author and original readers.

8. Metaphorical Meaning

The eighth premise states that metaphor presents meaning different from and in addition to literal meaning. Chapter 5 describes and supports Ricoeur's treatment of metaphor to validate this premise. In so doing, it contrasts metaphor with other figurative forms of expression, and it explains how Ricoeur's description of metaphor is different from the way that other commentators on Mark 13 use metaphor.

As described by Ricoeur, metaphor is a transgression of linguistic conventions which creates multiplicity (but not infinity) of meaning. It exists in addition to and not instead of conventional (i.e. literal) meaning. It is not to be confused with substitutionary literary tropes such as allegory. Metaphor creates an evocative tension between the "is" and "is not" of the elements of the statement, or between the world as described by the text and the world as experienced by the reader, thus opening multiple meanings.

9. Truth in Metaphor

For Mark 13 to be appropriated as a true text by today's reader, it is not enough that the text presents metaphorical as well as literal meaning; the metaphorical meaning must be true in some sense. As Chapter 5 explains, truth in this sense is not defined by the text's accord with history or with prior conceptualizations, but by metaphor's existential disclosure or manifestation of what had been previously hidden or forgotten. This truth comes from new world configuration that the metaphor creates. Metaphor's capacity for truth depends upon the literal falsity of the metaphorical statement. As the first-order of reference of the statement fails (i.e. is recognized to be false), the second-order of reference becomes recognizable. The reference, or "about what," of the text is a newly revealed world toward which the reader can be oriented. The sort of truth that metaphor presents allows the reader to apprehend the world or self in a new way that was not available within the structures of previous linguistic and conceptual categories and frameworks. Metaphor's equation of two different concepts creates new thought because of a new configuration of the world in which previously unrecognizable implications become apparent.

10. Mark 13 as Metaphor

Chapter 6 supports the claim of premise 10 that Mark 13 is a metaphorical text as it is encountered by today's reader. Two conditions must be met for Mark 13 to function metaphorically and not to be dismissed as simply false; I argue that they are. First, the prediction must be something other than the near-future occurrence of certain events. Latent within the text are regular or ongoing happenings (changes of season and generational change) and the impossibility of knowing when events will take place in the future. The meaning that particular circumstances happen regularly but not predictably is able to be foregrounded. A metaphorical extension of the meaning is that events or conditions related to the final predicted events present themselves on a continuing basis. Second, the text's predictions today are different from the original prediction of literal events. The evident meaning of the text no longer deals solely with collapsing skies and the descent of the Son of Man, but also with the dynamics of the reader's lived world. To consider the metaphorical possibilities of the described events, particularly those dealing with transcendent beings and celestial cataclysm, recognizing the text's status as a limit-expression (i.e. the description of an experience at the limits of human perception) is helpful.

Metaphorical tension is present in Mark 13 in two ways: inherent to the text itself, and in its split reference. First, there is an inconsistency between vv. 30 and 32 about the timeline for the predictions. Before the passing of the generational deadline, these two sayings could be reconciled easily: v. 30 provided a broad prediction, and v. 32 cautioned against a too-precise application of the prediction. After the passing of the deadline (even in its broadest sense), we recognize a tension between the two logia that was not discernible until after the failure of the v. 30 prediction. This tension is not a contradiction but an evocative "is/is not" metaphor. The text's claim that Jesus is able to predict future events, even generally, must be reconciled with his purported admission of ignorance in order for the text not to collapse into absurdity (Jesus says the predicted events will happen within a certain time, but then says that he does not know when they will happen).

Mark 13 operates as metaphor in a second way. Events described by the text are a split reference: the literal events as understood when the text was written, and the metaphorical meanings recognized by today's reader. The metaphor of Mark 13 is the difference between history as predicted by the text and history as experienced by today's reader. That is, the literal events predicted by the text serve as a first order of reference, and the figurative meanings recognizable today are a second order of reference. Mark 13, as encountered today, violates convention by claiming events will happen in a time period when they did not. In this case, the discourse is metaphoric because it brings together a configuration of the world that does not match historical events. It is false at the first level of reference, but it creates new ways to understand self and world at the second level of reference. Today Mark 13 no longer functions as a prediction of certain literal events in the near-future but as a description of the world that would not be possible in straightforward expression.

When Mark 13 is read as metaphor there is a recurring feature to the text's predictions, expressed through its emplotment of regular ongoing events. When the text was written, the parable of the fig tree of v. 28 and the generational prediction of v. 30 indicate an imminent but imprecisely predictable occurrence. After the imminence of the events is no longer possible because the deadline has passed, the ongoing or recurring nature of these tropes becomes recognizable: summer comes each year, and generations follow each other. The text's prediction of a punctiliar and fully completed occurrence in the future provides understanding in the present of a continuing progression of events. Chapter 7 (pp. 169–172) develops this theme more fully.

11. Different Meaning Today from When Mark Was Written

Premise 8 explains that metaphor presents meaning different from and in addition to literal meaning. Premise 10 demonstrates that Mark 13 is metaphorical as it is encountered today. Therefore, Mark 13 provides meaning today in addition to the literal meaning that was apparent when it was written.

I describe a metaphorical meaning in which human experience is affected by powers which appear to be dominant, are deceptive, cause calamity, and persecute. Despite the apparent dominance of these forces, they are curtailed and are undone on a regular basis, while forces of vindication and unification prevail. This description is not meant to be a complete exposition of the text's metaphorical meaning; the evocative nature of metaphor makes full description impossible. Nor is it meant to replace literal meaning; metaphor is a second order of reference which depends upon first order of reference. It is metaphor rather than fiction or myth because fictive discourse purports to present truth without configuring reality. Thomas More's *Utopia* and Isaac Asimov's science fiction novels are true in that they explore aspects of the human condition, but they are not presentations of reality. In contrast Mark 13, like other apocalyptic texts, purports to describe the certainty of a coming reality.

12. Potential Truth for Mark 13's Metaphorical Meaning

Premise 9 states metaphorical truth has the capacity to be true. Premise 10 states that Mark 13 is metaphor. Therefore, it follows that Mark 13's metaphorical meaning is able to be true. This premise is stated as potentiality rather than certainty because metaphorical meaning is also able to be false.

13. Potential Truth of Mark 13's Meaning Today

Premise 11 states that Mark 13 presents meaning which is different from the meaning that was apparent when the text was written. Premise 12 states that the metaphorical meaning of Mark 13 is able to be true. Therefore, Mark 13 has the potential to present meaning today that is true.

14. True Descriptions are Different from False Descriptions

The premise that a true description of the world is different from a false description is presumed to be true; what is false is different from what is true.

15. Appropriation of Metaphor Is Different from Appropriation of Literal Meaning

The penultimate premise states that a reader's appropriation of Mark 13's meaning as metaphor is different from her appropriation of the meaning that was apparent when it was written. This follows from premise 5, which states that the originally apparent meaning of the text is false, and from premise 13, which states that the metaphorical meaning of Mark 13 that is discernible today is able to be true. Because a true description is different from a false description, as premise 14 states, Mark 13 can be appropriated in a new and different way.

16. Mark 13 Is Able To Be Appropriated in a New Way

Chapter 7 concludes this project by presenting options for how today's reader is able to appropriate Mark 13 in a new and different way, as a metaphorical text. It begins by identifying cues for appropriation from the text's apocalyptic genre, from its place within Mark's gospel as a whole, and from the structure of the discourse. Mark 13 describes a world in which negative forces continually and perpetually affect the world. When appropriated, Mark 13 reveals that the identity of these negative powers may be surprising and shocking, and that the efficacy of these forces is more apparent than real. The negative powers are limited and repudiated by what Mark presents as God's positive force. This actual power, which is not always readily discernible, mitigates the influence of the negative forces and ultimately triumphs over them. The interaction between apparent negative forces and concealed positive forces continues in a regular recurrence. When appropriated, Mark 13 summons the reader to recognize the true nature of the negative powers and the presence of the positive, and to respond appropriately. This description is not meant to be all-encompassing, because metaphor offers multiplicity of meaning. But it is one metaphorical possibility which emerges from the text.

NOTES

1. Paul Ricoeur, "What Is a Text? Explanation and Understanding," in *From Text to Action: Essays in Hermeneutics, II*, trans. Kathleen Blamey and John B. Thompson (Evanston, IL: Northwestern University Press, 1991), 100–17.

2. Ricoeur, "Language of Faith," in *The Philosophy of Paul Ricoeur: An Anthology of His Work*, eds. Charles E. Reagan and David Stewart (Boston: Beacon Press, 1978), 223–31.

3. Ricoeur, "Appropriation," in *Hermeneutics and the Human Sciences: Essays on Language, Action, and Interpretation*, trans. John B. Thompson, ed. John B. Thompson (Cambridge & New York: Cambridge University Press, 198) 192.

4. Ricoeur, "Appropriation," 182–87, 191; *Paul Ricoeur, Time and Narrative*, Volume 3, trans. Kathleen McLaughlin (Chicago: University of Chicago Press, 1988), 179.

5. Paul Ricoeur, *Interpretation Theory: Discourse and the Surplus of Meaning* (Fort Worth: Texas Christian University Press, 1976), 71–88; Paul Ricoeur,

"Explanation and Understanding: On Some Remarkable Connections between the Theory of Texts, Action Theory, and the Theory of History," in *From Text to Action: Essays in Hermeneutics, II*, trans. Kathleen Blamey and John B. Thompson (Evanston, IL: Northwestern University Press, 1991), passim.

6. Dan R. Stiver, *Ricoeur and Theology* (London, New York: Bloomsbury, 2012), 42–4.

7. Ricoeur, *Time and Narrative* 3 100–101; Paul Ricoeur, "The Hermeneutical Function of Distanciation," in *From Text to Action: Essays in Hermeneutics, II*, trans. Kathleen Blamey and John B. Thompson (Evanston, IL: Northwestern University Press, 1991), 85–6; Paul Ricouer, "Toward a Hermeneutic of the Idea of Revelation," in *Essays on Biblical Interpretation* (Philadelphia: Fortress Press, 1980), 102, Paul Ricouer, "The Canon between the Text and the Community," in *Philosophical Hermeneutics and Biblical Exegesis*, eds. Petr Pokorný and Jan Roskovec. *Wissenschaftliche Untersuchungen zum Neuen Testament* (Tübingen: Mohr Siebeck, 2002), 11–12; cf. Stiver *Ricoeur and Theology*, 80.

8. Paul Ricoeur, "The Model of the Text: Meaningful Action Considered as a Text," in *From Text to Action: Essays in Hermeneutics*, II, trans. Kathleen Blamey and John B. Thompson (Evanston, IL: Northwestern University Press, 1991), 155; Ricoeur *Interpretation Theory* 7; Ricoeur *Time and Narrative* 3 178–79.

9. Cf. pp. 45–46 for my argument that the Olivet Discourse is an apocalyptic text.

10. David F. Strauss's Life of Jesus of 1836 provides the first serious critical challenge to the reliability of the Olivet discourse. Strauss notes that in it Jesus temporally links the destruction of Jerusalem with the "end of all things." Although Jerusalem fell nearly eighteen (and now more than nineteen) centuries ago, the eschaton has not yet occurred, leading Strauss to conclude that this prediction was erroneous. He dismisses the "mountain-top" theory to explain this dilemma, which claims that events in the future present a false sense of proximity with each other in the same way that peaks in a far-off mountain range may appear to be closer than they are. According to Strauss, this would merely provide a reason for Jesus' error but would not remove it. Similarly, he rejects the notion that Jesus offers this prophecy to exert moral pressure upon his listeners, as this would save Jesus from being charged with error, only to accuse him of being a fraud. While Strauss's work focused upon the authenticity of the discourse as a saying of Jesus, his critique touches on the credibility of the discourse itself (in Beasley-Murray, Jesus and the Last Days 3–4, "The Vision on the Mount" 39–40).

Writing five decades ago, Cranfield notes that the majority of exegetes hold the view that early Christians expected the parousia within a few decades at most, and that the failure of this expectation caused at least some degree of embarrassment and disappointment. He cites numerous theories about the origin of the mistaken expectation and suggests that the early church confused the "Christ event" as being one "moment" instead of two: the first containing the elements of incarnation, crucifixion, resurrection, and ascension, the second consisting of the parousia, "drawn together by an overwhelming magnetism and yet for a time are held apart" (1954, 286–88; *Gospel* 408). I question this perspective, as indeed Cranfield himself seems to with his division of one event into two moments, because although there may a theological unity in the work of Christ, the length of time between the ascension and parousia is far too great to consider them as the same event. The early church's confusion over the delay of the parousia comes from this very issue. They considered the parousia to be part of the "event," and struggled to understand why it was missing.

Most recently, Marcus points out the serious apologetic dilemma of the discourse. It seems to indicate that Jesus expected the eschaton, with its cosmic upheaval and with the triumphant return of Jesus, to happen very soon. The fact that these events have not taken place, even after a significant period of time, motivates scholars to counter this apparent mistake of Jesus. Marcus summarizes their attempts as belonging to two groups. The first, or "conservative" set of explanations explain the apparent error as "prophetic perspective." Just as an artist includes both nearby objects and distant mountains in a landscape painting, Jesus discussed events that would occur in both the near and distant future. The second, or "liberal" group of theories parse out the discourse by only attributing to Jesus those predictions which actually were fulfilled. The others came from Jewish or early Christian sources (Mark 8–16 864–65).

11. James Stuart Russell, *The Parousia: A Critical Inquiry into the New Testament Doctrine of Our Lord's Second Coming* (London: T. Fisher Unwin, 1878, Grand Rapids: Baker Book House, 1983), v–vi, 60–4. However, Russell asserts that the disciples did in fact experience the predicted events. Motivated by his theological commitments, he argues that historical evidence is secondary to the "affirmations of inspiration" which come from the Bible. Historical evidence must be considered through the lens of the Biblical text, not vice versa. Mark 13 explains that the parousia will occur within a lifetime of Jesus' ministry. Russell therefore seeks to demonstrate that the apocalyptic predictions were indeed fulfilled. In particular, he explains that the elect actually were removed from the world in an unrecorded rapture (Preface to the New Edition).

12. Russell, *The Parousia*, 54–59.

13. Peter Bolt, "Mark 13: An Apocalyptic Precursor to the Passion Narrative," *Reformed Theological Review* 54 (1995), 20–6; cf. Dean B Deppe, "Charting the Future or a Perspective on the Present? The Paraenetic Purpose of Mark 13," *Calvin Theological Journal* 41.1 (2006), 96; cf. Jan Lambrecht, *Die Redaktion der Markus-Apokalypse: Literarische Analyse und Strukturuntersuchung*. Analecta Biblica. Vol. 28 (Rome: Pontifical Bible Institute, 1967), 253; cf. Dale C., Allison, Jr., *Constructing Jesus: Memory, Imagination, and History*. Grand Rapids : Baker Book House, 2013), 60–61; cf. Elizabeth Struthers Malbon, "Literary Contexts of Mark 13," in *Biblical and Humane: A Festschrift for John F. Priest*, eds. Linda Bennett Elder, David L. Barr and Elizabeth Struthers Malbon. (Atlanta: Scholars Pr, 1996), 115–16.

14. Robinson, John A.T., *Jesus and His Coming: The Emergence of a Doctrine* (London: Abingdon Press, 1957), 40–52.

15. First, darkness (σκότος) covered the land for three hours as Jesus died on the cross (15:33), fulfilling v. 24b's prediction that the sun will be darkened (σκοτισθήσεται) and the moon will fail to produce light. Second, the falling of the stars, understood as the collapse of heavenly beings, and the disruption of heavenly powers of v. 25 occurred during the crucifixion, as the spiritual order of the world was transformed. The tearing of the temple curtain (15:38), which hearkens to the tearing open of heaven during Jesus' baptism (1:10; both passages use σχίζω), demonstrates

the upheaval of the heavens. Jesus' exorcisms during his ministry further indicate the present reality of spiritual transformation or upheaval. The later emendation of 16:17–18 intensifies this presentation of reality as spiritual powers are bestowed upon the disciples. The coming of the Son of Man refers to Jesus' return as a resurrected being, if with Robinson we understand his "coming" as an ascent to heaven rather than a descent to earth. Finally, the gathering of the elect from across the world was a self-evident fact for the readers of Mark, as they witnessed the inclusion of individuals from across the known world into the community of the church. Cf. Allison *Constructing Jesus* 60–61 for a similar discussion.

16. Cf. Caird (252–256) for a similar summary of responses to Schweitzer's "thoroughgoing" (or "consistent") eschatology.

17. e.g. 1 Thessalonians 4:13–5:11, Revelation passim, Didache 16.

18. Robinson, *Jesus and His Coming*, 59–63.

19. Ibid., 134–36, 176–78; cf. Thomas Francis Glasson, *The Second Advent: The Origin of the New Testament Doctrine* (London: The Epworth Press, 1963), 233.

20. John A.T. Robinson, *In the End, God* (London: Harper & Row, 1968), 68–73.

21. Robinson, *Jesus and His Coming*, 160–71.

22. Ibid., 95–96.

23. Ibid., 9–10.

24. Ibid., 40–52, 160–71.

25. N.T. Wright, *Jesus and the Victory of God. Christian Origins and the Question of God. Vol. 2.* (Minneapolis: Fortress Press, 1996), 345–46.

26. Ibid., 361, cf. ibid., 354–58.

27. Paul R. Eddy, "The (W)Right Jesus: Eschatological Prophet, Israel's Messiah, Yahweh Embodied," in *Jesus and the Restoration of Israel: A Critical Assessment of N. T. Wright's Jesus and the Victory of God*, ed. Carey C Newman (Downers Grove IL: InterVarsity Press, 1999), 44.

28. Wright, *Jesus and the Victory of God*, 367–68.

29. Dale C., Allison Jr, "Jesus and the Victory of Apocalyptic," in *Jesus and the Restoration of Israel: A Critical Assessment of N. T. Wright's Jesus and the Victory of God*, ed. Carey C Newman (Downers Grove IL: InterVarsity Press, 1999), 131.

30. Dale C., Allison Jr, *Jesus of Nazareth: Millenarian Prophet* (Minneapolis: Fortress, 1998), 152–71.

31. Allison, "Jesus and the Victory of Apocalyptic," 135–37.

32. Charles E. B. Cranfield, *The Gospel According to Saint Mark: An Introduction and Commentary*, ed. C. F. D. Moule (Cambridge: Cambridge University Press, 1959), 404–5.

33. G.B. Caird, *The Language and Imagery of the Bible* (London: Duckworth, 1980), 258–60.

34. Ibid., 266–67.

35. Edward Adams, "Historical Crisis and Cosmic Crisis in Mark 13 and Lucan's Civil War," *Tyndale Bulletin* 48.2 (1997): 332.

36. Michael P. Theophilos, *The Abomination of Desolation in Matthew* 24.15 (London: Continuum, 2012), 227–28.

37. George Raymond Beasley-Murray, *Jesus and the Kingdom of God* (Exeter, England & Grand Rapids: Eerdmans, 1986), 343.

38. James D. G. Dunn, "Jesus and the Kingdom: How Would His Message Have Been Heard?" in *Neotestamentica Et Philonica: Studies in Honor of Peder Borgen*, eds. David A. Aune, Torrey Seland and Jarl Henning Ulrichsen (Leiden & Boston: Brill, 2003), 26–32.

39. Ernst von Dobschütz, *The Eschatology of the Gospels* (London: Hodder and Stoughton, 1910), 22–31.

40. E.g. Romans 8:18–25, Philippians 3:20–21, 1 Thessalonians 4:13–18, 2 Peter 3:3–10, Revelation 22:7–21.

41. Rudolf Bultmann, *Jesus Christ and Mythology* (New York: Scribner's, 1958), 25–6.

42. Ibid., 80–81.

43. Rudolf Bultmann, "New Testament and Mythology," in *New Testament and Mythology and Other Writings*, 1941, trans. Schubert Miles Ogden, ed. Schubert Miles Ogden (Philadelphia: Fortress, 1984), 19.

44. C. H. Dodd, *The Parables of the Kingdom* (New York: Scribner, 1961), 47–48.

45. Ibid., 163–64.

46. Ibid., 33–5.

47. Ibid., 52–5.

48. Ibid., 159–60.

49. Ibid., 22–4.

50. The Seed Growing Secretly (Mark 4:26–29), the Sower (Mark 4:2–8), the Tares (Matthew 13:24–30), the Dragnet (Matthew 13:47–48), the Mustard Seed (Mark 4:30–32), and the Leaven (Matthew 13:33).

51. Dodd, 140–56.

52. Dale C. Allison, Jr. and W. D. Davies, A Critical and Exegetical Commentary on the Gospel According to Saint Matthew Vol. 3, Commentary on Matthew 19–28 (International Critical Commentary. Edinburgh: T & T Clark, 1997), 327–31.

53. Robert Eisler in George Raymond Beasley-Murray, *Jesus and the Last Days: The Interpretation of the Olivet Discourse* (Peabody, Mass: Hendrickson 1993), 90–1.

54. Francis Dewar, "Chapter 13 and the Passion Narrative in St Mark" *Theology* 64 (1961): 103.

55. James G. Crossley, *The Date of Mark's Gospel: Insight from the Law in Earliest Christianity* (London & New York: T & T Clark International, 2004), 29–35; Beasley-Murray, Jesus and the Last Days 367; Glasson, The Second Advent,180–84; Frederick J. Murphy, *Apocalypticism in the Bible and Its World: A Comprehensive Introduction* (Grand Rapids: Baker Academic, 2012), 240.

56. Joel Marcus, "The Jewish War and the Sitz Im Leben of Mark," *Journal of Biblical Literature* 111.3 (1992): 454–55; Joel Marcus, *Mark 8–16: A New Translation with Introduction and Commentary* (The Anchor Bible. Vol. 27A. New Haven and London: Yale University Press, 2009), 870–71.

57. Theophylact and Augustine in Thomas Aquinas, *Gospel of Mark*, trans. William Whiston, Catena Aurea (London: J.G.F. and J. Rivington, 1842), 260; Russell, *The Parousia*, 73; Howard in Beasley-Murray, *Jesus and the Last Days*, 242–44; Robert H. Gundry, *Mark: A Commentary on His Apology for the Cross* (Grand Rapids: Eerdmans, 1993), 774–75.

58. John Chrystostom, Homilies on the Gospel of St. Matthew, in *A Select Library of the Nicene and Post-Nicene Fathers of the Christian Church*, ed. Philip Schaff (Edinburgh & Grand Rapids: T & T Clark & Eerdmans, 1998), 452–53; William A. Such, *The Abomination of Desolation in the Gospel of Mark: Its Historical Reference in Mark 13:14 and Its Impact in the Gospel* (Lanham, Md: University Press of America, 1999), 94–7.

Chapter 2

Appropriation

To consider the merits of the claim that today's reader is able to appropriate Mark 13 as a true text, we must understand what it means for a reader to appropriate a text, why she would be motivated to do so, and how a text can be true. Before examining the issues raised by Mark 13, the hermeneutical problem associated with them, and a Ricoeur-oriented resolution of this problem, I define appropriation more fully and consider the Olivet discourse's appeal for today's reader; that is, why she would seek to appropriate it. This chapter begins by describing appropriation along the lines of Ricoeur's work. Next, it considers the appeal (i.e. the desirability for appropriation) of Mark 13. It then describes how non-historical texts in general, and apocalyptic texts in particular, are able to be true. The chapter concludes with an examination of Ricoeur's claim for the distinctiveness of Biblical texts, and his failure to argue successfully against the challenge presented by the Yale School to his claim. Despite this failure, Ricoeur's description of appropriation provides broad parameters which are helpful for this project.

DEFINITION OF APPROPRIATION

Appropriation is the engagement of a text by a reader in such a way that her prior commitments are affected by that engagement. As Ricoeur puts it, "appropriation is the process by which the revelation of new modes of being ... *gives* the subject new capacities for knowing himself. ... The reader isbroadened in his capacity to project himself by receiving a new mode of being from the text itself."[1] McLean asserts that hermeneutical inquiry, with appropriation this defined as its goal, sets it apart from the Enlightenment-inspired historical-critical approach that dominates the field of Biblical studies. Whereas hermeneutics seeks to engage the reader with the text, historical-critical studies "defamiliarize" the text and create distance between it and the reader. Pursuing an interpretive strategy with appropriation as its goal offers an alternative to what McLean calls the "nihilism" produced by the subject-object Enlightenment model.[2]

As Ricoeur develops the concept of appropriation, he speaks of the "world" of the text and the "world" of the reader. He describes these worlds as the *Welt* or world of being, rather than as the *Umwelt* or situation of the individual. In Heideggerian terms, Ricoeur's "world" of the text is the lived world of Dasein. The "world" of the text is not a reconstruction of the author's being-in-the-world, but the world of the text itself. Properly speaking, a text cannot have a world in this sense because a text is not a Dasein. Rather, the text projects a world to the reader, who then must decide whether or not to allow the world projected by the text to challenge her prior understanding of her being-in-the-world.[3] Understanding a text, therefore, is to hold the world of the text against one's own lived world in such a way that the reader's self- and world-understanding moves beyond the immediate situation and the reader is able to explore "new dimensions of our being-in-the-world."[4] As Ricoeur puts it, "to interpret a work is to display the world to which it refers by virtue of its 'arrangement,' its 'genre,' and its 'style.'"[5] That is, the purpose of hermeneutics is to recognize its "world," or the configuration of reality which it offers. DiCenso explains that Ricoeur's description of the reader's world relates to the cultural and linguistic construct within which humans operate. The world of the reader refers not to the objective, physical environment of the reader, but the reader's projection of self into that world. In the same way, DiCenso explains, the world of the text is that which is disclosed or revealed by the text's representation of reality or possibilities for reality.[6] To avoid confusion of the term "world" as it is used to describe both the reader's lived experience and the configuration of possibilities by the text, Klemm suggests the term "ontological world" to refer to the first option, while retaining "text-world" for the second. But this ought not to be understood as a separation of what Ricoeur treats as a unity: a world that is objectively presented by the text and one that is projected by the reader in response to the text. The text crafts ways for being in the world. Klemm argues that the text-world shapes an ontological world, which the reader can then explore as a possibility for authentic existence.[7]

The reader benefits from the challenges that texts present because they provide her with the opportunity to explore new ways to understand her world and to re-examine previous understandings. McLean explains that neither the text's world nor the reader's world is subsumed into the other, nor that the purpose for textual interpretation is simply to understand the world of the text, but that the creative interaction of the two enables the reader to advance her self-understanding.[8] Ricoeur explains that in appropriation, the reader "receive[s] an enlarged self from the apprehension of proposed worlds" presented by the text; she does not impose her world construct upon the text.[9] Similarly, McCarthy defines appropriation as "the criticism of an autonomous ego, and the imaginative appropriation of the self through the textual form of the Other."[10] The effect of this engagement by the reader with the text may take one of several various forms. First, it may confirm her previous commitments with information or a configuration of the world which supports them. Second, it may clarify what the reader already knew in a less defined way. Third, appropriation can challenge her previous commitments with new information or perspectives that counter those prior commitments. Fourth, appropriation makes a more comprehensive understanding possible by associating concepts which had not previously been drawn together. And fifth, it may rearrange her categories of knowing. These five examples of the effect of appropriation upon a reader are not intended to be exhaustive but to demonstrate several possible results from a textual encounter. Appropriation may challenge or change the reader's preconceptions, or it may confirm or strengthen them.

For textual engagement to be considered appropriation, the issues must be both relevant and significant for the reader. A Nebraskan corn farmer may be able to read and understand a manual describing the operation of a submarine periscope, but it would be neither relevant or significant to her (unless submarines are a hobby interest for her or she has a relative or friend in the Navy). Our same farmer may read a newspaper article reporting that a key ingredient of her favorite toothpaste is now being imported from Malaysia instead of Indonesia. This would be relevant to her, but not significant. The farmer may read and comprehend these texts, but she will not appropriate them because they address issues which for her are trivial. They do not inform her understanding of self and of her construal of the experienced world. The relevance and significance of a text for a reader may not be initially evident; as she encounters the text its relevance and significance for her may become discernible. An assessment of the relevance and significance of a text upon a reader is necessarily subjective, because they will differ from person to person. If the corn farmer had a son serving on a Navy submarine, or if her crop prices would be affected by a change in trade policies with Indonesia, the texts would be relevant and significant and therefore appropriable. Thus, the ability of a reader to appropriate Mark 13 is affected by her self-identity and her world configuration. She will consider Mark 13 to be relevant and significant, and thus appropriable, if she considers it to be a component of a text that has authoritative status for her, of if individuals and communities that do so are important to her either professionally or personally.

For a reader to be able to appropriate a text she does not impose her world framework upon the text and evaluate the text's conformity to this framework, but she is willing to consider the text's presentation of the world in its own light. Ricoeur compares his concept of appropriation with Gadamer's description of play, in which the individual loses herself in the world constituted by the parameters of the game. Play is impossible until the individual is open to, accepts, or enters into the space defined by the game's rules. Ricoeur states, "In entering a game we hand ourselves over, we abandon ourselves to the space of meaning which holds sway over the reader." Just as a player must enter into the world created by the game, a reader must enter into the world created by the text for appropriation to be possible. In so doing, the reader is changed by experiencing the text's world. As Ricoeur expresses it, "Play is an experience which transforms those who participate in it."[11]

Ricoeur labels the alternative to appropriation "the narcissism of the reader: to find oneself in a text, to impose and rediscover oneself." Appropriation involves a "relinquishment" of oneself instead of a "taking possession" of the text.[12] A personal anecdote may serve as an example for the openness necessary for appropriation. A controversial issue arose at a school I attended, and at an open forum to address it someone suggested a dialogue between the two factions. One individual responded, "I'm willing to dialogue with them, but I'm not going to change my mind!" This person is analogous to a reader who refuses to set aside her prior commitments when approaching the text; she would evaluate it only as it conformed or failed to conform with those commitments. The individual who suggested dialogue between the school's rival factions represents the call for appropriation as an engagement between two understandings of the world: the world-configuration of the text and the world understanding of the reader. For appropriation to be possible, the reader cannot insist that Mark 13 conform to her norms and standards in order to appropriate it; she must be willing to consider the possibility that her encounter with the text will change her and her world-conceptions. This willingness does not require the reader to accept that the text is true; only to consider that it might be.

It is implicit in the definition of appropriation that the text is an "other" that confronts the reader. The text presents a voice from outside of the reader's situation. The alterity of the text is not only a hermeneutical challenge, but it makes reading valuable. The text is "other" in that it comes from a linguistic and conceptual framework that is different from that of the reader. The otherness of the text must not be so great as to make comprehension impossible (e.g. written in a language that the reader does not know, or based upon a conceptual system that has no points of connection with hers).[13] Before the discovery of the Rosetta Stone, the otherness of ancient Egyptian hieroglyphs was so great that they were incomprehensible texts. It was necessary for a sufficient level of commonality to be present in order for these texts to be readable. As Ricoeur explains, "'Appropriation' is my translation of the German term *Aneignung*. *Aneignung* means 'to make one's own what was initially 'alien'. It takes the place of the answer in the dialogical situation.'"[14] The reader neither rejects nor accepts the message of the text out of hand, but engages with it as a distinct voice such that a productive dialectic creates new understanding for her. Ricoeur writes, "Even when we read a philosophical work, it is always a question of entering into an alien work, of divesting oneself of the earlier 'me' in order to receive, as in play, the self-conferred by the work itself."[15] As Amherdt puts it, this dialectic is possible only because of the difference between the text's and the reader's perspectives, which creates new understandings.[16] The interaction may be confirmatory, challenging, or re-orienting.

Ricoeur explains that when reading the New Testament, we encounter its world(s) as "strangers" because of the "distance" or disjuncture between its culture and ours. As we seek to make it our own, we have two choices. First, we can follow an approach like Bultmann's "demythologization," which assumes the validity of our own culture and attempts to conform the New Testament text to modern concepts. As Ricoeur puts it, we as moderns "have a certain standard of what is physical, historical, true, false, believable, and unbelievable." Our culture provides the norm to which the text must be made to conform. Instead, Ricoeur argues for a process of "transferring ourselves into another universe of meaning and thereby putting ourselves at a kind of distance with regard to *our* actual discourse." We cannot relinquish the world understanding which permeates us, but we are able to question it and "struggle with the presuppositions of [modern] culture," in order to make possible an interrogation of a text which does not share those presuppositions. Hermeneutics is an endeavor to allow the text and the world that it projects to present a challenge to one's world. To do so, Ricoeur explains that we must question our assumptions that alienate us from the text's world. Such self-suspicion for moderns encountering the New Testament involves a suspicion of the extension of rationality which objectifies everything.[17]

As Taylor points out, Ricoeur counters the objection that we are trapped in our cultural and social traditions by arguing that the dialectic of explanation and understanding provides an opportunity for "distanciation" which allows us to recognize and critique our ideologies from the perspective which the text offers. However, we are not trapped in our social and cultural contexts; our encounters with an other through the world of the text offers us new possibilities for self- and world- understanding.[18] Relying on Ricoeur's work, Evans explains that on the one hand, the text challenges the reader's understanding of self and world by opening new possibilities for truth. On the other hand, the reader approaches the text with critical suspicion in order to question its ideologies and assumptions.[19]

According to Pellauer, Ricoeur considers hermeneutics to be based on the hope that the text has something to say to the reader, despite the difference between its world and that of the reader. Pellauer refers to this hermeneutical wager as the expectation that the message of the text is relevant in other contexts.[20] Distanciation provides not only the threat of unintelligibility but the prospect of change. It is through the reader's interaction with the text that previously held understandings of the world can be challenged, refuted, transformed, or confirmed by it. As Rogers notes, Ricoeur asserts that the reader is changed by her encounter with the textual world to such an extent that she becomes a different person.[21]

Appropriation depends upon the reader's openness to what is manifested or revealed by the text. First, this manifestation or revelation can disclose what had been forgotten or lost because of the conceptualizations and understandings of the world that that reader and her community possess. The text challenges and disrupts these prior concepts by presenting a new perspective on the world which enables the reader to perceive what had previously been impossible to discern. Second, the text also brings new truth into being. By forming a novel configuration of the world, it opens up new possibilities for life in that world. The imaginative work of a text is a productive one which transforms the reader by creating a new way for her to be in the world. The world, and the truth about the world, becomes different because the text shows it in a new way.

THE APPEAL OF THE TEXT

Today's reader must have motivation and justification in order to appropriate a text such as Mark 13. As previously explained, the text's description of the world must be relevant and significant in order for it to be appropriated. Relevance and significance are subjective parameters, in that the world situation and the reader's particular predispositions and preconceptions determine to a large extent what is relevant and what is significant. In addition to the relevance and significance of the text for the reader, I explore the possibility that Mark 13 is also true. A text is true when the reader does not reject the clarification, challenge, information or conceptualizations presented by the text as false. Textual truth extends beyond a verifiable description of historical events and includes information and perspectives about the world. Truth is more than accord with world referents but includes possibilities for world understandings. Texts which are explicitly fictive are able to be true because their truth value does not depend upon accord with historical events.

Shakespeare's *Romeo and Juliet* offers truth whether or not there existed in history two star-crossed young lovers, two feuding families, or even a city named Verona. The appropriation of Asimov's science fiction stories does not fail because the robots he describes do not exist. In both of these examples, the texts provide insights about the human condition, such as the power of love to overcome barriers and what it means to be a self-reflective being.

This section explains how texts are able to make truth claims that do not depend upon accord with verifiable past or present world reality. It considers the special nature of truth claims of apocalyptic texts such as Mark 13 as a particular form of fictive literature. It then examines and critiques Ricoeur's arguments for the distinctive nature of the Bible. I offer the conclusion that while non-historical texts in general and apocalyptic texts in particular are able to describe what is true, Ricoeur fails to demonstrate that the Bible necessarily offers a true world description based solely on factors inherent to the text itself.

Truth in Non-Historical Texts

Ricoeur explains that narrative provides innovation for human thought. It offers a perspective from which the world is viewed in a particular way. This "seeing as" is an emplotment of truth in order to organize time into meaningful wholes. Ricoeur describes this organization by emplotment as being valid for both historical as well as fictive narratives. In both cases, narratives creates a mimesis of reality. In fact, Ricoeur asserts that narrative provides a "three-fold mimesis," describing its aspects as pre-figuration, con-figuration, and re-figuration. Mimesis$_1$, or pre-figuration, is the lived world or event of the producer of the text. In the case of fiction, this lived world is not ostensive, but is an alternate possibility of what may be. Mimesis$_2$, or con-figuration, is the creation of a text as the emplotment of the prefigured world which provides a "seeing as if" of the world. Mimesis$_3$, or re-figuration, occurs in the process of reading the text as the worlds of the reader and the text intersect.[22]

For a text to express truth, it does not need to be a verifiable configuration of world happenings. Fiction, as well as history, is able to present truth. For Brabant, the difference between history and fiction is the degree of emphasis on either representation of the objective world or construction of a possible world.[23] When Ricoeur distinguishes between history and fiction as two forms of narrative, he does not employ conventional understandings of history as "true" and fiction as "not true." He describes historical narrative as a "standing-for" of the past which no longer exists because of the passage of time, but which has created "traces" that have been preserved, from which the narrative constructs the past. Fictional narrative, while not "standing-for" anything in history, converges with the world of the reader in such a way as to alter the reader's perception of that world. The fictional narrative in this way comes to "stand for" the reader's world through its dialectic with the reader's prior world-understanding.[24] Van der Heiden explains that fiction creates a distance for the reader from her everyday world, making it possible for another world to be disclosed. This other world, however, discloses aspects of the reader's world to which she would otherwise be blind.[25]

Ricoeur describes the difference between historical and fictional discourse as the difference between texts of first-order reference and those of second-order reference. The world, or reference, of the text is true not only if it relates to the ostensible, objective world, but as it is an expression of the lived world of the Dasein. For Ricoeur the aim of hermeneutics is not to discern the author's intentions nor to analyze textual structure and genealogy, but "to explicate the type of being-in-the-world unfolded *in front of* the text:" what the text actually presents, rather than the principles from which it develops. He seeks to re-describe the proposed world of the text in such a way that the reader projects her possibilities into it.[26] Caird likewise warns against considering figurative speech not to be true. He provides examples of hyperbole, understatement, irony, synecdoche (using a part to refer to the whole), metonymy (identifying a subject by naming an object associated with it), circumlocution, and legal fiction (such as treating an individual as a corporation) as non-literal speech acts that express truth.[27]

As Stiver notes, history and fiction are more similar than one may typically assume. Both require the author to construct a narrative out of the possibilities available to him. The process of configuring this story involves the author's creative imagination. To express truth, histories must conform to traces from the past, while fictions must conform to the lived experience of human existence. Further, it is a fallacy to conclude that absolute and final truth statements of any sort are possible, whether historical or fictive, because the pursuit of truth necessarily includes the ongoing project of knowing oneself.[28] That is, historical discourse attempts to present a reliable account of the past. Fiction as defined by Ricoeur, on the other hand, refers not to "that which is not true" (e.g. there never were feuding families named Montague and Capulet in Verona), but to "that which does not require a referent within the realm of historical human experience." Myth serves as an example of such a fictive text that expresses truth. It does not describe world occurrences, but it nonetheless provides understanding about the world and the human condition. That is, historical texts direct the reader toward a referent in the real world, while fictive texts direct her to a referent in a possible world. The fictive text is true if its referent captures the condition of human experience.

Historical narrative addresses truth as adequation or verification: conformity to existing norms and that which can be confirmed through observation. This observation includes the examination of the traces of past happenings which continue to exist, such texts and institutions. Fictive discourse manifests truth by revealing what would not otherwise be recognizable. Ricoeur points out that revelation, as a form of poetics, displays that which is otherwise hidden: "a proposed world, a world I may inhabit and wherein I can project my inmost possibilities."[29] Following Heidegger's understanding of truth as disclosure rather than proof, Ricoeur explains that revelation involves the process of "being made manifest, torn out of concealment." He relates this concept with his understanding of narrative and poetics as a re-description of the world in order to expose new aspects of it for the audience's contemplation.[30] But fiction does more than reveal what had been hidden by prior organizing paradigms of the world; it creates new truth by showing the world in a different way. According to Taylor, Ricoeur considers ideology and utopia, two forms of fictional discourse, to be "processes of imagination" which are invented through the creativity and invention of metaphoric re-categorization of the world. Each in their own way presents expressions of social possibilities for world-understanding. Ideologies function for Ricoeur as pictures seeking to be reproduced and preserved in the lived world. Utopias are imagination-as-fiction which seek to produce "possibilities above and beyond the given." They are alternative descriptions for reality that suggest a new way of being in the world. As Taylor suggests, utopia is a dream seeking actualization. The very presentation of possibility by the utopian text can shatter existing conceptions of the world.[31]

A presentation of truth through fictive texts (i.e. texts which do not depend upon world referents) is not simply a defective or limited presentation which could be more fully or completely described by historical texts (i.e. those with world referents). Fiction is able to make truth claims which are different from those that history offers. Following Ricoeur, Reinsdorf asserts that "Literature, freed from slavish adherence to fact, can and does reach further and deeper into human experience to reveal what is 'true,' which is not the facts of that experience, but the truths of human nature."[32] Truth, in this sense, is not about the facts of the world but the essence of being human. In describing Ricoeur's hermeneutics, Vanhoozer[33] and Gorospe[34] explain that fiction differs from history in that it creates new truth for the lived world of the reader, rather than describing what was already known. In fiction, the imaginary challenges and transforms understandings of that which is true As Ricoeur explains, the task of hermeneutics is "to explicate the sort of being-in-the-world unfolded in front of the text." For fictive and poetic texts, this world of being is different from the world of history, and it is this distanciation between the actual and the potential (i.e. possible but not necessarily true) which allows the reader to reorient her understanding of her lived world. The mimesis of the world which poetic discourse configures allows the reader to re-configure her awareness of being-in-the-world. She is able to imagine life as being different from what it actually is. In the same way, Ricoeur argues, religious texts reveal a new world with historical, cosmic and personal dimensions.[35] The reader is able to determine if the text's world is able to transform her lived world by her engagement with it.

There is a difference between fiction's operation as the presentation of possibility and its disclosure of reality. When it functions as possibility, fiction is a reconsideration of human potentialities, which is valuable as it requires the reader to rethink the inevitability of present structures. Some utopian texts, for example, evoke the reader's imagination for how things may be but are not. But when fiction functions as disclosure, it draws attention to aspects of human actualities. For example, *Romeo and Juliet* is a fictive text that describes the nature of love. The focus of this project is primarily upon fiction as disclosure rather than possibility. This is a critical difference if Mark 13 does something more than offer a fantasy to dream about. The predictions of vindication, glorification, and in-gathering are able to inspire hope only if the reader has reason to believe that they will be fulfilled in some way or if they are true descriptions of the current human condition. As Vanhoozer notes, "texts may project evil or false visions of the world." He cites examples in which the text's world "dehumanizes," or "legitimizes an authority that exceeds what the society is willing to accord it."[36] Fictional texts are able to present false world descriptions, but they are also able to be true in the sense that they reveal a new and different way to understand reality. The following section explains how apocalyptic texts are able to disclose new aspects of the human condition in this way, and how a reader can appropriate them.

Appropriation of Apocalyptic Texts

I explain below (pp. 45–46) that the Olivet discourse is an apocalyptic text. While Ricoeur does not describe this genre in anything more than a cursory way (a gap which is also present in the secondary literature related to Ricoeur), it is a form of poetic or fictive discourse with special features that allow it to present truth claims in a manner different from other genres. I provide an overall description of the apocalyptic genre and continue with a discussion of its distinctive temporal nature: a description of the future which purports not to be fictive but to be a configuration of historical referents. This section concludes with an argument that Mark 13 is an example of apocalyptic and that we can understand its truth claims in light of an understanding of this genre.

Description of Apocalyptic

In his seminal study of apocalyptic, J. Collins offers a formal definition of it as "a genre of revelatory literature with a narrative framework, in which a revelation is mediated by an otherworldly being to a human recipient, disclosing transcendent reality which is temporal." He explained that this is not meant to be a set of characteristics that must be met fully in each instance of the genre, but that it defines a framework for which particular texts can be evaluated.[37] J. Collins,[38] Grayston,[39] Hartman,[40] Koch,[41] Lacocque,[42] and Murphy[43] each offer a set of criteria to define the apocalyptic genre. To generalize from their descriptions, apocalyptic texts are pessimistic about the current situation and are marked by visions provided by spiritual or heavenly mediators which provide the author with insights not otherwise accessible to humans. These visions typically describe God's coming judgment against the powers of evil in the world, a cosmic catastrophe, the vindication of God's elect, and the establishment of a new paradise under God's rule. The visions usually are attributed to significant religious leaders from the past in order to gain credence, are highly symbolic[44], present a dualist worldview, contain few ethical injunctions, describe the influence of spiritual beings upon the affairs of humans, frequently include the figure of a mediator,[45] and describe history as a predetermined course of events under God's control.[46] Wright,[47] Caird,[48] and Beasley-Murray[49] represent critical consensus that Biblical apocalyptic texts express Jewish nationalistic hopes in situations of social and political powerlessness. Slater argues that apocalypticism is a social movement as much as it is a theological concept, seeking the reversal of the social order.[50] Apocalyptic discourse is an appeal to the eventful in-breaking of the divine into the time-space world at a time and under circumstances when conditions seem impossible for people to move out of hopelessness, oppression, and evil and into hope, unity, and goodness. Restoration or redemption is not possible from within the system itself, but require input that is not part of the time-space nexus. Apocalyptic hope seeks the intervention of something new that is not currently part of the military, political, diplomatic, economic, social, and religious frameworks. J. Collins points out that while apocalypses as a whole describe a "transcendent" eschatology, not all of them describe an "end of history" judgment.[51]

Ricoeur, in contrast, does not treat apocalyptic as a separate genre, but rather as either a combination of different genres,[52] or as a form of prophecy.[53] Like many Biblical scholars,[54] he describes apocalyptic as the embarrassing cousin in the family of Biblical genres. It is at best a derivative form that cheapens and degrades the much richer prophetic, and to a lesser extent wisdom, genres. That which had been addressed to humanity as a whole has become narrowly nationalistic. That which had been a call to ethical conduct now encourages passivity. Evocative symbols become simplistic allegories. Apocalyptic texts are limited to their particular historical context and represent the wistful dreams of oppressed people. Instead of motivating them to action and challenging them to self-reflection, apocalypticism provides an escapist hope that God will step into the realm of history and act for them. Their evil and oppressive enemies will be destroyed and they, the righteous elect, will be glorified. Apocalyptic literature is an opiate for self-satisfied people to castigate their enemies and congratulate themselves. J. Collins argues that Biblical scholars generally have a negative prejudice about apocalyptic literature because of its association with "fanatical millenarian" movements that use texts such as Daniel and Revelation to advance viewpoints that "more rational" academics find distasteful. They reject the texts because of the ways that they have been used and label them theologically suspect and historically derivative from the prophetic genre, which is conceptually and poetically superior.[55] Murphy adds that both academic and mainstream moderns object to apocalyptic because of its strange symbolism, its interpretive challenges, its failed predictions, and its problematic moral dualism.[56] J. Collins also points out that efforts to identify the source(s) of the apocalyptic genre emphasize its derivative nature. In contrast, he argues that the importance of the genre is determined not by the traditions or genres upon which it draws, but by the ways in which it combines, builds upon, or produces innovations from them. Apocalyptic literature is to be read in its own light, and not as a cheap knock-off of some higher, purer form. As Collins puts it, "The new product is more than the sum of its sources."[57]

When apocalyptic literature is not considered as a sad imitation of some other genre, a fuller interpretation of these texts is available. As J. Collins points out, identification of the apocalyptic genre is necessary if one wishes to employ form criticism as an exegetical approach. Having a "generic framework" of the genre allows the exegete to recognize the world-view of the texts that conform to it.[58] When freed from the perspective of being a derivative of prophecy, apocalyptic texts can be recognized to be appropriate for contexts of political, economic, and/or religious oppression.[59] This sets them in contrast to prophetic texts such as Amos, which are addressed to people with relative prosperity and power. For such people, a challenge for self-reflection and reform in order to be more faithful to God is apt. But when the audience is painfully aware of its suffering at the hands of the Seleucid or Roman Empire, a message of hope and a promise of deliverance is more suitable. People in despair need a message of hope to stir them to action, instead of a message of condemnation and punishment.[60] Stiver explains that readers who are oppressed and victimized by the powerful recognize them to be texts that engender "tremendous faith, courage, and hope." Apocalyptic texts are abused by those who seek to use them as a means of escape from their desperate circumstances rather than as a guide for engaging with them. According to Stiver, such misreadings tend to be based upon inappropriate literal interpretation of the texts. But when apocalyptic is recognized as symbolic discourse, it provides hope and promise in times of struggle.[61]

Second and more importantly, however, apocalyptic imagery is misunderstood when it is taken to be a spiritual figure for a historical circumstance; the triumph of God in the trope is then understood to indicate his future victory over historical oppressors. For example, the boastful little horn of Daniel 7 represents Antiochus Epiphanes, and the destruction of the horn, and the body from which it sprouts indicates the collapse of the Seleucid Empire. The text is merely a rhetorically ornamented device to predict Antiochus' demise.[62] On the other hand, apocalyptic texts can be read as what they purport to be: the unveiling or disclosure of spiritual realities which find, or will find, expression in the world of time and space. They offer insight into the events of history by noting their correlation to aspects of the spiritual world which are otherwise hidden from human perception. While the apocalyptic vision may arise from a particular historical situation (such as Antiochus' campaign against the Jews), it is not limited to that situation. It offers insight into subsequent similar historical situations, which it claims are also reflections in the physical world of dynamics in the spiritual world.[63] Thus Caligula can also be understood to be the boastful little horn; the same spiritual forces and figures from two centuries ago are apparent in the world once again.

The inclusion of apocalyptic as a distinct genre strengthens Ricoeur's strategy for interpretation of the Bible as a constellation of incomplete descriptions coming from multiple genres which operate together to testify to a common referent. It offers its own particular contributions toward the common testimony of the Biblical texts to the referent of the "Wholly Other" (cf. pp. 47–48). Apocalyptic is particularly well suited to Ricoeur's presentation of religious discourse because these texts explicitly direct the reader's attention to that which is foreign to human experience. It interprets historical events as traces of the activity of that which exists outside the boundaries of human experience. The Bible's apocalyptic texts claim that the spiritual dimension of the divine and the demonic (i.e. that which is beyond human experience) influence historical events. Interpreters who fail to recognize this referent-beyond-experience will conclude that apocalyptic literature is simply a banal treatment of worldly events. Diaz argues similarly in her Ricoeurian treatment of another apocalyptic text: "The visions [of Revelation] occur in a narrative form, have an enduring quality, and provide . . . tension between real and fictive life." In particular, she notes the juxtaposition of the ordinary and extraordinary as issues of typical life are presented with images that evoke the "other-worldly."[64] As J. Collins puts it, "Their abiding value does not lie in the pseudoinformation they provide about cosmology or future history, but in their affirmation of a transcendent world."[65]

Interpretation of apocalyptic texts as metaphor is more appropriate that the traditional consideration of them either literally or as allegory, as Murphy argues. Read literally, apocalyptic becomes simplistic description of objects external to the self that cannot fuel self-reflection or evoke the otherworldly. Read allegorically, apocalyptic texts are nothing but ciphers for objective world events and figures, unable to offer insight about "an unseen world that affects and is affected by this world."[66] Ricoeur proposes an alternate reading strategy that avoids these deficiencies. According to Amherdt, he explains that apocalyptic texts refer to the kingdom of God. The presence of paradox, hyperbole, and intensification disorients the reader from conventional world understanding and opens her to new descriptions of reality. These texts also employ temporal strategies which challenge understandings of the present by describing a future world.[67] Ricoeur further argues that apocalypticism presumes that the past is relevant and instructive for the present. "The establishment of an analogical relation between one situation and the other underlies the very operation of apocalyptic discourse." It is faithful to the norms of the genre itself for a modern reader to discern analogies between the worlds of the text (i.e. that of the actual author and that of the purported one) and her own situation. However, Ricoeur argues against the "detective game" of assigning a one-to-one correspondence between each apocalyptic image and a historical person or feature. Doing so ignores the evocative power of symbols to elicit new contextual understandings for readers in other historical settings.[68]

The world-configurations which apocalypse describes are a pertinent example of how fictive discourse discloses truth. As Frye notes, there is a similarity in the Greek between apocalypse (ἀποκάλυψις) as an uncovering or opening, and truth (ἀλήθεια) as an unveiling or removal of forgetfulness. Both words offer a sense of drawing attention to what has been repressed or hidden. What is shown is not merely what will occur in the future, but is also a deeper sense of the present situation. Frye points out, however, that while apocalypse exposes the significance of what is typically hidden, it does so in a way that preserves mystery and openness.[69] Apocalyptic narrative, in contrast to both history and traditional fiction, purports to emplot a truth claim about something that is not otherwise knowable to the reader. Like history, it makes a direct truth claim about world happenings, albeit about events that have not yet happened because they are in the future. Like fiction, the text has no world referent because it falls beyond the limits of human experience (or, in Gadamerian terms, is beyond the reader's horizon). However, unlike traditional fiction, the truth claims of apocalyptic depend upon the reader's acceptance that the text describes world happenings. The happenings that apocalyptic texts claim to describe are in the future, and so a consideration of how these texts describe time is appropriate.

The Temporal Nature of Apocalyptic

Apocalyptic texts relate to time differently from more conventional narratives. Ricoeur's consideration of time in relation to narrative is informative as we seek to understand this feature of apocalypticism. Following Aristotle, he distinguishes narrative-as-history from narrative-as-poetry by explaining that history is a description of what happened, whereas poetry is a description of what could happen.[70] Apocalyptic writing is a form of poetry which describes not what could have happened (in the past), but what will happen (in the future). If an apocalyptic text offers a presumably ostensive reference relating to time, such as Mark 13:30's temporal referent based upon "this generation," a reader from our later perspective could conclude that the apocalyptic "what will happen" has become a historical statement of "what did happen." In the case of Mark 13, this would be a false historical statement: "all these things" which were predicted to have happened within the time of the generation did not take place. However, if the text continues to be read today as poetry rather than as history, with the only difference being that it can now be understood as "what could have happened" rather than "what could happen," the text continues to evoke meaning for the reader.

Read as history (i.e. a configuration of reality, albeit of a future and not a past reality) apocalyptic can be validated or invalidated when events that are future at the time when the text was written become past for the reader: when the referent of the text has taken place. If the text configures an event that does not happen, it is false. On the other hand, apocalyptic texts which are read as poetry evoke events and a world that may be, which is different from events that have happened and the world as it currently is. If the descriptions offered by apocalyptic pass from future possibilities to events that do not happen, apocalyptic becomes a more conventional poetic text; it describes what could have been. When this happens, the forward-looking quality of the text continues to encourage expectation for what may still lie in the future for the reader, even if the ostensive referent of the text now lies in the reader's past. To encounter the world of the apocalyptic text is to encounter a world that is perpetually in the future because it is in the future for the text itself. The challenge for the reader is to accept the text's world as that which is future, even if the text contrives an ostensive reference to that which is past for the reader.

Ricoeur points out that narrative does not always follow the "arrow of time" by moving progressively through chronology from the beginning through the intervening points of time to the end. Narrative can operate from a "sense of an ending" and configure events in light of where they lead. According to Ricoeur, such narratives "read time itself backwards," in which the conclusion organizes the preceding events.[71] Apocalyptic narratives configure the world according to an expected conclusion of history, and they describe events according to how they lead to this culmination. They are distinctive because the terminus of the narrative lies in the future, both in the sense of a future which the narrative anticipates and in the sense of the future which has not yet happened. As Dunn explains, apocalyptic discourse does not adhere to the temporal flow of past to present to future, as other narrative styles do.

Because these texts interject the future into the past and present, the reader is not able to construct a comprehensive temporally-oriented narrative.[72] Likewise, in his description of apocalyptic texts, Dušek explains, "In most of them, there is a certain tension between the present and the future. The present refers to the future and, in such a way, the future interprets the present. The present is often characterized by a *secret* that shall be manifested as *true* in the future and by the presence of a *mendacious* that should be avoided as the *false* in the future."[73]

As Ricoeur puts it, history can be narrated only by virtue of the "traces" which remain from past events.[74] But apocalyptic texts claim to be configurations of traces of the future which can be found in the present. Because temporally progressive human experience cannot recognize traces of the future, these texts depend upon non-human agency to make the perception of these traces possible. Typically, these agencies depend upon a fantastic spiritual journey, such as Enoch's, or the mediation of a heavenly being, such as Daniel's messenger, to escape the limits of temporal progression and report about the future. For Mark 13, Jesus functions as the super-human mediator who can testify about what lies beyond human experience.[75]

The radical disjuncture between the present of the reader and the future of the apocalyptic text does not prevent the text-world from interacting with the reader-world. If we accept the premise that apocalyptic texts are chronicles of a future which is as fixed as the past is, we limit the potentials for understanding that the texts offer. When eschatologies are read only as narratives of the future, they are not able to suggest a configuration of the reader's world in the present. Ricoeur notes von Rad's assertion that apocalyptic texts present the future as fully determined in advance, and that they present an understanding of history which encourages the reader to become a passive observer of what God has already decided to do. However, Ricoeur agrees with LaCocquethat such a strict determinism is undercut by the illocutionary feature of the apocalyptic text itself. The text's identification of that which had been hidden and its exhortation for its readers to understand and act in a certain way is part of the process by which this predetermined future is actualized. He also notes that apocalyptic texts contain an inherent mystery and openness. Even though they claim that the future is already set, their presentation of that future is indeterminate.[76]

As Chmielewski puts it, the future impinges upon present action in two ways. First, the expected future is that toward which production in the present is directed: the future in this sense offers a teleology to shape action. Second, the unexpected or surprising future touches present action, in what Chmielewski calls "insuring or hedging defenses."[77] The unexpected, in this sense, is not truly unexpected because past experience has taught us to prepare for it. Nonetheless, the future impinges upon the present even in a non-teleological sense such as this. Apocalypse offers a third form of the future affecting the present. It leads people to expect the unexpected: to move the future's effect upon the present from Chmielewski's second sense to the first. If the future is moving toward a vindication of God and his people in the face of forces which appear to prevent such vindication, as apocalyptic texts claim, the present can be marked by confidence rather than despair and by actions of resistance rather than resigned submission. The present can be shaped in view of a future which apocalyptic texts present. However, because apocalyptic texts disclose a future which is radically disjunctive from the past and present, it does not conform to either of Chmielewski's categories. It is not a future which is informed by the past experience, including the experience of surprise and the unexpected, because of the discontinuity between the past and the future. Further, the testimony of the future which apocalyptic texts present is not merely a prediction of what will happen; it is a re-description of the present situation for the reader. It is a future which does not simply reside in the future (for example: "the time will come when God transforms the cosmos"); it is a future which re-orients the present. In the case of the Olivet discourse, the seemingly permanent and irresistible forces of the present are described as neither permanent nor irresistible. Because they will end, and because God's power is already at work to limit and subvert them, we are able to act differently in the face of them.

Ricoeur bases his bifurcation of narrative into historical and fictional primarily upon the historical presence or absence of the referent of the text. This distinction is problematic for texts which describe future events as if they are as concrete and real as conventional histories. The discourse of Mark 13, for example, does not function purely as a fictional narrative that offers a possible but unreal world: a utopia to be held in creative tension with the lived world of the reader. Nor, however, does it function as an emplot-ment of actual events: the presentation of real-world facts in a particular way so as to challenge the reader to schematize the world in a new fashion. Mark 13 does not do the former because it purports to be a description of reality. Nor does it do the latter because the events which it describes have not happened yet; that which is potential is not real, although traces of it may be evident in the present. Mark 13 purports to be a reverse history: a telling of events in the future whose reality is as certain as events in the past like the Babylonian conquest and the Maccabean revolt. We can read *Romeo and Juliet* and be challenged by the world it presents even if the Montagues and Capulets do not exist and never did. The claim that these texts make upon the reader does not rest upon the real-world presence of the referent, but the claim of Mark 13 does. Its description of the vindication of the elect and of the downfall of destructive powers at the coming of the Son of Man provides hope and a motivation for perseverance through distress only if it is a description of future historical reality.

If apocalyptic is a text which speaks of a time that is future in relation to the time of its writing but is past for today's reader, what is the temporal relationship between the world of the text and the modern reader? If the story is about something which will happen in the future, it can be read before the events have actually happened. And, assuming that these events do take place (i.e. there is a pre-figuration of the text that makes it history instead of fiction), the story can also be read after they have taken place. However, the text itself cannot tell the reader where she stands temporally in relation to the event. Ostensive references in the text (such as dates or pointers like "next year" or "after the winter") are necessarily artificial once the text has gained its autonomy from the context of its production. In the case of Mark 13, "this generation" never passes away because there is always a generation. It is the same trick of ostensive reference by which "tomorrow" never arrives because when the next day comes, it is no longer "tomorrow" but "today." It is in the reader's process of re-figuring the narrative in her temporal setting that she must determine whether it is still about a future happening, it has already taken place, or the events are taking place at the time of the reading.

Temporal designation of the text's world need not be considered in this linear fashion, however. As Brabant puts it, "There is a cosmological time that cannot be reconciled seamlessly within phenomenological time."[78] Rather than considering time to be an objective fourth dimension of reality, it is best understood as an aspect of an individual's lived world. For a veteran suffering from Post-Traumatic Stress Disorder, the horrors of combat are not in his past; he experiences them existentially as being in the present. The subjective experience of time does not always conform to a progression of past, present, and future. Our unfortunate war veteran experiences in the present that which objectively is in the past. Conversely, that which is in the future objectively can be experienced as being in the present; this is the approach of apocalyptic texts such as Mark 13.[79] While any reasonable observer may note that the stars continue to hang placidly in the night sky and that God's elect continue to be dispersed across the globe, a reader who apprehends the world of Mark 13 experiences in the present a world which objectively lies in the future. Wallace makes a similar point when he relies upon Ricoeur's hermeneutics to propose a literary unity across the Gospel of Mark in which predicted events (that which will happen) actually occur (that which did happen). The result is a sense that the events of Jesus' ministry are the fulfillment or overflow of cosmic hope. Events which were predicted, not with the force of expectation or aspiration but with the conviction that the future is as real as the past, unfold according to the text's description of them.[80]

Ricoeur's call for the reader to project herself into the world of the text takes an interesting twist with apocalyptic texts because they point to a world that has not yet happened. The role of the reader in such a projection is a call to watch (βλέπετε), in order to understand future events (i.e. future in relation to the event of the text's production, but present in relation to the reader) and figure them according to the narrative structure provided by the text. To project oneself into the world of an apocalyptic text is to ask the question: How do present events conform, or fail to conform, to the world that the text produces? Or again, how can the narrative be a frame or structure by which these events can be understood? In this sense, because the text directs our attention to that which is not yet actual, it is an incomplete discourse. It purports to present events that have not yet happened. It calls upon the reader to complete its own meaning-production.

Mark 13 as an Apocalyptic Text

For the preceding discussion of apocalyptic texts to be relevant to this project, it is necessary to demonstrate that Mark 13 functions as apocalyptic. The preceding description of the genre allows for this evaluation. A number of scholars measure the Olivet discourse against the features of the apocalyptic genre to determine whether it qualifies an example, and the results are decidedly mixed. Nickelson,[81] Hartman,[82] Brandenburger,[83] and Beasley-Murray[84] each outline characteristic features of apocalyptic and conclude that Mark 13 conforms sufficiently to these criteria. Other scholars who conduct this same exercise, however, reach less conclusive results. Grayston,[85] Slater[86] and Gundry[87] note that it lacks several essential aspects of apocalyptic literature, such as a conflict between good and evil, a new cosmology, and a comprehensive chronology. Pesch characterizes the Olivet discourse as an anti-apocalyptic, proposing that Mark adapts an apocalyptic pamphlet to mitigate its eschatological fervor after the temple's destruction.[88] A. Collins identifies Mark 13 as a scholastic dialogue with prophetic or apocalyptic content,[89] functioning as a farewell address.[90] Shively contends that Mark 13 is not an example of the apocalyptic genre, because it bears too much affinity with other genres. She does concede, however, that it is an expression of "an apocalyptic imagination."[91]

Any attempt to define Mark 13 as an apocalyptic text should be recognized as relative rather than absolute. A particular instance of apocalyptic writing will not conform completely to the genre's parameters. J. Collins, who subdivides the genre into two sub-types, lists six features of "historical" apocalypses;[92] Mark 13 includes five of these six features.[93] An evaluation of Mark 13 based on Lacocque's description of apocalyptic[94] also reveals that this discourse matches the overall characteristics of the apocalyptic genre, albeit with some modifications.[95] Under J. Collins' definition of apocalyptic,[96] Mark 13 qualifies as an example of apocalyptic literature. It has a narrative framework, a revelation is provided to the human disciples, and Jesus is the otherworldly mediating agent.[97] The discourse provides both temporal and spatial descriptions of a supernatural (i.e. non space-time) world. The most significant distinctions between Mark 13 and more typical apocalyptic texts are that there is no description of a vision and the human agents are normal people, either still alive or only recently deceased, rather than religious notables from antiquity. Instead of viewing these considerations as criteria for rejecting the discourse's apocalyptic credentials, I recognize these variations from the norms of the genre as a way that the text challenges the audience with new understandings.[98] While Jesus neither describes a vision of his own nor provides one for the four inquiring disciples, a text need not conform to all aspects of a genre to be counted as an example of it. And while Peter, James, John, and Andrew are not in the same league with notables such as Moses, Abraham, and Enoch, two of them were significant figures in the early Christian movement and their teaching and leadership provided much of the impetus for it. Setting them in an equivalent role with religious all-stars from the past serves to promote their importance, and by extension the legitimacy of their message.

Ricoeur on the Bible's Distinctiveness

Ricoeur attempts to demonstrate that the Biblical canon is distinctive: that is, that it presents a true configuration of the world.[99] If he succeeds, and if he can show that all of the elements of the whole share this trait, then Mark 13 can be appropriated as a true text. As this section demonstrates, a major flaw in Ricoeur's Biblical hermeneutics lies in his failure to demonstrate that the reader is justified in accepting the truth of the text, based on a quality inherent to the canon as a whole. He offers several options, each of which is problematic because they are not features of the text itself or because they depend upon the reader's prior commitment to the text. This section examines each of them. Because Ricoeur is unable to argue successfully for the distinctiveness of the Bible in this regard, appropriation of Mark 13 as a true text depends upon either a non-Ricoeurian argument for the truth of the Biblical canon, or an argument for the truth of Mark 13 specifically and not the Bible generally. In Chapter 6, I argue the latter: that Mark 13 is able to be true because of its status as a metaphor.

This section evaluates four of Ricoeur's arguments for the Bible's ability to make truth claims: its acceptance by a faith community, its distinctive referent, its expression of limit experiences, and its function as a polyphonic description of God. None is able to demonstrate the ability of the Bible to present truth claims in a manner that is inherent to the text, rather than dependent upon the prior commitments of the reader.

The Text of a Faith Community

Ricoeur explains that when a text has been identified as canonical, the community which provides such an identity commits itself to the text as authoritative. He explains that such faith-oriented reading is the activity of a circle comprising the text, the reading of the text, and the community which provides a tradition regarding the text.[100] While the community's sense of the text as a canonical authority informs the reader's approach, it does not control the reader's understanding because of the presence of multiple traditions within the community regarding the text.[101] Kenny notes that Ricoeur's program for reading religious texts depends foundationally upon the religious community, most notably for the identification of the textual canon which figures importantly in his work.[102] According to Dickinson, Ricoeur identifies the canon as the collection of texts that nurture "happy memory," as discovered by a community. The constantly changing nature of community precludes the fixed identity of a canon and makes possible its "continuing creation" instead.[103] Thus the canon becomes a product of the community rather than an authority for it. Kelsey explains in addition that this approach "ascribes no property to the texts whose presence in them could be checked out independently of the judgment itself."[104] An argument for the truth claim of the Bible as the Scripture of a faith community depends upon that community's commitment to the text's authority, not upon an inherent feature of the text to describe truth.

Distinctive Referent

Ricoeur bases his most significant argument for the distinctive nature of the Bible upon the special nature of its referent.[105] He explains that religious texts direct the readers' attention away from "immediate signification toward the Wholly Other." Ricoeur asserts that interpretations of religious texts must recognize them as a "point of encounter with the infinite."[106] He describes the reference of the text as the "extralinguistic reality" of "lived experience that is brought to language." In religious discourse, the referent is God. Ricoeur claims that religious texts uncover or reveal that which cannot otherwise be perceived in ordinary life experience, that is, traces of God in the world.[107] Following Marin, Ricoeur suggests that structuralist explanations of Biblical texts reveal a "hole" in the text: "an extra-linguistic being [designated] by the *residues* of the system" of the text. That is, inherent to the text is an openness which cannot be fully explicated by structural analysis. The text refers to an Other that is not contained within the linguistic code.[108]

Ricoeur explains that religious language (i.e. discourse about God) differs from other forms of discourse because of the unique referent of "God" to which it is directed. This reference to God, or "naming of God," as Ricoeur put is, occurs both through the description of God by means of conventional schemas (e.g. God as monarch, judge, parent, and servant), but also through limit-expressions (discussed below) which subvert conventional configurations. These limit-expressions undermine the tendency to turn the conventions into "idols:" understandings of God that are limited to the conventional categorizations used to describe him and that limit God to these categorizations in the process.[109] However, Ricoeur's description of the unique referent of the Bible depends upon two premises that he fails to support. First, he assumes the existence of a Wholly Other (conventionally named God). Second, he asserts rather than demonstrates that the texts of the Biblical canon are united by a shared referent rather than by some other consideration, whether inherent to the text or imposed upon it. Without support for these premises, Ricoeur's argument for a unique Bible referent fails.

Limit Expression

For Ricoeur, a religious text is the expression of a limit experience. A limit experience is an encounter with the Wholly Other at the boundaries of human existence. These liminal experiences disrupt ordinary human knowing in a totalizing and universal manner and suggest the presence of beings or forces beyond human experience which impinge upon it. In conventional religious discourse, the referent for these limit expressions is "God," and the spiritual or supernatural is that which is beyond ordinary experience. Regarding religious discourse, Ricoeur writes, "I speak of the Wholly Other only insofar as it addresses itself to me; and the kerygma, the glad tidings, is precisely that it addresses itself to me and ceases to be Wholly Other. Of an absolutely Wholly Other I know nothing at all. But by its very manner of approaching, of coming, it shows itself . . . as Wholly Other by annihilating its radical otherness."[110] Human discourse can address only what is part of human experience. In order for that which lies beyond human experience to be part of human discourse (assuming that there is something beyond human experience), it must enter human experience. Whatever it reveals of itself indicates that there is a "that-which-is-beyond-human-experience." Such a revealing is an intrusion into human experience and discourse by something from outside. The purported double-voiced nature of Biblical texts (i.e. the voice of the human author and that of the divine) allows the texts to bear testimony "from somewhere else" beyond human experience.[111]

According to Ricoeur, our ability to conceive of the absolute and unconditioned is not based upon what we experience, but on our ability to imagine an order of reality beyond our experience. Religious discourse provides a logic of meaning at odds with the logic of correspondence between the thing and the thing signified. "The logic of limit-expressions" does away with the normal sense of reference of language in order to open the way for a "new dimension of reality" beyond that which would otherwise be perceived. The mundane or "surface" meaning of the text is reversed so dramatically that the text can no longer be read at that level: one must either discard it as nonsense or discern a new orientation for meaning.[112] Religious texts violate conventional patterns of discourse in such a way as to redefine human experience. Ricoeur describes the referent of such texts as "human experience centered around the *limit-experiences* which would correspond to the *limit-expressions* of religious discourse." Biblical hermeneutics is the attempt to describe the world of these texts which are expressions of human experience at the borders of that experience and testify to that which lies beyond those borders.[113] For Ricoeur, limit experiences are literally extra-ordinary; they cannot be comprehended by association with ordinary life. Citing the experiences of survivors of the Nazi death camps as an example, he writes, "The experience to be transmitted is that of an inhumanity with no common measure with the experience of the average person." Ricoeur considers this to be a "crisis of testimony:" how can one describe or inscribe an experience that is utterly foreign to one's audience?[114] While a Holocaust survivor's experience is quite different from that of an individual who purportedly experiences an apocalyptic vision, they share the quality of having gone through an experience which is incomprehensible for other people.

Ricoeur explains that limit-experiences impose a total demand upon the entire person, and that they offer a schema that is universally significant.[115] Limit experiences are points at which contingent human experience connects with a universal human condition in a way that reorients the individual's self-awareness. This reorientation moves the individual beyond her own experience to an awareness of that which is beyond her contingency.[116] As Amherdt describes it, Ricoeur's understanding of religious discourse is one of disorientation from normal world-understanding to provide a reorientation to the superabundance of God. Limit-expressions are the eruption of the extraordinary, strange, and implausible into ordinary existence. These expressions refer to the experience of the "kingdom of God" as the Wholly Other or the transcendent. The limit expressions of the gospels, and the parables in particular, describe the extravagance of the kingdom of God through the violation of conventional narrative standards.[117]

The apocalyptic genre is particularly well suited for the expression of a limit experience and does so more intentionally than the other Biblical genres which Ricoeur identifies. Apocalyptic texts explicitly describe the impingement of the transcendent (i.e. that which is beyond human knowing and experience) upon the sphere of ordinary existence. Typically for these texts, this impingement takes the form of a spiritual being interacting with an individual, a person's experience of "heavenly" places (i.e. not part of the perceivable world), and/or descriptions of future events. Each of these is extraordinary, in the sense that it is not characteristic of typical human experience. As limit-experiences, they describe the totalizing influence of universal forces upon contingent situations.

Ricoeur's explanation that religious texts are limit-expressions depends upon the effect that these texts may have upon a reader and not upon a distinctive quality inherent to them. One cannot claim that a text is universalizing and transformative because it is a limit-expression. Instead, one may recognize that it is a limit-expression because it is universalizing and transformative. A text's identification as a limit-expression does not make it distinctive; its distinctiveness means that it is a limit-expression. Ricoeur's discussion of the Bible as a limit-expression describes what it means to say that it is distinctive. But it does not demonstrate that the Bible is distinctive.

Multiple Naming of God

Ricoeur explains that because of the special nature of the Bible's referent, it employs a variety of language strategies or genres to describe it. Each genre provides an incomplete description of God, but the constellation of different genres are able to do together what each is unable to do alone.[118] For Ricoeur, religious language is "a polyphonic language maintained by the circularity of the forms." God-referential discourse appears in multiple genres in order to provide "meaningful contrasts" through which a referent can be discerned that cannot be fully understood through a single genre.[119] Ricoeur explains that "God is named in turn as the target of and the vanishing point outside each discourse and the whole of them."[120] According to him, each genre delivers content in ways different from the others. The reader must therefore engage with the various Biblical genres together in order for the common referent to be understood. The prescriptions of the Torah, for example, depend upon an awareness of their relationship with the God of the exodus to whom narrative texts refer. The prophetic proclamation is in dialectic relationship with these commands, and so on.[121]

Within the Bible, Ricoeur identifies five genres or "forms of discourse" which offer a "pluralistic, polysemic" testimony to the reference of this faith: prophetic, narrative, prescriptive, wisdom, and hymnic discourse.[122] In "The Self in the Mirror of the Scriptures," Ricoeur explains that this list of Biblical genres serves as examples of what can be found in the Bible without being comprehensive.[123] Although he typically employs this five-fold explanation of Biblical genres, Ricoeur also accepts Jewish tradition by describing the

Old Testament as Torah, Prophets, and Writings (Tanakh).[124] And, following Perrin, he identifies parables, proverbs, and eschatological sayings as three different genres of Jesus sayings that mutually support each other in their description of the kingdom of God.[125]

For Ricoeur, there is an important relationship between the mode in which something is said (i.e. its literary genre) and what is being said in that mode. That which is expressed through prophecy, for example, cannot be conveyed through narrative. Each genre expresses content appropriate for that particular genre. They operate together, in tension, to refer to what cannot be expressed fully in either mode by itself. As Ricoeur puts it, "Religious language appear[s] as a polyphonic language sustained by the circularity of its forms."[126]

Ricoeur suggests that a text is able to be read in different and even opposing ways, depending upon its genre identification. He explains that the Song of Songs can be read both as a wisdom text that describes nuptial love and as a prophetic text that deals with God's love for his people. The first is a literal reading; the second is metaphorical. For Ricoeur, the intersection of these readings does not mean that the reader must choose one over the other. To the contrary: the power of the text comes from its ability to bring together both meanings in such a way that both influence the other and provide evocative new truth as a result. He further points out that violations of genre identification (wisdom and prophetic literature in the case of the Song of Songs) do not confound the reader's quest for meaning but enrich it. "Let us therefore allow these texts to project themselves on one another and let us gather those sparks of meaning that fly up at their points of friction."[127] The use of multiple genres to describe a referent, however, confirms neither the uniqueness of the referent nor the truthfulness of the texts. For example, my wife can be described by her medical chart, a school transcript, and by a love poem I write for her. Each individually is an incomplete description of her, but when they are taken together they give a fuller testimony. This use of multiple genres to describe my wife does not demonstrate that she is a unique referent. More importantly, texts from different genres that refer to the same referent are not necessarily all true, even if some of them could be proven to be so. There could be errors in my wife's medical chart even if the school transcripts are accurate and my love poem is appropriately evocative.

Each of Ricoeur's four arguments for the distinctiveness of the Bible is lacking. The fact that it is an authoritative text for a faith community speaks only to that community's experience of the text. Ricoeur does not succeed in demonstrating that the Biblical texts share a significant and perhaps unique referent. His exposition of Biblical texts as limit-expressions is a description of what it means to call them distinctive and not an argument for their distinctiveness. Finally, a single referent can be described in multiple genres without being transcendent. With Rogers,[128] Kelsey,[129] Amherdt,[130] and McCarthy,[131] I conclude that Ricoeur's arguments for the appropriation of the Bible depend upon his theological commitments, and not upon features of the text itself.

The Challenge of the Yale School

Frei and other members of the "Yale School," including Frei, Kelsey, and Lindbeck, object to Ricoeur's Biblical hermeneutics on three counts. They charge first that Ricoeur privileges theory over text, second that he fails to account for the distinctive nature of the Bible, and third that his consideration of the world of the texts is divorced from the real or historical world. This section explores the second and third of these concerns in order to determine whether Ricoeur is able to demonstrate that the Bible presents truth.[132]

For Ricoeur to counter the critique of the Yale School that he fails to describe why the Bible is a distinctive text, he must demonstrate that there is something inherent to the text itself which warrants its appropriation. In fact, not only does Ricoeur provide no argument that the Bible is a distinct and special discourse, but he claims that such an argument is not possible.[133] However, while Frei charges that Ricoeur fails to explain the distinctiveness of Biblical texts, Fodor counters that Frei does so in a way that turns the Bible and its readers into a ghetto of its own making. It operates as an isolated system with no possible connection with texts outside itself.[134] Frei's understanding of the Bible prevents conversation with others who do not accept the authority of the Bible. Fodor explains that Frei at this point is open to the same charge that he levels against Ricoeur: imposing prior philosophical or theological standards upon the text.[135] Even if we accept Fodor's critique of Frei's argument for Biblical distinctiveness, however, it does not rescue Ricoeur's argument. Frei raises the issue; his inability to deal with it adequately does not dismiss the issue itself. The approaches of both Ricoeur and his Yale detractors require a prior commitment to the nature of the Biblical text. For the members of the Yale School, it is their insistence that the Bible is unique and must be dealt with uniquely. For Ricoeur, it is the distinctive nature of the text's referent. The best defense Ricoeur can offer is a circular argument: the multiple naming of God in the Biblical canon indicates that the referent is something outside of human experience, which must therefore be referred to in multiple ways.

Ricoeur and Frei also disagree about how the Bible presents truth. As Vanhoozer explains, Frei claims that the truth of the Bible, and of the gospels in particular, depends upon a literal sense that its descriptions correspond to reality. For Ricoeur, what matters most is the text's testimony to truth beyond the literal that creates a potential.[136] Frei complains that Ricoeur disconnects the text from reality, relegating it to its own self-enclosed virtual world. In the case of the New Testament, the words and actions of Jesus become nothing more than descriptions of what is consistent with the world-description of the text and not of real-world activity. Frei understands this to mean that the emphasis for meaning-production lies with the reader and not the text, even though this runs counter to Ricoeur's explicit explanations.[137] Ricoeur and Frei agree that the reference of the text should be understood clearly through its sense.[138] But for Frei, a text refers to the extra-linguistic world and not to a configured world of the text.[139] He asserts that the literal Jesus story is the central motif of the Christian New Testament, and figurative components such as parables are to be understood as they relate to the primary literal story. The "plain meaning" of the text is the literal meaning, not a spiritualized one.[140] Frei argues that Jesus' identity comes from the story presented by the text itself, not from "tearing asunder the person and his story."[141]

Frei argues for literal understanding of the Bible but not for acceptance of its historicity. Without making any claims about the historicity of the New Testament's description of Jesus, Frei argues that his identity can be recognized through the "history-like" nature of its narratives, which distinguishes them from myth.[142] Fodor explains that Frei's contention is not that the literal sense of the gospels must match actual events, but that concern over the historicity of the text should not overshadow its literal meaning. For Frei, the message of the text comes from its literal meaning, regardless of how it accords with actual events. When we concern ourselves with the congruence of history with the narrative, or with figurative rather than literal meaning, we step away from that which the Bible presents. For Frei, Fodor explains, it is the story that matters, not the story's congruence with history or figurative meanings which can be construed from it.[143]

A defense of Ricoeur's hermeneutics on this challenge begins with an inquiry into the importance of the text's relationship to the real world. For Ricoeur, what matters most is not the text's ability to report reality but to manifest truth. Amherdt questions the distinction between the Yale School's characterization of the Bible as "history-like" and Ricoeur's description of it as poetics. "History-like" is not history; the Yale School does not claim that the Bible records events as they actually happened. And Ricoeur's understanding of poetics does not draw a sharp distinction between history and fiction; the text's ability to evoke something new is more important than its accord with world happenings.[144] Ricoeur fails to explain how the text's presentation can be considered to be an insight into reality, apart from the readers' sense of being captivated by it. Similarly, however, Frei fails to explain how a text's "history-like" presentation relates to the reader's lived world. Byrd notes that Ricoeur's hermeneutics deals not with the historicity of the Biblical narrative, but with the way that the experience of the text is able to become the experience of the reader.[145] Reinsdorf charges that while

Frei claims that the Biblical text presents an account for the reader, he does not explain how the text persuades the reader to accept its account.[146] Fodor argues that Frei tends to conflate meaning and truth when reading the Bible; the fact that the text means something does not lead to the conclusion that the meaning is truth. This betrays Frei's commitment to the text's authority, which guides his project. For him, the text does not open a possibility for the reader to encounter but describes a certainty which binds the reader.[147] Fodor's challenge to Frei applies equally to Ricoeur. While Ricoeur presents a different argument for the world which the text presents, he is also unable to show how the text's description could be true.

Wallace summarizes the issue of the truth of the Biblical texts well when he points out that there is no proof of the God-referent of these texts. The reader may potentially presuppose that the God to which these texts testify is real, but this testimony can only be validated and not verified.[148] Ultimately, Ricoeur is unable to demonstrate how the success of a wager, i.e. the initial guess about the text, can be determined. The truth, or lack of truth, in Mark 13 can only be discerned or evaluated as the reader engages with the text; it cannot be determined prior to the act of reading the text. But as the opening section of this chapter explains, this reading must be conducted with an attitude of openness to the world that the text presents, and not with an insistence that the text must conform to her prior world conceptualization.

While Ricoeur offers a helpful description of how a reader is able to appropriate a fictional text as truth, he does not provide a way for the reader to determine the truth of Mark 13 specifically or of the Bible generally. The best one can do is to be open to the possibility that it is able to be true, and to determine if this possibility is validated or negated by explanatory efforts. The following chapter engages in this analysis in order to determine if Mark 13 is able to be true.

NOTES

1. Ricoeur, "Appropriation," 192.
2. B. H. McLean, *Biblical Interpretation and Philosophical Hermeneutics* (Cambridge, New York: Cambridge University Press, 2012), 302–05.
3. Paul Ricoeur, "Metaphor and the Main Problem of Hermeneutics," in *The Philosophy of Paul Ricoeur: An Anthology of His Work*, eds. Charles E. Reagan and David Stewart (Boston: Beacon Press, 1978), 139–43.
4. Ricoeur, "Model of the Text," 148–49.
5. Paul Ricoeur, *The Rule of Metaphor: Multi-Disciplinary Studies of the Creation of Meaning in Language*, trans. Robert Czerny (Toronto: University of Toronto Press, 1977), 220.

6. James J. DiCenso, *Hermeneutics and the Disclosure of Truth: A Study in the Work of Heidegger, Gadamer, and Ricoeur* (Charlottesville: University of Virginia, 1990), 127–30; cf. Theo L. Hettema, *Reading for Good: Narrative Theology and Ethics in the Joseph Story from the Perspective of Ricoeur's Hermeneutics*, in Studies in Philosophical Theology (Kampen, Netherlands: Kok Pharos, 1996), 32; Kevin J. Vanhoozer, *Biblical Narrative in the Philosophy of Paul Ricoeur: A Study in Hermeneutics and Theology* (Cambridge: Cambridge University Press, 1990), 89.

7. David E. Klemm, *The Hermeneutical Theory of Paul Ricoeur: A Constructive Analysis* (Lewisburg PA & London: Bucknell University Press & Associated University Presses, 1983), 86–90.

8. McLean, *Biblical Interpretation*, 245.

9. Ricoeur, "Appropriation," 182–83.

10. John McCarthy, "Script to Scripture: Multivalent Textuality," *Annali di Storia dell'Esegesi* 30.2 (2013): 355.

11. Ricoeur, "Appropriation," 186–87.

12. Ibid., 191.

13. Bultmann considers this to have been the case for New Testament texts, and offers his project of demythologization as a way to make the texts comprehensible for moderns (Jesus Christ, 11–16).

14. Ibid., 185; cf. Ricoeur, "What Is a Text," 118–19; *Ricoeur Interpretation Theory*, 43.

15. Ricoeur, "Appropriation," 190.

16. François-Xavier Amherdt, *L'herméneutique Philosophique de Paul Ricoeur et Son Importance pour L'exégèse Biblique: en Débat avec la New Yale Theology School* (Paris: Cerf; Saint-Maurice: Saint-Augustin, 2004), 131–33.

17. Ricoeur, "Language of Faith," 223–31; cf. Mark I. Wallace, *The Second Naiveté: Barth, Ricoeur, and the New Yale Theology* (Macon, GA: Mercer University Press, 1990), 59–60.

18. George H. Taylor, "Editor's Introduction," in *Lectures on Ideology and Utopia*, ed. George H. Taylor (New York: Columbia University Press, 1986), xxiv–xxvii.

19. Jeanne Evans, *Paul Ricoeur's Hermeneutics of the Imagination* (New York: Peter Lang, 1995), 134. Vanhoozer challenges the possibility for this dialectic between reader-world and text-world to take place. While Ricoeur explains that the reader is not to project her own understanding onto the text and is to abandon prior self-understandings in order to encounter the challenge of the text's possibilities for understandings, Vanhoozer points out, "there are as many worlds [of the text] as there are interpretations." That is, the reader's interaction with the text may devolve into a form of self-reaffirmation, in which the reader interprets the text according to his prior self- and world-understandings, such that the world of the text becomes a cipher of the reader's world and self. Vanhoozer argues that Ricoeur's hermeneutics is just as subjective as that of the Romantics, albeit in a more nuanced and sophisticated way. He doubts that Ricoeur offers a way for interpretation to move beyond the subjectivity of the self (Vanhoozer, Biblical Narrative,138–141). We may answer Vanhoozer's charge by highlighting the place of explanation in Ricoeur's description of the interpretive process. A proper suspicion must be applied not only to the text,

56   *Chapter 2*

but to the reader's understandings. An interpreter can never escape her subjectivity and cultural/social/linguistic framework. But a critical awareness of these factors may allow her to encounter a text that is radically other, such that she is able to discern new understanding.

20. David Pellauer, "Reading Ricoeur Reading Job," *Semeia* 19 (1981): 74; cf. Wallace, *Second Naiveté*, 27; Amherdt, *L'herméneutique Philosophique*, 79–80, 378–85.

21. William E. Rogers, "Ricoeur and the Privileging of Texts: Scripture and Literature," *Religion & Literature* 18.1 (1986): 4–6.

22. Paul Ricoeur, *Time and Narrative*, Volume 1, trans. Kathleen McLaughlin (Chicago: University of Chicago Press, 1984), 52–77; cf. *Stiver, Ricoeur and Theology*, 47–50.

23. Christophe Brabant, "Ricoeur's Hermeneutical Ontology," in *Paul Ricoeur: Poetics and Religion*, eds J. Verheyden, T.L. Hettema, P. Vandecasteele (Leuven : Uitgeverij Peeters, 2011), 465.

24. Ricoeur, *Time and Narrative* 3, 100–101; cf. Hettema, *Reading for Good*, 43.

25. Gerrit Jan van der Heiden, *The truth (and Untruth) of Language: Heidegger, Ricoeur, and Derrida on Disclosure and Displacement* (Pittsburgh: Duquesne University Press, 2010), 83–85.

26. Ricoeur, "Hermeneutical Function," 85–6; cf. Keith D'Souza, "Ricoeur's Narrative Development of Gadamer's Hermeneutics: Continuity and Discontinuity" (PhD. dissertation, Marquette University, 2003), 30–1; Richard Rorty, "Is There a Problem About Fictional Discourse?" in *Consequences of Pragamatism* (Essays: 1972–1980) (Minneapolis: University of Minnesota Press, 1982), 134.

27. G.B. Caird, *Language and Imagery*, 131–43.

28. Stiver, *Ricoeur and Theology*, 48–9, 79–80, 120–23.

29. Ricoeur, "Toward a Hermeneutic," 102.

30. Ricoeur, "Canon" 11–12; cf. Gerald Bruns, "Against Poetry: Heidegger, Ricoeur, and the Originary Scene of Hermeneutics," in *Meanings in Texts and Actions: Questioning Paul Ricoeur*, eds. David E. Klemm and William Schweiker (Charlottesville, Va: Univ Press of Virginia, 1993), 36–8; Dan R. Stiver, *Life Together in the Way of Jesus Christ: An Introduction to Christian Theology* (Waco: Baylor University Press, 2009), 27–8, 88–9, 268.

31. Taylor, "Editor," xxviii–xxix.

32. Walter Reinsdorf, "How Is the Gospel True?" *Scottish Journal of Theology* 56.3 (2003): 341.

33. Vanhoozer, *Biblical Narrative*, 67–9.

34. Athena Evelyn O. Gorospe, "The Ethical Possibilities of Exodus 4:18–26 in Light of Paul Ricoeur's Narrative Theory: A Filipino Reading," (Th.D dissertation, Fuller Theological Seminary, 2006), 82–3.

35. Paul Ricoeur, "Philosophy and Religious Language," trans. David Pellauer, in *Figuring the Sacred: Religion, Narrative, and Imagination*, ed. Mark I. Wallace (Minneapolis: Augsburg Fortress, 1995), 42–4.

36. Vanhoozer, *Biblical Narrative*,105–8.

37. John J. Collins, *The Apocalyptic Imagination: An Introduction to Jewish Apocalyptic Literature*, 2nd ed. (Grand Rapids: Eerdmans, 1998), 4–5.

38. J. Collins, *The Apocalyptic Imagination*, 6–7.

39. K. Grayston, "The Study of Mark 13," *Bulletin of the John Rylands Library* 56 (1974): 379–80.

40. Hartman, *Prophecy Interpreted*, 23–49.

41. In J. Collins, *The Apocalyptic Imagination*, 12–13.

42. André LaCocque, *The Book of Daniel*, trans. David Pellauer (Atlanta: John Knox, 1979), 5–6; André LaCocque, Daniel in His Time (Columbia: Univ of South Carolina Press, 1988), 82–4.

43. Murphy, *Apocalypticism*, 6–14.

44. Reynolds asserts that not all apocalyptic literature is symbolic (Bennie H. Reynolds, *Between Symbolism and Realism: The Use of Symbolic and Non-Symbolic Language in Ancient Jewish Apocalypses 333–63 B.C.E.* (Göttingen: Vandenhoeck & Ruprecht, 2011), passim).

45. Cf. Lars Hartman, *Prophecy Interpreted: The Formation of Some Jewish Apocalyptic Texts and of the Eschatological Discourse Mark 13*, trans. N Tomkinson (Coniectanea Biblica. Lund: Gleerup, 1966), 54–70.

46. Cf. Robert J. Miller, "Introduction," in *The Apocalyptic Jesus: A Debate*, ed. Robert J. Miller (Santa Rosa, CA: Polebridge Press, 2001), 6; Dunn "Jesus and the Kingdom," 12–13.

47. N.T. Wright, *The New Testament and the People of God* (Minneapolis: Fortress Press, 1992), 280–88.

48. Caird, *Language and Imagery*, 261–65.

49. Beasley-Murray, *Jesus and the Kingdom of God*, 39–42.

50. Thomas B. Slater, "Apocalypticism and Eschatology: A Study of Mark 13:3–37," *Perspectives in Religious Studies* 40.1 (2013): 8.

51. J. Collins, *Apocalyptic Imagination*, 11.

52. Ricoeur, "Toward a Hermeneutic," 88.

53. Ibid., 76–7.

54. e.g. Lacocque, Daniel in His Time, 84–7, 127–28; George Raymond Beasley-Murray, "The Vision on the Mount: The Eschatological Discourse of Mark 13," *Ex Auditu* 6 (1990): 44; Marian Kay Diaz, "Creation, Prophecy and Fulfillment: A Ricoeurian Study of Revelation 22:1–5" (master's thesis, Catholic Theological Union, 1996), 47–8; J. Collins *Apocalyptic Imagination*, 1–2; Norman Perrin, *Jesus and the Language of the Kingdom: Symbol and Metaphor in New Testament Interpretation* (Philadelphia: Fortress Press, 1976), 26–7, 30–1, 44.

55. J. Collins, *Apocalyptic Imagination* , 1–2.

56. Murphy, *Apocalypticism*, 379–84.

57. J. Collins, *Apocalyptic Imagination*, 20–1

58. Ibid., 8.

59. Cf. Ibid., 37–39; Wright, *New Testament and the People of God*, 287–88.

60. Cf. J. Collins, *Apocalyptic Imagination* , 41.

61. Stiver, *Life Together*, 438–40, 471.

62. Cf. e.g. C.L. Seow, *Daniel* (Louisville, KY: Westminster John Knox Press, 2003), 106; W. Sibley Towner, *Daniel* (Atlanta: John Knox Press, 1984), 95.

63. Cf. Murphy, *Apocalypticism*, 381.

64. Diaz, "Creation," 11.

65. J. Collins, *Apocalyptic Imagination* , 282.

66. Murphy, *Apocalypticism*, 380–82.

67. Amherdt, L'herméneutique Philosophique, 268–69.

68. Paul Ricoeur, "Foreword," trans. David Pellauer, *The Book of Daniel*, ed. Andre LaCocque(Atlanta: John Knox, 1979), xxi–xxiii.

69. Northrop Frye, *The Great Code: The Bible And Literature* (New York: Harcourt Brace Jovanovich, 1982), 135–36; cf. André LaCocque, "Apocalyptic Symbolism: A Ricoeurian Hermeneutical Approach," *Biblical Research* 26 (1981): 11–12.

70. Ricoeur, Rule of Metaphor, 39.

71. Ricoeur, *Time and Narrative* 1, 67–8.

72. Dunn, "Jesus and the Kingdom," 33–5.

73. Jan Dušek, "Saying 'True' According to A.J. Greimas," *Philosophical Hermeneutics and Biblical Exegesis*, eds. Petr Pokorný and Jan Roskovec. (Tübingen: Mohr Siebeck, 2002), 97.

74. Ricoeur, *Time and Narrative* 3, 100, 116–24.

75. Cf. Ronald Lee Nickelson, "The Meaning and Significance of Astronomical Disturbances as Depicted in Mark 13:24–27 and Synoptic Parallels" (PhD diss., Trinity Evangelical Divinity School, 1997), 32–3.

76. Ricoeur, "Foreword," xxiv–xxvi, cf. Lacocque, "Apocalyptic Symbolism," 9.

77. Philip J. Chmielewski, "Toward an Ethics of Production: Vico and Analogy, Ricoeur and Imagination" *Philosophy & Theology* 9.3–4 (1996), 405.

78. Brabant, "Ricoeur's Hermeneutical Ontology," 464.

79. Ricoeur provides a similar discussion in his description of Augustine's *intentio* and *distentio* (Time and Narrative 1, 16–22).

80. Wallace, Second Naiveté, 45–46; cf. Mark I. Wallace, "Parsimony of Presence in Mark: Narratology, the Reader and Genre Analysis in Paul Ricoeur," *Studies in Religion/Sciences Religieuses: A Canadian Journal: Revue Canadienne*, 18.2 (1989): 207–08.

81. Nickelson, "Meaning and Significance," 13–33.

82. Hartman, *Prophecy Interpreted*, 239.

83. Egon Brandenburger, *Markus 13 und die Apokalyptik* (Göttingen: Vandenhoeck & Ruprecht, 1984), 13–16, cf. 131–47.

84. Beasley-Murray, *Jesus and the Last Days*, 375–76.

85. Grayston, "Study of Mark," 379–80.

86. Slater, "Apocalypticism and Eschatology," 16.

87. Gundry, Mark, 751–52.

88. Rudolf Pesch, *Naherwartungen: Tradition und Redaktion in Mark 13* (Düsseldorf: Patmos-Verlag, 1968), 218–23; cf. Werner Georg Kümmel. *Promise and Fulfilment: The Eschatological Message of Jesus*, trans. Dorothea M. Barton (Naperville, IL: A. R. Allenson, 1957) 97, Edward Adams, *The Stars Will Fall from Heaven: Cosmic Catastrophe in the New Testament And Its World* (London, New York: T&T Clark, 2007), 135.

89. Adela Yarbro Collins, "The Eschatological Discourse of Mark 13," in *The Four Gospels 1992: Festschrift Frans Neirynck, eds. Frans van Segbroeck and Christopher M. Tuckett* (Louvain: Peeters, 1992), 1128–129.

90. Adela Yarbro Collins, "The Apocalyptic Rhetoric of Mark 13 in Historical Context," *Biblical Research* 41 (1996): 8–10.

91. Elizabeth E. Shively, *Apocalyptic Imagination in the Gospel Of Mark: The Literary and Theological Role of Mark 3:22–30* (Berlin, New York: De Gruyter, 2012), 187–88.

92. J. Collins, *Apocalyptic Imagination*, 6–7.

93. *Ex eventu* prophecy, persecution, eschatological upheaval, cosmic transformation, and resurrection or an afterlife. It does not include the condemnation of wicked people and of supernatural beings, unless one reads vv. 24–27 as a description of such condemnation (cf. Shively 203).

94. Lacoque, *Book of Daniel*, 5–6, Lacoque, *Daniel in His Time*, 82–4)

95. If we accept the premise that this discourse was written immediately before, during, or after the Jewish war, then Jesus serves as the historical figure of renown to whom the discourse is attributed. The course of historical events covers only four decades: less than typical for apocalyptic texts, but appropriate nonetheless.

96. J Collins, *Apocalyptic Imagination*, 4–5.

97. Although a presentation of Jesus as spiritual emissary is more fitting for John's gospel, even in Mark Jesus' other-worldly identity is a subject of speculation and explanation (cf. 1:1, 1:9–11, 8:27–30, 15:39. We may also argue that 1:24, 2:10, 2:27–28, 3:23–27, 5:7, 6:49, 8:38, and 9:2–8 indicate that Mark's gospel presents Jesus as an other-worldly figure). Mark and his audience understand Jesus to be a heavenly figure *par excellence*, the fact that he was not recognized as such by his disciples during his ministry notwithstanding. Jesus himself is the heavenly being who imparts spiritual insight upon the four disciples. The appropriate analogy between this and other apocalyptic texts is not between Jesus and Daniel, for example, as recipients of heavenly mysteries. Rather, Jesus functions as a heavenly messenger such as Gabriel, and the four disciples are the recipients like Daniel (cf. Nickelson 32–3; contra Slater 16).

98. Cf. J. Collins, *Apocalyptic Imagination*, 4–5.

99. Cf. Theodoor Marius van Leeuwen, "Texts, Canon, and Revelation in Paul Ricoeur's Hermeneutics," in *Canonization and Decanonization: Papers Presented to the International Conference of the Leiden Institute for the Study of Religions* (Lisor), Held at Leiden 9–10 January 1997, eds. Arie van der Kooij, Karel van der Toorn and Joannes Augustinus Maria Snoek (Leiden: E J Brill, 1998), 399–402.

100. Paul Ricoeur, "Biblical Readings and Meditations," trans. Kathleen Blamey, in *Critique and Conviction: Conversations with François Azouvi and Marc De Launay* (Cambridge & New York: Polity Press & Columbia University Press, 1998), 143–45.

101. Cf. Wallace, *Second Naiveté*, 114–22

102. Peter Kenny, "Conviction, Critique and Christian Theology: Some Reflections on Reading Ricoeur," in *Memory, Narrativity, Self and the Challenge to Think God: The Reception within Theology of the Recent Work of Paul Ricoeur*, ed. Maureen Junker-Kenny and Peter Kenny (Münster: Lit Verlag, 2002), 108–10.

103. Colby Dickinson, "The Absent Notion of 'Canonicity' in Paul Ricoeur's Memory, History, Forgetting," in *Paul Ricoeur: Poetics and Religion*, eds J. Verheyden, T.L. Hettema, P. Vandecasteele (Leuven: Uitgeverij Peeters, 2011), 495–99.

104. David H. Kelsey, *The Uses Of Scripture In Recent Theology* (Philadelphia: Fortress, 1975), 109.

105. cf. Amherdt, *L'herméneutique Philosophique*, 322–24.

106. Paul Ricouer, "Biblical Hermeneutics," *Semeia* 4 (1975): 108–09.

107. Paul Ricoeur, "Naming God," trans. David Pellauer, in *Figuring the Sacred: Religion, Narrative, and Imagination*, ed. Mark I. Wallace (Minneapolis: Augsburg Fortress, 1995), 220–23; cf. Ricoeur, "Toward a Hermeneutic," 94–5.

108. Ricoeur, "Biblical Hermeneutics," 63.

109. Ricoeur, "Naming God," 232–33.

110. Paul Ricoeur, *Freud and Philosophy: An Essay on Interpretation*, trans. David Savage (New Haven: Yale University Press, 1970), 525.

111. Paul Ricoeur, "The Hermeneutics of Testimony," in *Essays on Biblical Interpretation* (Philadelphia: Fortress Press, 1980), 131.

112. Paul Ricoeur, "Manifestation and Proclamation," in *Figuring the Sacred: Religion, Narrative, and Imagination*, trans. David Pellauer, ed. Mark I. Wallace (Minneapolis: Augsburg Fortress, 1995) 57–61; cf. Ricoeur, "Naming God," 228–30.

113. Ricoeur, "Biblical Hermeneutics," 32–5; cf. David E. Klemm, "Philosophy and Kerygma: Ricoeur as Reader of the Bible," in *Reading Ricoeur*, ed. David M. Kaplan (Albany: SUNY, 2008), 62–63.

114. Paul Ricoeur, *Memory, History, Forgetting*, trans. Kathleen Blamey and David Pellauer (Chicago, IL: University of Chicago Press, 2004), 175–76.

115. Ricoeur, "Biblical Hermeneutics," 123–24.

116. Ibid., 127–30; cf. Ricoeur, "Naming God," 234–35; David Tracy, "Religious Classics and the Classics of Art," in *Art, Creativity, and the Sacred: An Anthology in Religion and Art*, ed. Diane Apostolos-Cappadona (New York: Crossroad, 1984) 243–44; David Tracy, *The Analogical Imagination: Christian Theology and the Culture of Pluralism* (New York: Crossroad, 1981), 160–65; Vanhoozer Biblical Narrative, 257–66, and Klemm Hermeneutical Theory, 112–13.

117. Amherdt, *L'herméneutique Philosophique*, 274–80; cf. Ricoeur, "Biblical Hermeneutics" 138.

118. Ricoeur, "Philosophy and Religious Language," 45.

119. Paul Ricoeur, "Philosophical Hermeneutics and Biblical Hermeneutics," in *From Text to Action: Essays in Hermeneutics*, II, trans. Kathleen Blamey and John B. Thompson (Evanston, IL: Northwestern University Press, 1991), 92; cf. Klemm, *Hermeneutical Theory*, 112–13; Amherdt, *L'herméneutique Philosophique*, 303–05.

120. Paul Ricoeur, "Experience and Language in Religious Discourse," in Phenomenology and The "Theological Turn": The French Debate, ed. Dominique Janicaud, Jean-François Courtine, Jean-Louis Chrétien, Michel Henry, Jean-Luc Marion, and Paul Ricoeur (New York: Fordham University Press, 2000), 139–44.

121. Ricoeur, "Naming God," 224–28; cf. James Fodor, *Christian Hermeneutics: Paul Ricoeur and the Refiguring of Theology*, (Oxford: Oxford University Press, 1995), 239–40; Gorospe "Ethical Possibilities," 69–70.

122. Ricoeur, "Toward a Hermeneutic," 73–90.

123. Paul Ricoeur, "The Self in the Mirror of the Scriptures," in *The Whole and Divided Self*, trans. David Pellauer, eds. David E. Aune and John McCarthy (New York: Crossroad, 1997), 210–13.

124. Ricoeur, "Experience and Language," 139–44; cf. Ricoeur, "Philosophy and Religious Language," 39.

125. Ricoeur, "Biblical Hermeneutics," 101–06, Ricoeur, "Manifestation and Proclamation," 57–9. Van Leeuwen objects to this flexibility of genre identification, arguing that it can be changed only at the expense of altering the entire structure of the canon. "To add new genres to the system is to alter it." The dynamics of the interplay between genres will be affected, just as the addition of a new supporting thread to a spider web redefines the tensions between the existing threads. He points out that the interrelated system of texts that is the Hebrew Tanakh is very different from the system of texts that is the Christian Old Testament, even though they are the same books. The introduction of the New Testament into the system redefines the place of the original books within that system. Van Leeuwen notes that the introduction of new genres or texts could supplement or increase the joint testimony which the existing genres and texts provide. Additional genres and books further the revelatory nature of the Bible. If the constellation of testimonies can become even fuller and more evocative with the addition of more texts and genres, then the inclusion of additional texts ought to continue. However, the concept of canon as a closed system of interdependent texts would be lost (405–08).

126. Ricoeur, "Philosophy and Religious Language" 40–1; cf Ricoeur, "Toward a Hermeneutic," 90–91; Wallace, *Second Naiveté*, 57.

127. Andrè Lacocque, and Paul Ricoeur, *Thinking Biblically: Exegetical and Hermeneutical Studies*, trans. David Pellauer (Chicago & London: University of Chicago Press, 1998), 301–03.

128. Rogers, "Ricoeur and Privileging," 7–9.

129. Kelsey, *Uses of Scripture*, 74–7.

130. Amherdt, *L'herméneutique Philosophique*, 286–88, 448–53.

131. McCarthy, "Script to Scripture," 357–59.

132. The first challenge that Ricoeur inappropriately privileges theory over text is valid inasmuch as he approaches the Bible with a philosophical framework. But the challenge fails in that reading is impossible without a foundation of some sort. Stiver notes the theoretical foundations that Frei and Lindbeck themselves also used. However, the point for consideration is the degree to which the interpretive strategy controls the reading of the text, rather than the text itself. As Stiver puts it, does the Biblical world or the modern world take priority (Ricoeur and Theology 86–7)? Ricoeur's insistence on the reader's interaction with the text as an equal subject rather than as an object, and his use of multiple interpretive strategies which are guided by the text's genre, indicate that his hermeneutics is guided by the text rather than theory.

133. Ricoeur, *Freud and Philosophy*, 524.

134. Hans W. Frei, "The 'Literal Reading' of Biblical Narrative in the Christian Tradition: Does It Stretch or Will It Break?" in *Bible and the Narrative Tradition*, ed. Frank McConnell (New York: Oxford University Press, 1986), 289.

135. Fodor, *Christian Hermeneutics*, 273.

136. Vanhoozer, *Biblical Narrative*, 165–68.

137. Frei, "Literal Reading," 43–7.

138. Amherdt, L'herméneutique Philosophique, 488–89.

139. Frei, "Literal Reading," 72–3.

140. Ibid., 36–43.

141. Hans W. Frei, *The Identity of Jesus Christ: The Hermeneutical Bases of Dogmatic Theology* (Philadelphia: Fortress Press, 1975), 87, 90–91; cf. Frank Kermode, *The Genesis of Secrecy: On the Interpretation of Narrative* (Cambridge, Ma: Harvard University Press, 1979), 118–20.

142. Frei, Identity, 139–46; cf. Amherdt, *L'herméneutique Philosophique*, 480–81.

143. Fodor, *Christian Hermeneutics*, 262–69, 271–73; cf. William Wesley. Elkins, "Learning to Say Jesus: Narrative, Identity, and Community: A Study of the Hermeneutics of Josiah Royce, Hans Frei, George Lindbeck, Paul Ricoeur and the Gospel of Mark" (PhD diss., Drew University, 1993), 88–98; Reinsdorf, "How Is the Gospel," 331–32; Kermode, *Genesis of Secrecy*, 104.

144. Amherdt, *L'herméneutique Philosophique*, 559–63.

145. Joseph Byrd, "Paul Ricoeur's Hermeneutical Theory and Pentecostal Proclamation," *Pneuma* 15 (1993): 210–11.

146. Reinsdorf, "How Is the Gospel," 333–34.

147. Fodor, *Christian Hermeneutics*, 279–83.

148. Wallace, *Second Naiveté*, 28. For Ricoeur's description of the difference between manifestation and adequation, cf. Ricoeur, *Time and Narrative* 3, 100–01, Ricoeur, "Hermeneutical Function" 85–6, Ricoeur, "Toward a Hermeneutic" 102, Ricoeur, "Canon" 11–12.

Chapter 3

The Issues of Mark 13

Ricoeur explains that the process of appropriation includes the mode of explanation, which is a critical analysis of the text that challenges innocent acceptance of the text's surface presentation.[1] I describe the explanatory mode of interpretation more fully in pp. 107–109. This chapter presents the work of explanation as described in Ricoeur's methodology, and it provides support for the fourth premise of the project's argument: "The meaning for Mark 13 that was apparent when it was written is a literal prediction that certain events will happen relatively soon." In order to do so, it substantiates three assertions. First, Mark 13 was understood literally and not figuratively at the time that it was written. Second, it predicts nine future events. And third, it states that all of these nine events will take place during the lifetime of the first Christian generation. In addition to supporting these assertions, I discuss the significance of these predictions at the time that they were made, and the purpose for making them. I conclude by identifying issues which were present but not discernible at the time when the text was written, but which today's reader is able to recognize.

Mark 13 predicts nine events, to each of which I assign a letter for ease of reference.

A. The Jerusalem temple will be destroyed (v. 2)
B. The Christian community will experience deception (vv. 5b-6, 21–23).
C. Calamities will strike the world (vv. 7–8, 17–20).
D. Christians will be persecuted (vv. 9, 11–13).
E. The Christian gospel will be preached to all peoples (v. 10).
F. A profoundly (and perhaps uniquely) evil figure will emerge (vv. 14–16).
G. The cosmos will be disrupted (vv. 24–25).
H. A spiritual being will be universally perceived (v. 26).
I. God's people will be gathered together (v. 27).

PRESENTED AS LITERAL EVENTS

The argument that Mark 13 predicts literal events can be outlined by the following premises:

1. The meaning for Mark 13, when written, is a literal prediction of certain historical events. (Thesis to prove)
2. It is likely that the meaning for Mark 13, when written, is a prediction of certain literal events. (One cannot argue for the certainty of the thesis, but only for its probability)
3. When Mark 13 was written, other texts of the same genre existed which predicted the same or similar events. (Can be demonstrated historically)
4. The predicted events of these other texts were understood in those conditions to be literal happenings. (Can be demonstrated historically)
5. It is likely that texts of the same genre in the same milieu that make similar claims will be understood similarly. (Presumed)
6. It is likely that the claims of Mark 13 were understood in the same way that claims of other similar texts were understood. (From 5).
7. Texts similar to Mark 13 were understood to make predictions of literal events. (From 4)
8. It is likely that the predictions of Mark 13 were understood literally in its writing-conditions. (From 6 and 7)
9. It is likely that the meaning for Mark 13 in its writing-conditions is a prediction of certain literal events. (From 8)

As I explain in pp. 6–12, many modern commentators claim that the Olivet discourse was written and was originally understood as a figurative text. In particular, they argue that the unprecedented events of vv. 24–27 (G, H, and I) were originally read as representations of events other than celestial chaos, the appearance of a heavenly figure, and an angelic round-up of God's elect. These claims, however, do not find support in the available evidence. I argue against these claims and contend with Allison and Adams that the literal fulfillment of these events would have been the likely understanding of the text when it was written. This is necessarily a probability argument because of unknown variables. Given the evidence available to us, however, the more reasonable conclusion is that Mark 13 was read literally. The evidence to support this contention comes from Old Testament allusions found in the text, from prevalent Jewish understandings of the time, from evidence of early Christian expectation of a literal parousia, and from the presence of similar expectations in other cultures.

The first point of evidence for a literal reading of Mark 13's predictions comes from the Old Testament texts to which the discourse refers.

Theophilos explains that prophetic texts use the imagery of a darkened sky and falling stars ubiquitously to describe military defeat (133–34). Allison concedes Wright's similar observation that many of these texts are meant to be read figuratively but are mistakenly taken literally. But Allison points out that many Old Testament and Second Temple texts which seem fantastic to modern readers were understood to describe future literal events. Further, there are no textual cues in Mark 13 to lead a reader to interpret vv. 24–27 metaphorically. To the contrary: these verses appear in context with predictions of events such as wars, earthquakes, and famines that can only be read literally. Allison supports his contention by citing examples of unusual celestial descriptions in the Old Testament that were certainly meant literally.[2] Adams likewise disputes Wright's claim that vv. 24–25 serve as figurative descriptions of the devastating implications of the temple's destruction. While he agrees that some Old Testament passages describe socio-political turmoil with images of cosmic upheaval, Adams points out that in other Old Testament texts "global/ cosmic disaster language has a more exclusively eschatological reference."[3] For Adams, the images of vv. 26–27 (i.e. coming in clouds, with power and glory, accompanied by angels, and gathering people from the nations) are consistent with Old Testament descriptions of the coming of God. Mark applies this descriptions of theophany to the parousia of Christ.[4] Adams refers to Mark 8:38 to support his claim that v. 26 refers to Christ's parousia and not to his heavenly glorification, as Wright and France assert. He points out that this verse is drawn not only from Daniel 7:13, which describes a heavenly glorification, but also to Zechariah 14:5, which speaks of God coming to the earth.[5]

Allison contends that Second Temple Jews typically understood predictions of cosmic cataclysm literally. What sounds fantastic or absurd to the sensibilities of our modern reader was perfectly plausible for first century Jews. He argues that the concept of gigantic distant celestial bodies raining upon the earth was conceivable for the ancients because of their familiarity with meteor showers.[6] He also demonstrates that Jews struggled with unfulfilled apocalyptic predictions before Jesus' career and that their disenchantment with and reworking of these predictions demonstrates that the predictions had been read literally.[7] Adams explains that Second Temple Jewish texts used images of celestial upheaval to describe the end of the world, not socio-political events. In particular, he identifies similarities between vv. 24–27 and 1 Enoch 1:3b-9, 102:1–3 and Testament of Moses 10, explaining that cosmic upheaval in these texts refers to literal occurrences as a theophany. He does not claim that Mark 13 depends upon these passages, but that it "conforms to a well-established and probably well-known Jewish eschatological pattern": that is, that literal celestial catastrophe will occur when God comes.[8]

Allison strengthens the argument that Mark 13 was initially read literally by pointing out similarities between this text and other early

Christian texts that were also read literally. In particular, he notes that 1 Thessalonians 4:13–18 bears strong affinity to the Markan passage and is quite evidently meant to be read literally.[9] He points out that early Christians resorted to reworking apocalyptic prophecy which did not find its expected literal fulfillment.[10] Further, he claims that the lack of a fully articulated apocalyptic agenda in the text does not indicate the absence of such literal expectation. He explains that because the culture was familiar with eschatological thought and apocalyptic symbolism, the textual traditions do not provide a comprehensive description of it. Mark's themes would have been commonly understood by his contemporaries, and the text is therefore silent about topics for which there would have been broad consensus.[11] Like Allison, Adams argues that early Christian readers would have understood vv. 26–27 to refer to the return of Christ because of their pervasive belief in this future event.[12]

Allison and Adams find cues within the Olivet discourse itself that support the contention that it should be read literally. Allison points out that the discourse predicts events such as war, famine, and earthquake which are quite obviously intended literally. If other elements of the discourse are read literally, vv. 24–27 should be as well.[13] And Adams considers the presence of v. 31 in the discourse to indicate that the end of the world was a concept that Mark accepted. Therefore, interpretations that vv. 24–27 predict the eschaton cannot be dismissed on the grounds that it is a foreign notion for Mark.[14]

Allison's cross-cultural research of apocalyptic expectation provides further support for his contention that Second Temple Jews and early Christians had them as well. He refers to the widespread predictions of physical calamities from many cultures and eras and demonstrates that they are invariably understood by their societies, and by the scholars who study them, to be expectations of literal events associated with "supernatural judgment and repair of a fallen world." He finds it disingenuous to argue that while such expectations of literal physical catastrophe are so widespread, first century Jews and Christians would necessarily have meant them metaphorically.[15]

DESCRIPTIONS OF THE EVENTS

Analysis of the structure of Mark 13 demonstrates that the text predicts nine events. As Beasley-Murray,[16] Gundry[17] and Grayston[18] observe, vv. 1–4 provide the introductory framework for the discourse, consisting first of an exchange between an unnamed disciple and Jesus as they exit the temple, and second of a subsequent inquiry on the subject by four disciples. While the discourse has an introductory framing narrative, no concluding narrative frame follows.

While scholars differ on the major elements of the discourse, its division by Lambrecht,[19] Beasley-Murray,[20] Pesch,[21] Cranfield,[22] Grayston,[23] and Marcus[24] into three sections best reflects the textual evidence: vv. 5–23, vv. 24–27, and vv. 28–37.[25] Gundry[26] and Cranfield[27] offer two options for subdividing each major section. Gundry identifies the repeated call for watchfulness (Βλέπετε) and warnings against deception as markers that separate "signs which precede but do not indicate nearness" and "signs which precede and indicate nearness." Cranfield explains that vv. 5–23 consists of three signs of the eschaton that identify its sections. First, deceivers will claim the status of Messiah. The more eagerly believers anticipate the parousia, the more likely they are to be duped by these deceivers. Second, the run-up to the parousia will be characterized by suffering. Some of this suffering will affect all of humanity (wars, earthquakes, and famine), but some of the distress will be unique to believers. Third, a historical crisis instigated by the "abomination of desolation" will precede eschatological upheaval.

I propose a structure for the Olivet discourse that is informed by the analysis of other scholars. With Grayston,[28] Pesch,[29] Lambrecht,[30] and Deppe,[31] I recognize a chiastic structure for vv. 5–23. I subdivide vv. 28–37 as Cranfield[32] and Lambrecht[33] do[34]. Like Marcus,[35] Hartman,[36] and C. Black,[37] I consider vv. 5–27 to be the culmination of Jesus' answer to his disciples' question about what "all these things" will be, and vv. 28–37 to answer their question about when these events will occur. While France understands vv. 5–13 to be a description of preliminary events that are not related to the eschaton and v. 14 to begin the description of signs heralding the immediate approach of the end,[38] I accept Marcus' explanation that the predicted events of vv. 5–23 had already taken place by the time Mark's gospel was written, and that vv. 24–27 describe the coming eschaton.[39] I conclude that Mark 13 is structured as follows:[40]

I. Precipitating Logion (1–2)
II. Subsequent Questions by Disciples (3–4)
III. Extended Answer by Jesus (5b-37, introduced by 5a)
    A. Description of Life as a Disciple (5b-23)
        1. Warning against deceivers (5b-6)
        2. Destructive forces on earth (7–8)
        3. Persecution of believers by civil and religious authorities (9–10)
        4. The presence and guidance of the Holy Spirit (11)
        5. Persecution of believers within families (12–13)
        6. Time of calamity (14–20)
        7. Warning against deceivers (21–23)
    B. Parousia of the Son of Man (24–27)
        1. Destruction of World Powers (24–25)

2. Appearance of the Son of Man (26)
3. Ingathering of the Elect (27)
C. Timeline of Events (28–37)
   1. Parable of Fig Tree: Imminence (28–30)
   2. Permanence of Words of Christ (31)
   3. Timeline unknown (32–33)
   4. Parable of householder: Watch (34–37)

The description of life as a disciple in the present age (vv. 5b-23) is arranged chiastically, with elements 1 and 7 (deception), 2 and 6 (calamity), and 3 and 5 (persecution) balancing each other respectively. This draws attention to the most significant element of the description: v. 11's assurance of the guiding presence of the Holy Spirit in the midst of distress.[41] Because of this chiastic balance, I consider the discourse's double descriptions of deception, calamity, and persecution to be predictions of three events or conditions, rather than six. V. 10's prediction of international proclamation of the Christian message is a subordinate feature of the persecution element[42] and stands as a predicted event of its own. Similarly, the figure of the abomination of desolation is a feature of the calamity motif, but one that is significant enough to warrant individual consideration. These five predictions, together with the prediction of the temple's destruction in the opening framework for the discourse and the three predictions in the second section (vv. 24–27), comprise the nine predicted events of the chapter. I argue that events A-F (the destruction of the temple and those events described in vv. 5–23) occurred during the first century, and that events G-I (those described in vv. 24–27) have not.

A: Temple Destruction

Mark presents the prediction of the temple's destruction in v. 2 as the precipitating statement that leads to the rest of the predictions. The prediction is significant for two reasons: the destruction of the temple was understood to mean the destruction (or at least the significant disruption) of creation, and it serves as an indictment against the religious practices and the power structures associated with the building.

Beasley-Murray,[43] Cranfield,[44] Gundry,[45] and Bolt[46] explain that the temple of Jerusalem was recognized to be a unique group of buildings, not only because, as Beasley-Murray put it, "the temple complex in Jerusalem was probably the most awesome building in the ancient world," but because it represented God's care for the Jewish nation. Commentators share a broad consensus that a prediction of the destruction of the temple represented for first century Jews and Christians a prediction of the eschaton.[47]

Additionally, the destruction of the temple was understood to be God's judgment against the temple practices. Patristic, medieval, and early modern Christian commentators claim that the destruction was God's punishment of the Jewish people for rejecting Jesus as the Christ,[48] and while modern critical scholars do not share their sentiments, they do agree that Mark presents the destruction of the temple as God's rejection of the temple cultus. Marcus[49] and France[50] associate the prediction of v. 2 with 11:12–21 and conclude that Jesus condemns the presence of commercial activity within the temple complex and the nationalistic sentiments associated with it. Beasley-Murray asserts that Jesus' prediction of the temple's destruction is related thematically to Ezekiel 9–11, in which God's presence leaves the temple because proper worship there has ended. God's judgment of the temple extends to the city of Jerusalem as a whole. The logion of 13:2 ought rightly to be understood as a pronouncement of eschatological judgment against the people.[51]

This first of the nine predictions found in Mark 13 appears to have been fulfilled by the Roman destruction of the temple in 70. However, Kümmel agrees with patristic sentiments[52] that the prediction was not fulfilled because the temple was not torn down entirely; the western retaining wall still stands, and the temple was burned, not demolished stone by stone.[53] Kloppenborg dismisses such objections as "needlessly pedantic."[54] Marcus rebuts Kümmel's point with an explanation that later Jewish commentators describe the total destruction of the temple by the Romans.[55] We may therefore accept that this first prediction was fulfilled.

B: Deception

The first section of the Olivet discourse (vv. 5b-23) begins and ends with warnings about deception. Such speculates that these pericopae were originally combined and that Mark split them in order to form a pair of sayings to accentuate the force of the second.[56] A. Collins, however, asserts that the types of deception described in these passages is too different to be about the same circumstances.[57] The discourse predicts that leaders will arise and attempt to lead Christians astray. Commentators describe this deception in several ways: the leaders claim that they are acting on Jesus' behalf, that they are Jesus returned, that they have divine authority independent from Jesus, and even that they themselves are God.[58] A. Collins,[59] Gundry,[60] and Marcus[61] each explain that the first century was rife with figures claiming to be the messiah or to have divine inspiration and power. For these reasons, we may accept these persons as the fulfillment of the Olivet discourse's prediction of deceptive leaders. In fact, the fulfillment of this prediction Jesus supposedly made was already apparent at the time of the gospel's writing.

C: Calamity

The second layer of the chiasm of vv. 5b-23 (vv. 7–8 and 14–20) predicts that calamities will strike the earth. While v. 8b predicts earthquakes and famine, the prevailing theme of the predictions is warfare. Such,[62] A. Collins,[63] Marcus,[64] and Brandenburger[65] explain that the predictions of warfare in vv. 7–8 were fulfilled by military conflict that was prevalent in the Roman Empire during the 60's, culminating in the Jewish War.[66] Beasley-Murray[67] and Calvin[68] consider these verses to refer to a more pervasive war-like atmosphere throughout the world. Vv. 14–20, the second element of chiastic pairing on calamity, is more specific and describes events associated with the Roman assault of Jerusalem.[69] Commentators generally accept the theory that the command to flee describes the refugees leaving Jerusalem at the time of the Roman siege, but they disagree on how this flight specifically took place. Marcus[70] accepts the traditional explanation that this flight refers to the exodus of Jewish Christians to the Transjordanian city of Pella, but Gundry,[71] Wright,[72] and Beasley-Murray[73] dispute this. Each does, however, consider the summons to flee to relate to the siege of Jerusalem. Such contends that the prediction of flight evokes memories of the Maccabean Revolt and of reaction to Caligula's plan to desecrate the temple,[74] and that the command to flee refers to events after the fall of Jerusalem.[75] The prediction deals with specific practical concerns related to ease and speed of escape,[76] and Theophylact even suggests that v. 17 is a subtle reference to the cannibalism to which Jerusalem citizens resorted during the Roman siege.[77] Despite Adams' contention that these predictions are specifically eschatological and that first century events cannot be considered to be fulfillment of the prediction,[78] and despite the lack of consensus about exactly how the discourse's prediction relates to actual events, we may safely consider it to have been fulfilled.

D: Persecution

The third element of the chiasm addresses persecution and can be found in vv. 9–10 and 11–13. I contend that v. 11 stands at the center of the chiasm and emphasizes Mark's promise of God's intervening presence in difficult situations. I address this theme more specifically on p. 161. It does, however, relate directly to the theme of persecution which precedes and follows this verse. The first part of the chiasm describes official persecution of Christians, and the second predicts persecution and conflict that arise within the family unit. The pervasive persecution of Christians in the first century is widely accepted to be historical fact, as Russell states.[79] Lambrecht,[80] Cranfield,[81] Gundry,[82] and Theophylact[83] consider familial persecution to be a greater hardship than what Christians faced at the hands of religious and civil authorities because of the family's unparalleled importance in the social structure. Gundry points out that family members turned against each other either to avoid persecution, because of antipathy to the gospel, or both. Marcus[84] and van Iersel[85] propose that the prediction of familial conflict does not only describe persecution among literal kinship groups, but also within church communities. Marcus cites the fact that Christians frequently referred to each other as "brother," and van Iersel notes that Jesus' entourage functioned as a family unit. In this latter instance, Judas' betrayal serves as a prefiguration of what would happen in the early church. Evidence supports the conclusion that this prediction was fulfilled.

E: Worldwide Proclamation

An assessment of the fulfillment of v. 10's prediction that the Christian message will spread to all nations depends upon one's identification of "all the nations" (πάντα τὰ ἔθνη). Marcus,[86] Gundry,[87] Such,[88] Kümmel,[89] and Chrysostom[90] argue that because "all the nations" refers only to those nations known to Mark and his readers, that is, those of the Roman Empire and the Near East, the worldwide spread of the gospel would have been complete, or nearly so, by the time the gospel was written. Origen disputes this claim, citing a number of people groups beyond the borders of the Roman Empire which had not received it the Christian message,[91] and Calvin represents commentators who understand the global spread of the gospel not to be limited to the known world of the first century, but to the entire planet.[92] Allison appears to agree, noting that at the time, some believed that the parousia depends on the fulfillment of this prediction.[93] Notwithstanding these objections, I accept the contention that this prediction was fulfilled as well.

F: The Abomination of Desolation

In order to determine whether or not v. 14's prediction of the coming of the abomination of desolation (τὸ βδέλυγμα τῆς ἐρημώσεως) was fulfilled, I first consider the identity of this figure. As Beasley-Murray[94] and Theophilos[95] explain, this is an echo of a phrase that appears in Daniel (9:27, 11:31, and 12:11) which refers to the actions of Antiochus Epiphanes, and which came to be used to describe someone who destroys in a sacrilegious manner, horrifying the people and devastating the temple and the city of Jerusalem in the process. Marcus asserts that it was a well-known expression for Mark's readers,[96] and Crossley adds that it was typically used in the first century to refer to Rome.[97] As Wenham notes, early Christians believed that the coming of the abomination would precede the cataclysmic return of Jesus.[98]

Drawing upon the juxtaposition in v. 14 of the neuter noun "abomination" (βδέλυγμα) with the masculine participle "standing" (ἑστηκότα), Dewar asserts that the abomination is a person rather than an object.[99] Wenham agrees, and he suggests that the "abomination" reference was originally impersonal and was developed into a personal reference.[100] Pesch also notes the personification of the abomination trope but reverses it by claiming that the abomination is the personification of the temple's destruction.[101] Additionally, although he contends that the abomination is an object and not a person, Such points out that the present tense of the participle ἑστηκότα indicates an ongoing or permanent condition of "standing," or of being in place.[102] The abomination endures beyond what would be possible if it were a conventional human being. It is a person, but something more than or different from how persons are typically identified. I suggest two options: first, it may be an office that is filled by a person. For example, we may speak of the President of the United States being the commander-in-chief in an ongoing sense without referring to a particular individual such as Barack Obama or George W. Bush. The person is the individual who fills the office. Alternately, we may consider this enduring personal abomination as a spiritual figure, such as a demonic power or a pagan god.[103]

Commentators have offered a dizzying array of candidates to fill the role of τὸ βδέλυγμα τῆς ἐρημώσεως.[104] Robert Eisler[105] claims that the abomination refers to Pilate's placement of Roman standards in Jerusalem in 19, but Such[106] and Crossley[107] refute this notion. While Crossley suggested that Caligula's plan to desecrate the temple in 40 may have been a popular association with this title in the first century,[108] Allison and Davies[109] and Brandenburger[110] assert that it was used to describe the temple's destruction in 70, and Gundry claims that by the time Mark was written the Caligula episode had faded from memory.[111] A strong consensus of commentators agree that the abomination refers in some way to the Roman destruction of the temple, but they offer a broad range of options for how it specifically does so. Theophylact and Augustine identify the abomination as the overall event,[112] Russell explains it refers to the Roman standards that were erected on the temple grounds after the fall of Jerusalem,[113] Roskam understands the abomination to be a reference to the presence of Roman soldiers in the temple at the time of its destruction,[114] Howard proposes that it is the legion standards which they carried,[115] and Chrysostom assumes that the abomination of desolation was the statue of Titus which was erected in the temple.[116] Theophilos contends that the abomination of Israel's rejection of the Messiah resulted in the desolation of the temple's destruction.[117]

Each of these theories, however, ignores the fact that the abomination describes a person rather than an event. Other commentators provide theories which take this into account. Such explains that Titus' acclamation as a god-like "Imperator" by his troops after their victory qualifies as an abominable offense.[118] Marcus contends that the abomination refers not to a pagan presence in the temple, but to the occupation of the temple by Jewish nationalists. He proposes that the most suitable candidate for the abomination title is Eleazar son of Simon, who turned the temple into a garrison for his fighters.[119] Other scholars identify the abomination not as a historical figure but as an eschatological reference. Allison and Davies contend that the abomination refers to an eschatological Antichrist.[120] A. Collins explains that the abomination is not a pagan altar in the temple, but the deity to which it is dedicated. She claims that Mark offers this prediction as an eschatological event that was still in the future.[121]

I propose a different understanding of τὸ βδέλυγμα τῆς ἐρημώσεως which is similar to Eddy's assertion that 11:17 refers to corrupt temple leadership.[122] The context of the discourse within the gospel indicates that the entire temple-based religion had become detestable to Jesus. The fig tree episode (11:12–14, 20–24), the disputations with temple officials (11:27–12:27), the praise of personal devotion over temple ritual (12:28–34, esp. v. 33), and the condemnation of the conduct of temple officials (12:38–40), all of which immediately precede the discourse, are ample evidence of Jesus' opposition in the Gospel of Mark to the temple, its rituals, and its officials. Shively likens Jesus' relationship with the temple, its leaders, and its practices with his struggle against Satanic powers throughout Mark's gospel.[123] The temple practices were themselves the abomination. As Marcus points out, Jesus' departure from the temple in 13:1 parallels the withdrawal of the divine presence from the temple in Ezekiel 10, and his condemnatory language prior to his exit warrants such an interpretation.[124] As in Ezekiel, the abomination is not an external presence that is foisted upon the temple practitioners, but is the practice of those who purport to be faithful devotees to God. The discourse's personification of the abomination means that it directs an accusation of blasphemy to the high priest himself. He who claims to be acting on God's behalf is actually subverting and distorting God's intentions. The repeated calls for watchful awareness, particularly in relation to deceivers, supports this interpretation of the abomination; only an insightful observer will recognize that one who acts publicly on God's behalf actually opposes him. The prediction of the abomination refers to the temple cultus in general and to the high priest in particular. Mark's identification of the temple and/or high priest as the abomination of desolation would have been shocking and scandalous, inverting the entire Jewish understanding of proper religious conduct. This shock conforms with other scandalous sayings in Mark directed against the temple and its leaders (e.g. 11:17, 12:1–12, 12:38–40).

Alternately (or additionally, as multiple referents are appropriate for poetic discourse), Mark may personify the abomination as a demonic figure opposed

to God who orchestrates the corruption of temple ritual. The text claims
that there is a spiritual element to the worldly forces which challenge God.
Today's reader can understand the warning against an abomination of desolation to refer to an individual, or to a practice, which offers the appearance of
being faithful to God but which in actuality is opposed to him. It is promising
to consider this figure not only as a particular historical person or event, but
as the personification of the powers which work in opposition to God. Such a
meta-identification suits the apocalyptic nature of the discourse: a concealed
influence which affects the world in such a way as to cause destruction generally and tribulation for the elect in particular. I explore this theme more fully
in Chapter 7. At this point, however, I conclude that the appearance of an
abomination took place and fulfilled the prediction of v. 14.

G: Cosmic Disruption

The second section of the discourse (vv. 24–27) provides the final three predicted events of Mark 13. These are the events which did not occur as Mark
predicts. As I demonstrate on pp. 64–66, Mark presents event G as a literal
prediction of a historical happening. As originally understood, the text claims
that celestial objects will be darkened and fall from the sky.[125] Allison and
Davies explain that the occurrence of this event requires a violation of the
current natural order, noting that it is impossible for solar and lunar eclipses
to happen simultaneously.[126] Although Nickelson assumes that a literal understanding of vv. 24–25 necessarily indicates an event of divine judgment,[127]
Beasley-Murray[128] and Verheyden[129] explain convincingly that the cosmic
upheaval is caused by God's appearance in the world.

   Although vv. 24–25 predict the demise of the sun, moon, and stars in a
literal sense, this event deals with more than astronomical activity. Marcus,[130]
Allison,[131] Nickelson,[132] van Iersel,[133] and Theophylact[134] each explain that
first century cosmology understood the stars, sun, and moon not only to be
luminous objects in the sky but also to be spiritual beings. The prediction of
cosmic disruption therefore indicates both an upheaval in the natural order
as well as the defeat of evil spiritual forces by God. Gundry[135] and Hooker[136]
explain that the ancients perceived a unity between spiritual beings, celestial
and meteorological entities, and social forces. The predicted astronomical
chaos is an element of God's defeat of his spiritual and human enemies.
As Hooker puts it, "Roman armies were as much God's tools as were thunder-
bolts and falling stars." While today's reader may believe that social dynamics
depend solely upon human actions and motivations (either individually or
collectively), Mark and his readers believed that spiritual forces and beings
control human affairs. Mark's deliberate move to direct his readers' attention
to the collapse of heavenly bodies indicates judgment against social powers.

In doing so, he highlights the influence that these spiritual forces have upon human affairs.

The failure of Mark's prediction of G is obvious; we may safely assume that if calamitous events like these had happened, the historical record would indicate it.

H: The Appearance of the Son of Man

The eighth predicted event of Mark 13 is of the appearance of the "Son of Man" (ὁ υἱὸς τοῦ ἀνθρώπου). My analysis considers five elements to this verse: (1) those who will see the event, (2) the identity of the Son of Man, (3) the nature of his "coming," (4) cloud-riding, and (5) the nature and purpose for his coming. First, Gundry,[137] Lambrecht,[138] and Beasley-Murray[139] explain convincingly that Mark predicts a universal perception of the Son of Man's coming, although Marcus[140] and Augustine[141] claim that this is not the case. Second, as Crossley,[142] Hahn,[143] Shepherd,[144] Chronis,[145] Perrin,[146] Gundry,[147] and Murphy[148] explain, "Son of Man" is a title that originates from Daniel but was used by early Christians to refer to Jesus, and Allison[149] contends that Jesus used the term self-referentially.[150] Leim argues that Mark's conflates multiple figures from the Old Testament to describe Jesus. Thus, the "Son of Man" of v. 26 is not only the Danielic figure but is the appearance of God himself.[151] Third, Wright,[152] Glasson,[153] Dewar,[154] Robinson,[155] and Beasley-Murray[156] retain the original Danielic direction of movement in v. 26 and read it as a description of Jesus' ascension and enthronement in heaven, rather than as a descent to earth. However, Marcus,[157] Hartman,[158] Gundry,[159] and Blomberg[160] argue convincingly that Mark reworked the Daniel text and used it to describe the Son of Man's descent from heaven to earth. Fourth, Allison and Davies,[161] Crossley,[162] Marcus,[163] and Gundry[164] cite numerous instances from the Old Testament, from other ancient religious traditions, and from texts contemporary to Mark which indicate that the discourse's readers would have accepted predictions of literal cloud-riding by God or by God's agents. Fifth, despite arguments by Pesch,[165] Shively,[166] and Wenham,[167] the purpose for the Son of Man's appearance is not primarily to condemn the wicked but to redeem the elect.[168]

When the prediction of event H is understood this way, it is apparent that the prediction has not been fulfilled. If it had, it would have been a universal perception of Jesus' descent from heaven to earth on clouds for the purpose of redeeming the chosen ones. This has not happened.

I: Ingathering of the Elect

The last of Mark 13's predictions is that the "elect" will be gathered together from across the earth. Beasley-Murray laments the lack of specificity regarding the identity of these elect. It presumably refers to those who believe in God, but does not indicate whether or not it includes a resurrection of those who have died, or if it includes both Jews and Gentiles. However, Beasley-Murray concludes that this prediction includes those whom God has chosen from all nations together with the elect of Israel, to form "a single community under the lordship and in the fellowship of the Son of man."[169] Marcus suggests that the odd expression "from the ends of the earth to the ends of heaven" implies that the elect who are gathered together include both those still alive (i.e. those scattered to the ends of the earth) and those who have died (i.e. those who are in heaven).[170] Beasley-Murray understands this phrase to reflect the ancient cosmological understanding of the sky or heaven as a bowl placed over the earth. The "ends of the earth" and the "ends of heaven" are the points where the sky touches the earth.[171] The point to this expression is to emphasize the dispersion of the elect across the entire world and from every nation.

Gundry claims that "though this prediction of Jesus [concerning the ingathering of the elect] cannot count as a fulfilled one . . . Mark's recording of the fulfillments of many other predictions made by Jesus gives reason to believe that this grandest of all will also reach fulfillment."[172] He is overly optimistic on this point; the fact that someone has successfully predicted some events does not mean that all of their predictions are reliable. Theophilos presents the minority view that when ἄγγελοι is understood not to be spiritual beings but human missional emissaries, the fulfillment of this prediction is synonymous with Event E: the worldwide proclamation of the gospel.[173] Theophilos, however, undermines his argument by observing elsewhere that when ἄγγελοι appears in conjunction with the Son of Man (υἱὸς τοῦ ἀνθρώπου) it refers to heavenly beings.[174] I agree with the majority of scholars that Event I has not taken place; nor have events G and H. And as the following section explains, the time for Jesus' successful prediction of their occurrence has long since passed.

TIMING OF THE EVENTS

Events A through F have taken place as predicted, but events G, H, and I have not. Setting aside modern doubts about whether these three events could ever take place (a topic which extends beyond the scope of this project), the fact that they have not yet taken place does not mean that they never could nor will happen. The accuracy of the predictions is therefore undetermined at this time. If at some point in the future the stars collapse, everyone sees Jesus return, and the faithful are gathered together, we would be able to recognize that the predictions were accurate. However, the hermeneutical problem of Mark 13 is not just that the text predicts that certain events will take place; it predicts that these events will happen within a specified time. V. 30 predicts that "all these things" (ταῦτα πάντα) will take place within a "generation" (γενεὰ) of when Jesus is purported to have made the predictions. This statement, at its face, predicts that all nine events will occur within a few decades of Jesus' time, and certainly by the end of the first century at the latest. It is patently clear that events G, H, and I have not. Analysis of v. 30 focuses on two issues: the meaning of γενεὰ to understand when the events are predicted to occur, and the meaning of ταῦτα πάντα to understand which events are included in the prediction. I argue that the initially apparent meaning of v. 30 is the actual meaning: that all nine predicted events will happen during the first Christian generation.

As Beasley-Murray outlines, traditional church exegesis understands v. 30 to refer to return of Christ, and depends upon an understanding of γενεὰ (generation) as something other than the contemporaries of Jesus. Instead, these interpreters assert that the term relates variously to the Jewish people or even to humanity in general.[175] The majority of critical scholars reject this reading of the term and understand the verse to assert that the predicted events will take place within two or three decades.[176] Gundry explains that if "this generation" includes the time occupied by multiple lifetimes, the prediction becomes meaningless. Further, the prediction is made emphatically; it appears to be a predictive fact beyond dispute.[177] A strong consensus of modern critical scholarship agrees that γενεὰ clearly refers to Jesus' contemporaries.[178] Beasley-Murray points out that although the term had been used in earlier Greek literature to denote race or ancestry, it was never used in this way in the New Testament, and almost never in the Septuagint.[179] Rather, γενεὰ referred to Jesus' generation, and it typically carried a negative connotation.[180] He points out that if Mark was written during the Jewish War, Jesus' contemporaries were a dying breed. The author must therefore have believed that the prophecies had been fulfilled, or would be very soon. Marcus explains that Jewish and Greek literature of the time reckoned a generation to be forty years. Therefore, a prediction that events will happen within a generation of when Jesus was purported to have made it must be fulfilled by the mid-70's at the latest in order to be fulfilled.

The second issue concerning v. 30 addresses the events that are included in this generational deadline; what is the antecedent of "all these things" (ταῦτα πάντα) that will take place? If v. 30 only refers to events A-F, the prediction has been fulfilled. A number of scholars argue that this is the case, claiming that ταῦτα πάντα in v. 30 is parallel to ταῦτα in v. 29. As Gundry explains, v. 29 predicts that "these things" will take place before the coming of the Son of Man. He comments that "these things" cannot include the predictions of vv. 24–27, which describe the actual coming of the Son of Man, not signs of his coming.[181] Other commentators, however, dispute this assertion.[182]

Marcus explains that "these things" of v. 29 refers to the destruction of the temple and the other events which the Markan community was experiencing, and v. 30 to the eschaton and the return of the Son of Man. "When Jesus' disciples see 'these things,' they will know that the end is *near*, but when they see 'all these things" . . . they will know that is has *arrived*." He also notes that the similarities between Mark 9:1, Matthew 10:23, and v. 30 suggest an interrelationship between the three. Marcus uses their relationship with each other to reach the conclusion that v. 30's prediction includes the parousia.[183] Allison and Davies also understand ταῦτα πάντα to denote the entire escha-tological scenario for three reasons: expectation of an imminent parousia was ubiquitous among early Christians, a limitation of "all these things" to only some elements of the discourse flies in the face of the plain reading of the text, and the disciples' question in v. 4 implies an understanding that the temple destruction as an element of a larger nexus of events.[184]

This analysis of v. 30 demonstrates that the prediction includes all nine events, and that they are expected to take place within a generation, about forty years, from the time that Jesus was purported to have made the prediction.

On its initial reading, v. 32 appears to contradict v. 30. Jesus would not be able to state when the parousia would take place if only the Father knows when it will take place, and that he as the Son does not. Apart from theologi-cal difficulties stemming from Jesus' purported admission of ignorance which do not concern this project,[185] it seems contradictory for Mark to have Jesus state that the parousia will come within a generation, only to say two verses later that he does not know when it will come. However, as Beasley-Murray,[186] A. Collins,[187] Marcus,[188] Russell,[189] Murphy,[190] and Gundry[191] explain, Jesus claims to know that the eschaton will come within a general time period, even though he does not know precisely when it will happen. It is one thing to predict that the parousia will take place within the next forty years; it is quite another to claim to know the exact date that it will happen. Pesch[192] and Hahn[193] explain that these two logia are brought together so that the readers will gain hope from the assurance of the impending parousia but that they will not succumb to fanatical anticipation of it.

The contradiction between vv. 30 and 32, as they were understood when written, is more apparent than real. Taken together, Mark predicts that events A-I will take place within the next few decades, even though the exact timing is unknowable.

PURPOSE FOR THE PREDICTION

The Olivet discourse, as it was understood originally, makes its predictions in order to instill vigilance and to encourage hope in difficult situations.[194]

As Beasley-Murray notes, discernment or watchfulness is the major theme of the entire discourse, as evidenced by the repetition of the word βλέπετε (watch or beware) throughout. The closing parable of the householder emphasizes this theme.[195] Deppe,[196] Dupont,[197] Gundry,[198] and A. Collins[199] each maintain that the reason for this vigilance is to watch for Jesus' return. Beasley-Murray explains that the discourse is a summons for believers actively to be aware of and respond to God's activity around them. Waiting and watchfulness are not passive activities, but indicate participation in the tasks of discipleship.[200] According to Marcus, the call for wakefulness and vigilance ought to be understood as an exhortation to withstand the appeal of the demonic powers, to understand the true nature of the world, and to be prepared for God's in-breaking into it.[201] Vigilance also implies expectation. As Gundry puts it, the reader is to take on the role of the servants of the parable and be ready for the master's return.[202] Cranfield points out that this expectation does not imply withdrawal from the current situation, but engagement in the world with a recognition of God's presence in it.[203] Allison, using cross-cultural evidence from other eschatological prophecies, argues that Mark's call for watchfulness is a typical response when predicted events fail to occur.[204]

Cranfield,[205] Kümmel,[206] and C. Black[207] point out that the discourse provides its predictions not only to instill vigilance, but also to offer hope in difficult circumstances. The predictions, particularly of Jesus' return and of the ingathering of the elect, encourage perseverance for an anxious audience. Fast explains that the discourse does not offer an explanation for why its readers are experiencing hardships; it tells them how to conduct themselves in such situations.[208] Dewar[209] and Lightfoot[210] argue that this comfort and encouragement come not only from the prediction of the parousia, but also from the way that the discourse helps its readers to understand their suffering in light of Jesus' experiences. Just as he is purported to have been glorified after his crucifixion, believers will also be vindicated. As Malbon puts it, the message of the discourse is "The end is not now, not yet, not known; so keep alert, endure, and be saved."[211]

PAST AND PRESENT APPROPRIATION OF THE PREDICTIONS

I have demonstrated that the predictions of Mark 13 were for literal and historical events, rather than figurative expressions for personal or spiritual conditions. Six of the nine events took place during the first Christian generation. The discourse predicts that all nine of the events will take place during that time period, although it cautions against precise expectations for when they will occur. The original readers would have been able to appropriate these predictions as encouragement for vigilance and as a promise to instill hope during difficulty. These possibilities for appropriation were available to the original readers because at the time the text described a future world. These readers did not have to accept the world description of the Olivet discourse in order to appropriate it, as my previous treatment of appropriation explains (pp. 30–32). But they could still recognize it as a description of the world that challenged, re-oriented, or confirmed their prior conceptions.

Possibilities for the appropriation of this text changed, however, with the new historical circumstances of the readers. After the generational deadline had passed, the text no longer projected a literal world of the future; the future that it purported to have configured had arrived and it looked nothing like what the text configured. While it is true that events A-F did take place, their significance pales in comparison to the dramatic non-events G-I. This discrepancy between the text's world-description and the world conditions after the passing of the first Christian generation only enables the reader to appropriate the text's world as a possibility that could have been but is not. The text's meaning that was apparent when written was that these literal events would occur. Interpretive moves which claim figurative meaning cannot be supported by critical analysis of the text (i.e. the mode of explanation within Ricoeur's hermeneutics as I demonstrate on pp. 6–12). The text predicts that all the events will take place within the approximately four decades after Jesus was purported to have made the prediction. If the Olivet discourse were simply a fictive text, similar to Shakespeare's *Romeo and Juliet*, Sir Thomas More's *Utopia*, or Isaac Asimov's science fiction novels, the discrepancy between the text's world and the actual world would not affect its appropriation as dramatically. Today's reader could encounter, in the text's world, new perspectives on the actual world. In the case of Mark 13, this option for appropriation is not available because the text claims to refer to actual events, albeit ones in the future.

I contend that the options for today's reader to appropriate Mark 13 extend beyond understanding which arises from a text that makes a false prediction of the future. As I will argue in the next chapter, the meaning of Mark 13 is not limited to the meanings that were apparent for its original readers, in the historical circumstances under which the text was written. Following Ricoeur, I contend that meanings exist within the text that were latent in its original historical setting but are apparent now. Latent meanings are present within the linguistic constructs of a text in addition to those that are foregrounded by the conditions present in the context of its writing. When the reading-conditions of the text are different from the writing-conditions, latent meaning is foregrounded. It is not the case that the meaning of the text changes according to the circumstances in which it is encountered or with the preconceptions of the readers who engage with it. A reader who ignores or contorts what the text actually offers in order to make it conform with what she wants it to say is not appropriating the text but seeking for the text to confirm her prior commitments. The more important it is to the reader that the text say, or not say, something, the more likely she is to violate the boundaries of its meaning. In the case of Mark 13, some interpreters with a strong commitment to the authoritative nature or divine inspiration of the text refuse to accept that the discourse predicts events which did not happen, and they seek meanings for the text which do not accord with the text itself. Ricoeur's emphasis on the critical analysis of explanation disqualifies such hermeneutical maneuvers.

Other hermeneuts support Ricoeur's contention for latent meaning; that is, meaning that is inherent to a text but which is not discernible in certain historical settings. McLean contends that the fleeting nature of the historical situation that produced the text prevents the "latent reserve" of its meaning to be discerned at that time. It is only through subsequent interpretive work that the larger field of the text's reference becomes evident. As the reader engages with the text in conjunction with other texts, she is able to appropriate otherwise hidden meaning in it.[212] Grech explains that a written text "contains latent possibilities which are constantly actualized in history, and, in theological reversal can actually contradict [the author]."[213] The text does not move out of the situation of its production and change its meaning like a chameleon in a new environment. Rather, aspects of meaning which are inherent in the text itself become more recognizable. Similarly, Kermode writes of "the superiority of the latent over the manifest sense" in interpretation. He addresses Mark's gospel in particular, arguing that the meaning of the text is a mystery to be discerned rather than a plain sense to be accepted. The narratives "mean more than they seem to say" or even "other than [they] seem to say."[214] Kermode offers examples of this in non-religious texts as well. There is more happening in the text, a more significant meaning, than its straightforward sense.[215]

A text is able to contain meaning which is latent in some situations but is apparent in others. For example, Sophocles' play *Oedipus Rex* had latent meaning that describes an individual's emotional relationship with his parents which were not recognized until Freud's time. The tragic drama describes psychological dynamics that were unrecognized for more than two millennia. Theophilos identifies a similar latent feature in Jesus' discourse: v. 19's observation that the suffering will be worse than any suffered since creation, and that it will never be equaled in the future. Such an observation implies that there will in fact be a future in which there is suffering. This, as Theophilos puts it, "implies that there is a continuation of the space-time continuum."[216] This element of the text only emerges for consideration after the failure of predicted events to take place.

Today's reader is able to recognize two issues in Mark 13 that were not originally discernible. The first is the juxtaposition of vv. 30 and 32's logia. As I explain in p. 76–78, they could be reconciled easily before the passing of the deadline: v. 30 provides a broad prediction, and v. 32 cautions against a too-precise application of it. After the passing of the deadline, however, a tension between the two logia can be recognized which was not discernible until then. Jesus' purported ability to predict future events, even generally, must be reconciled with his admission of ignorance. The text presents a provocative ambiguity: how can a text describe Jesus' false claim to be able to predict the future, and at the same time portray him as disavowing the ability to make such predictions? Second, the parable of the fig tree of v. 28 and the generational prediction of v. 30 indicate an imminent but imprecise occurrence before the passing of the deadline. The ongoing or recurring nature of these tropes becomes evident after the imminence of the events is no longer possible: summer comes each year, and generations follow each other. In Chapter 7 I describe a continuing pattern of events that emerges from the text. For these issues to be aspects of the meaning of Mark 13 today, the text's meaning today must be different from, or in addition to, the meaning that was apparent in its original context. In the next chapter I present an argument to support this contention.

NOTES

1. Ricoeur, *Explanation and Understanding*, 142.
2. Allison, "Jesus and the Victory of Apocalyptic," 130–31; cf. Allison, *Jesus of Nazareth*, 162.
3. Adams, *The Stars Will Fall*, 156.
4. Ibid., 151–52.
5. Ibid., 147–50; cf. Crispin H. T. Fletcher-Louis, "Jesus, the Temple and the Dissolution of Heaven and Earth," in *Apocalyptic in History and Tradition*, eds. Christopher Rowland and John M. T. Barton (London: Sheffield Academic Press, 2002), 139–41.
6. Allison, "Jesus and the Victory of Apocalyptic," 130–31; cf. Allison, *Jesus of Nazareth*, 162.
7. Allison, *Jesus of Nazareth*, 165–66.
8. Adams, *The Stars Will Fall*, 156, 159–60.
9. Allison, "Jesus and the Victory of Apocalyptic," 135.
10. Allison, *Jesus of Nazareth*, 165–66.
11. Ibid., 130–31.
12. Adams, *The Stars Will Fall*, 152–53.
13. Allison, *Jesus of Nazareth*, 157–62.
14. Adams, *The Stars Will Fall*, 161–62.

15. Allison, "Jesus and the Victory of Apocalyptic," 137–39; cf. Allison, *Jesus of Nazareth*, 152–57.

16. Beasley-Murray, *Jesus and the Last Days*, 364–65.

17. Gundry, Mark, 733.

18. Grayston, "Study of Mark," 93.

19. Lambrecht, *Die Redaktion*, 267.

20. Beasley-Murray, *Jesus and the Last Days*, 364–65.

21. Pesch, *Naherwartungen*, 74–82.

22. Cranfield, "St Mark (1953)," 287, 301; Cranfield, "St Mark (1954)," 284.

23. Grayston, "Study of Mark," 373–75.

24. Marcus, *Mark 8–16*, 866–67.

25. For alternate descriptions of the discourse's structure, cf. Malbon, "Literary Contexts," 120; C. Clifton Black, "An Oration at Olivet: Some Rhetorical Dimensions of Mark 13," in *Persuasive Artistry: Studies in New Testament Rhetoric in Honor of George A. Kennedy*, ed. Duane F. Watson (Sheffield, England: JSOT Press, 1991), 74–5; Hartman, *Prophecy Interpreted*, 225; A. Collins, "Apocalyptic Rhetoric," 14–35; R. T. France, *The Gospel of Mark* (New York: Doubleday, 1998), 167, 174–75; Gundry, Mark, 733–34; Slater, "*Apocalypticism* and Eschatology," 9, and Brandenburger, *Markus 13*, 17–20.

26. Gundry, *Mark*,733–34.

27. Charles E. B. Cranfield, "St Mark 13," *Scottish Journal of Theology* 6 (1953): 287–90, 297–98; *Cranfield, Gospel*, 394–97.

28. Grayston, "Study of Mark," 373–75.

29. Pesch, *Naherwartungen*, 80.

30. Lambrecht, *Die Redaktion*, 273–78.

31. Deppe, "Charting the Future," 93.

32. Cranfield, *Gospel* 407; Charles E. B. Cranfield, "St Mark 13," *Scottish Journal of Theology* 7 (1954): 284.

33. Lambrecht, Die Redaktion, 280–85.

34. Pesch describes the structure of the third section as three exhortations nested between two parables (Pesch, Naherwartungen, 79, 81).

35. Marcus, *Mark 8–16*, 909.

36. Hartman, *Prophecy Interpreted*, 225.

37. C. Black, "An Oration at Olivet," 28–36.

38. France, *Gospel of Mark*,168; cf. Aquinas, *Gospel of Mark*, 260.

39. Marcus, *Mark 8–16*, 874.

40. Cf. Lambrecht, *Die Redaktion*, 286 for a similar outline.

41. Cf. Pesch, *Naherwartungen*, 80.

42. Marcus considers it to be an insertion which interrupts the logical flow of the discourse (Marcus, *Mark 8–16*, 883, 884), but Gundry claims that v. 10 fits logically into the discourse in its present location (Gundry, *Mark*, 768). Cf. Beasley-Murray, *Jesus and the Last Days*, 398; Pesch, *Naherwartungen*, 131, and David Wenham, *The Rediscovery of Jesus' Eschatological Discourse* (Gospel Perspectives, Sheffield: JSOT Press, 1984), 268–71, 273–75 on this point.

43. Beasley-Murray, *Jesus and the Last Days*, 383–84.

44. Cranfield, "St Mark (1953)," 189–90.

45. Gundry, Mark, 735–36.

46. Bolt, "Mark 13," 19–20.

47. Lambrecht, Die Redaktion, 87–8; Bolt, "Mark 13," 26; Kümmel, *Promise and Fulfilment*, 99–100; Adams, "Historical Crisis," 329; Adams, *The Stars Will Fall*, 140–41; Cranfield, "St Mark (1953)," 297–98; Cranfield, *Gospel According to Mark*, 401–02; C. Black, "An Oration at Olivet," 70; Fletcher-Louis, "Jesus, the Temple," 123–29; Pesch, *Naherwartungen*, 104; Russell, *Parousia*, 67; John Calvin, *Commentary of a Harmony of the Evangelists, Matthew, Mark, and Luke* (Edinburgh: Calvin Translation Society, 1843), trans. William Pringle. Vol. 3. 3 vols. (Grand Rapids: Baker, 1989), 117–18; and Cyril of Jerusalem, Mark, in Ancient Christian Commentary on Scripture, New Testament, vol. 2, ed. Thomas C. Oden, and Christopher A. Hall, (Chicago, London: Fitzroy Dearborn, 1998), 181. Beasley-Murray argues the opposite point, (Beasley-Murray, *Jesus and the Last Days* 382, 388).

48. Cf. e.g. Chrystostom, Homilies, 452; Pseudo-Jerome in Aquinas, *Gospel of Mark*, 255; Bede in Aquinas, *Gospel of Mark*, 254, 258; Calvin, *Commentary*, 116.

49. Marcus, *Mark 8–16*, 873.

50. France, *Gospel of Mark*,165.

51. Beasley-Murray, *Jesus and the Last Days*, 379–82; contra Allison and Davies, *A Critical and Exegetical Commentary*, 334.

52. E.g. Chrystostom, *Homilies*, 450; Theophylact in Aquinas, *Gospel of Mark*, 254.

53. Kümmel,. *Promise and Fulfilment*, 100–101.

54. John S. Kloppenborg, "Evocatio Deorum and the Date of Mark," *Journal of Biblical Literature* 124.3 (2005): 429–33.

55. Marcus. *Mark 8–16*, 868.

56. Such, *Abomination of Desolation*, 61–62; cf. Lambrecht, *Die Redaktion*, 100–05; Beasley-Murray, *Jesus and the Last Days*, 390–91.

57. A. Collins, "Apocalyptic Rhetoric," 27–8

58. Cf. Marcus, *Mark 8–16* 875, 879–80, 900–901; Gundry, *Mark*, 737; Origen in Harold Smith, *Ante-Nicene Exegesis of the Gospels, Translation of Christian Literature*, Series V (London: Society for Promoting Christian Knowledge, 1928), 141–44; A. Collins, "Apocalyptic Rhetoric," 14–18; and Beasley-Murray, *Jesus and the Last Days*, 392–94.

59. A. Collins, "The Eschatological Discourse," 1132–133.

60. Gundry, *Mark*, 761–62.

61. Marcus, *Mark 8–16*, 900–01.

62. Such, *Abomination of Desolation*, 169–71.

63. A. Collins, "Eschatological Discourse," 1133.

64. Marcus, *Mark 8–16*, 875–76.

65. Brandenburger, *Markus* 13, 46.

66. Cf. Theophylact and Bede in Aquinas, *Gospel of Mark*, 257.

67. Beasley-Murray, *Jesus and the Last Days*, 394–95.

68. Calvin, *Commentary*, 121–22.

69. France, *Gospel of Mark*,170, Beasley-Murray *Jesus and the Last Days*, 418.

70. Marcus, *Mark 8–16*, 895–96.

71. Gundry, Mark, 754–55.

72. Wright, *Jesus and the Victory of God*, 353.

73. Beasley-Murray, *Jesus and the Last Days*, 412–13.

74. Such, *Abomination of Desolation*, 55.

75. Ibid., 118–26.

76. Beasley-Murray, *Jesus and the Last Days*, 417–18; Gundry, Mark, 743; Allison and Davies, *A Critical and Exegetical Commentary*, 350; Marcus, *Mark 8–16*, 892.

77. In Aquinas, *Gospel of Mark*, 261.

78. Adams, *The Stars Will Fall*, 141–42.

79. Russell, *Parousia*, 69–72.

80. Lambrecht, *Die Redaktion*, 124.

81. Cranfield, "St Mark (1953)," 296; Cranfield, *Gospel According to Mark*, 400.

82. Gundry, *Mark*, 740.

83. In Aquinas, *Gospel of Mark*, 259.

84. Marcus, *Mark 8–16*, 537–39.

85. Bastiaan Martinus Franciscus van Iersel, "Failed Followers in Mark: Mark 13:12 as a Key for the Identification of the Intended Readers," *Catholic Biblical Quarterly* 58 (1996): 254–58, 260.

86. Marcus, *Mark 8–16*, 886.

87. Gundry, *Mark*, 739.

88. Such, *Abomination of Desolation*, 26–7.

89. Kümmel,. *Promise and Fulfilment*, 84.

90. Chrystostom, Homilies, 452.

91. In Oden, Mark, 183.

92. Calvin, *Commentary*, 128–29.

93. Allison, *Constructing Jesus*, 153.

94. Beasley-Murray, *Jesus and the Last Days*, 408–11.

95. Theophilos, *Abomination of Desolation*, 159–67.

96. Marcus, *Mark 8–16*, 889.

97. Crossley, *Date of Mark's Gospel*, 28–29.

98. Wenham, *Rediscovery*, 17–19.

99. Francis Dewar, "Chapter 13 and the Passion Narrative in St Mark," *Theology* 64 (1961): 103; cf. Lambrecht, *Die Redaktion*, 151–52; contra Theophilos, *Abomination of Desolation*, 18–19.

100. Wenham, *Rediscovery*, 193–95.

101. Pesch, *Naherwartungen*, 140–43.

102. Such, *Abomination of Desolation*, 87.

103. Cf. Gundry, *Mark*, 741.

104. Theophilus (*Abomination of Desolation*, 12–20) offers a detailed consideration of options that exegetes have provided.

105. In Beasley-Murray, *Jesus and the Last Days*, 90–1.

106. Such, *Abomination of Desolation*, 92.

107. Crossley, *Date of Mark's Gospel*, 37–38.

108. Ibid.

109. Allison and Davies, *A Critical and Exegetical Commentary*, 345–46.

110. Brandenburger, *Markus* 13, 24–5.

111. Gundry, *Mark*, 771.

112. In Aquinas, *Gospel of Mark*, 260.

113. Russell, *Parousia*, 73.

114. Hendrika Nicoline Roskam, *The Purpose of the Gospel of Mark in Its Historical and Social Context* (Leiden: Brill, 2004), 90–1.

115. In Beasley-Murray *Jesus and the Last Days* 242–44.

116. Chrystostom, Homilies, 452–53.

117. Theophilos, *Abomination of Desolation*, 123, 230.

118. Such, *Abomination of Desolation*, 94–97.

119. Marcus, "Jewish War," 454–55; contra Such, *Abomination of Desolation*, 93; A. Collins, "Apocalyptic Rhetoric," 24–5.

120. Allison and Davies, *A Critical and Exegetical Commentary*, 345–46; cf. Irenaeus and Hippolytus in Smith, *Ante-Nicene Exegesis*, 129–30; contra Beasley-Murray, *Jesus and the Last Days*, 414–16, Lambrecht, Die Redaktion, 151–52.

121. A. Collins, "Apocalyptic Rhetoric," 22–4.

122. Eddy, "The (W)Right Jesus," 46.

123. Shively, *Apocalyptic Imagination*, 193–94.

124. Marcus, *Mark 8–16*, 870–71.

125. Origen (in Smith, Ante-Nicene Exegesis, 150–51), Bede (in Aquinas, *Gospel of Mark*, 265), Calvin (Commentary, 146), Cranfield ("St Mark (1953)," 301–02 and Gospel According to Mark, 406), Dewar ("Chapter 13 and the Passion," 104), Nickelson ("Meaning and Significance," 36–83), and France (*Gospel of Mark*, 172–73) argue for figurative understandings of this prediction. However, I find the arguments provided by Allison and Davies (*A Critical and Exegetical Commentary*, 357–58) and Marcus (*Mark 8–16*, 906) to be more compelling.

126. Allison and Davies, *A Critical and Exegetical Commentary*, 357.

127. Nickelson, "Meaning and Significance," 114–15.

128. Beasley-Murray, *Jesus and the Last Days*, 374–75, 424–26.

129. Jozef Verheyden, "Describing the Parousia: The Cosmic Phenomena in Mk 13, 24–25," in *The Scriptures in the Gospels*, ed. Christopher M. Tuckett (Louvain: Peeters, 1997), 540–46.

130. Marcus, *Mark 8–16*, 906–7.

131. Allison, *Jesus of Nazareth*, 162.

132. Nickelson, "Meaning and Significance," 135–39.

133. Bastiaan Martinus Franciscus van Iersel, "The Sun, Moon, and Stars of Mark 13, 24–25 in a Greco-Roman Reading." *Biblica* 77.1 (1996): 86–90.

134. In Aquinas, *Gospel of Mark*, 265.

135. Gundry, *Mark*, 782–83.

136. In Beasley-Murray, *Jesus and the Last Days*, 186–87.

137. Gundry, *Mark*, 783.

138. Lambrecht, *Die Redaktion*, 179–80.

139. Beasley-Murray, *Jesus and the Last Days*, 428–29.

140. Marcus, *Mark 8–16*, 903–04, 908,

141. In Aquinas, *Gospel of Mark*, 266.

142. Crossley, *Date of Mark's Gospel*, 24–5.

143. Ferdinand Hahn, "Die Rede von der Parusie des Menschensohnes Markus 13," in *Jesus und der Menschensohn: für Anton Vögtle*, eds. Rudolf Pesch and Rudolf Schnackenburg (Freiburg: Herder, 1975), 262.

144. Michael B. Shepherd, "Daniel 7:13 and the New Testament Son of Man," *Westminster Theological Journal* 68.1 (2006): 106–11.

145. Harry L. Chronis, "To Reveal and to Conceal: A Literary-Critical Perspective on 'the Son of Man' in Mark," *New Testament Studies* 51.4 (2005): 461–66.

146. Norman Perrin, *Jesus and the Language of the Kingdom: Symbol and Metaphor in New Testament Interpretation* (Philadelphia: Fortress Press, 1976), 57–60.

147. Gundry, *Mark*, 784.

148. Murphy, *Apocalypticism*, 237–39.

149. Allison, *Constructing Jesus*, 293–303.

150. Contra Dodd (*Parables of the Kingdom*, 66–69), Albert Schweitzer (*The Quest of the Historical Jesus: A Critical Study of Its Progress from Reimarus to Wrede*. 1910, trans. W. Montgomery (New York: Macmillan, 1968), 282–85, Caird (*Language and Imagery*, 138–39).

151. Joshua E. Leim, "In the Glory of His Father: Intertextuality and the Apocalyptic Son of Man in the Gospel of Mark," *Journal of Theological Interpretation* 7.2 (2013): 224–28.

152. Wright, *Jesus and the Victory of God*, 361–62.

153. Glasson, *The Second Advent*, 25–31.

154. Dewar, "Chapter 13 and the Passion," 104–5.

155. Robinson, *Jesus and His Coming*, 40–52.

156. Beasley-Murray, *Jesus and the Last Days*, 430.

157. Marcus, *Mark 8–16*, 904–05.

158. Hartman, *Prophecy Interpreted*, 157–59.

159. Gundry, *Mark*, 784.

160. Craig Blomberg, "The Wright Stuff: A Critical Overview of *Jesus and the Victory of God*," in *Jesus and the Restoration of Israel: A Critical Assessment of N. T. Wright's Jesus and the Victory of God*, ed. Carey C Newman. (Downers Grove IL: InterVarsity Press, 1999), 32–3.

161. Allison and Davies, *A Critical and Exegetical Commentary*, 362.

162. Crossley, *Date of Mark's Gospel*, 23–4.

163. Marcus, *Mark 8–16*, 904.

164. Gundry, *Mark*, 784.

165. Pesch, *Naherwartungen*, 166–67.

166. Shively, *Apocalyptic Imagination*, 203.

167. Wenham, Rediscovery, 314–23.

168. Cf. Brandenburger, Markus 13, 60–4; Lambrecht, *Die Redaktion*, 190–91; Beasley-Murray *Jesus and the Last Days*, 430.

169. Beasley-Murray, *Jesus and the Last Days*, 433–34. Gundry explains that the prediction does not provide this specificity because of the discourse's emphasis on the coming of the Son of Man and not upon the fate of the believers (Gundry, *Mark*, 786).

170. Marcus, *Mark 8–16*, 905; cf. Origen, in Oden, *Mark*, 188.

171. Beasley-Murray, *Jesus and the Last Days*, 433; cf. Bede, in Aquinas, *Gospel of Mark*, 266–67.

172. Gundry, *Mark*, 745.

173. Theophilos, *Abomination of Desolation*, 137–45.

174. Ibid., 224–25.

175. Cf. Theophylact and Bede in Aquinas, *Gospel of Mark*, 268.

176. Beasley-Murray, *Jesus and the Last Days*, 443.

177. Gundry, *Mark*, 791.

178. Marcus, *Mark 8–16*, 911–12; Kümmel,. *Promise and Fulfilment*, 61; France, *Gospel of Mark*, 173; Allison and Davies, *A Critical and Exegetical Commentary*, 367–68; Beasley-Murray, *Jesus and the Last Days*, 444–45; Russell, *Parousia*, 18–21, 84–9.

179. Beasley-Murray, *Jesus and the Last Days*, 444–45. Focant, on the other hand, contends that γενεὰ refers to the Jewish race, thereby eliminating any temporal aspect from the predictions (Camille Focant, The Gospel According to Mark: A Commentary, trans. Leslie Robert Keylock (Eugene, OR : Pickwick, 2012), 550.)

180. Cf. Allison and Davies, *A Critical and Exegetical Commentary*, 367–68; Gundry, *Mark*, 790.

181. Gundry, *Mark*, 746; cf. A. Collins, "Apocalyptic Rhetoric," 31; Adams, *The Stars Will Fall*, 164–65; Cranfield, "St Mark (1954)," 284, 290–91; Cranfield, *Gospel According to Mark*, 407–09; Blomberg, "The Wright Stuff," 32–3; Focant, *Gospel According to Mark*, 549–50; Beasley-Murray, *Jesus and the Last Days*, 445–46.

182. Kümmel,. *Promise and Fulfilment*, 21, 60.

183. Marcus, *Mark 8–16*, 911; cf. Such, *Abomination of Desolation*, 167–68.

184. Allison and Davies, *A Critical and Exegetical Commentary*, 367–68.

185. Marcus *Mark 8–16*, 913–14; cf. Chrysostom 463–65, Theophylact, in Aquinas 269, 271, Augustine, in Madigan 273–74 and Oden 193–94, Hilary of Poitiers, in Madigan 259–62 and Aquinas 270, and Ambrose in Madigan 264–67.

186. Beasley-Murray, *Jesus and the Last Days*, 458–61.

187. A. Collins, "Apocalyptic Rhetoric," 33; A. Collins, "The Eschatological Discourse," 1137.

188. Marcus, *Mark 8–16*, 918.

189. Russell, *Parousia*, 89–90.

190. Murphy, *Apocalypticism*, 238.

191. Gundry, *Mark*, 747–48, 794.

192. Pesch, *Naherwartungen*, 181–95.

193. Hahn, "Die Rede von der Parusie," 243–44.

194. Marcus (*Mark 8–16*, 876) and Pesch (*Naherwartungen*, 229–31) also claim that it deals with apocalyptic excitement, but in different ways. Pesch argues that the discourse calmed fervor caused by the temple's destruction, but Marcus maintains that it aroused fervor instead. Cf. Beasley-Murray, *Jesus and the Last Days*, 45–6, 367–69 for further discussion of the discourse's warning to avoid deceptive apocalyptic teachings.

195. Beasley-Murray, *Jesus and the Last Days*, 389–90.

196. Deppe, "Charting the Future," 90–5.

197. In Beasley-Murray, *Jesus and the Last Days*, 216–17.

198. Gundry, *Mark*, 799–800

199. A. Collins, "Apocalyptic Rhetoric," 33–4.

200. Beasley-Murray, *Jesus and the Last Days*, 474–75.

201. Marcus, *Mark 8–16*, 921–23.

202. Gundry, *Mark*, 749. Cf. Bede in Aquinas, *Gospel of Mark*, 271; Beasley-Murray, *Jesus and the Last Days*, 475.

203. Cranfield, "St Mark (1954)," 297–98. Cf. Gregory in Aquinas, *Gospel of Mark*, 271.

204. Allison, *Constructing Jesus*, 149.

205. Cranfield, "St Mark (1954)," 294–95.

206. Kümmel,. *Promise and Fulfilment*, 97.

207. C. Black, "An Oration at Olivet," 81, 90–1.

208. Lesley D. Fast, "Rhetorical Dimensions of Speech Representation: A Study of the Speeches of Jesus in the Gospel of Mark" (PhD diss., McGill University [Canada], 2002), 106.

209. Dewar, "Chapter 13 and the Passion," 100.

210. In Beasley-Murray, *Jesus and the Last Days*, 99–101.

211. Malbon, "Literary Contexts," 122–23.

212. McLean, *Biblical Interpretation*, 238.

213. Prosper Grech, "Inner-Biblical Reinterpretation and Modern Hermeneutics," in *Philosophical Hermeneutics and Biblical Exegesis*, eds. Petr Pokorný and Jan Roskovec (Tübingen: Mohr Siebeck, 2002), 235.

214. Frank Kermode, *The Genesis of Secrecy: On the Interpretation of Narrative* (Cambridge, Ma: Harvard University Press, 1979), 2–3.

215. Ibid., 5–14.

216. Theophilos, *Abomination of Desolation*, 146.

Chapter 4

Textual Autonomy

This chapter provides support for the seventh premise of the argument that this project presents: "The meaning of a text is not limited to the meaning that was apparent when it was written." In order to support the contention that Mark 13 is able to be read metaphorically today, when it was originally read literally, it is necessary to demonstrate that in new contexts a text has the capacity to present meaning which was not initially evident. This meaning follows from the syntax, semantics, and pragmatics of the text itself; it is not a new meaning that derives from the historical perspective of the reader. The perception by today's reader of meaning other than or in addition to what was originally apparent is an appropriation of the text only if a text can mean something other than or in addition to what it meant when it was written: that is, the author's intended meaning, consistent with the presuppositions at the time of its writing, and as understood by its original audience. Otherwise, these issues are not present in the text itself, and engagement with them is not appropriation of the text.

To defend this claim I present and support Ricoeur's thesis that the meaning of a text is not limited to the intention of the author or to the context of its production. Appropriation of a text is an encounter with the world description of the text (cf. pp. 27–28). While it is a truism that an author intends to present meaning when he writes a text, the author may have failed in his attempt to express his intention; not all discursive acts accomplish what the author hopes. Additionally, and more relevant to this project, the text may present meaning in addition, and perhaps even in contradiction, to the author's intended meaning. Ricoeur argues that the meaning of the text comes from the text itself, and not from the author's intention or from the reader's expectations. Based on his definition of discourse as "someone says something to someone about something,"[1] I summarize Ricoeur's argument for textual autonomy thus:

1. A speaker or author initiates discourse ("someone says").
2. The speaker or author initiates discourse in order to convey meaning ("about something," or the reference of the text).
3. In order to convey this meaning, the speaker or author uses linguistic constructs ("something" that is said, or the sense of the text).
4. The linguistic expression of the speaker or author is received by an audience ("to someone," i.e. the listener or reader).
5. Because linguistic expressions of natural language do not possess a one-to-one correspondence between sense and reference in the manner of scientific, mathematical, or artificial languages, the meaning of the linguistic expression is not limited to the speaker or author's intended meaning.
6. The meaning(s) of the linguistic expression, or text, other than those that the speaker or author wished to convey, are also meaning(s) of the text.
7. In the case of written discourse, different meanings of the text are apparent in different reading contexts.
8. The reader engages in the explanatory mode of interpretation to determine the meaning(s) of the text.
9. While the meaning that is apparent to a reader may be the meaning that the writer wished to convey, a meaning other than the author's desired meaning is also able to be apparent.
10. The meaning of the text is determined neither by the author's intentions for creating the text, nor by the context of the reader, but by the linguistic constructs of the text itself, as it has been examined by the explanatory mode of interpretation.

Premises 1, 2, 3, and 4 are descriptions of discourse production. If premises 5, 6, 7, and 8 can be supported, premises 9 and 10 follow: meaning is not limited to the author's intended meaning, nor is it determined by the reading context, but comes from the text itself. The sections of this chapter provide support for each of these premises.

ADDITIONAL MEANING PRESENT IN THE TEXT

The fifth premise of Ricoeur's argument claims that when an author uses linguistic constructs to express meaning, the resultant text can express more than the single meaning of the author. For purposes of clarity, I assume that the author desired to express a singular meaning, and that he succeeded in

expressing it in the text. There are situations in which neither of these stipu-
lations apply, but for the purposes of this discussion I assume that they do.

Ricoeur explains that, in contrast to logical symbolism,[2] natural language
is polysemous. Words can have more than one meaning, and a communication act offers more than one meaning. Interpretation based on the context
of the word within the larger discourse is necessary to discern "the univocal
message the speaker has constructed on the polysemic basis of the common
lexicon."[3] He argues that this is a necessary feature of words; otherwise we
would need virtually infinite lexicons to assign a signifier for every possible
referent for every possible experience of that referent for every possible person doing the experiencing. Such a lexicon would be worthless in practical
terms because of its sheer size. Because of the polysemic meaning of words, a
word in isolation cannot properly be said to convey meaning; it can do so only
in the context of a sentence which provides predications of the word, in relation with the other words of the sentence.[4] And yet, even when a polysemic
word is placed in a textual setting, meaning still does not necessarily become
singular because polysemic meaning can also be present at the sentence level.
Ricoeur points out that meaning changes with the context and is never stable.
Further, even if there is a limited set of possible meanings for a discourse, it
is impossible to create a method for determining the appropriate meaning for
specific and ever-changing contexts.[5]

In support of Ricoeur's position, Wallace points out that the author's intentions have "passed over" into the text's literary structure. He explains that
authorial intention is discernible in the traces it left in the structure of the
text, but that reconstruction of intention is problematic because the autonomous text is able to convey extra-semiotic meanings (i.e. non-linguistic
reference) beyond the situation of its production. The reference of the text
can be more than what its author intended to present.[6] Bosco et al. also assert
that the "expressive meaning" of a speech act (i.e. its linguistic elements) is
not enough to determine the speaker's intention for the statement, and that
contextual cues beyond the discursive act itself are necessary for proper
understanding. They outline a number of physical and psycho-social factors
involved in the formation of discursive context, and they determine that a
variation of only one of these factors affects the understood meaning of the
statement.[7] Perception of intention can fluctuate even in the oral context, in
which speaker and listener share a setting which presumably can be used
by the speaker to construct a statement to convey his intentions. But in the
case of written discourse, the reader may not know the context of the text's
production and the author usually does not control the context in which
the reader encounters the text. The broad possibilities of meaning for the
text prevent the possibility of a singular meaning that matches the author's
intention.

Two examples illustrate how a text is able to present meaning other than the author's intention. First, Upton Sinclair intended for his book *The Jungle* to document the intolerable living conditions of immigrant workers in Chicago's meat-packing plants, but his descriptions of the filth in those plants led to the passage of the Meat Inspection Act of 1907 instead of worker reform. As Sinclair comments, "I aimed at the public's heart and by accident hit it in the stomach."[8] The second example is a personal one. In 1997 I traveled to Ghana and wrote my reflections on the trip in order to share my experience with others. I described the assistance my family received from a government official who put a vehicle and driver at our disposal. My intention for doing so was to point out the surprising generosity that we received from this and other individuals. The official, however, took offense at what I wrote because he read the description as an account of misuse of government resources. Without being aware of it, I had documented and disseminated an accusation against him.

Brandom provides another example to demonstrate how a statement includes the subsequent premises of that statement, even if the author was not aware of or in agreement with those subsequent premises. He imagines a colonel commanding his soldiers to cross a river within twenty-four hours. Inherent to that command is the injunction to do whatever lies within their ability and authority to effect that river crossing. The soldiers therefore cut down a copse of trees in order to construct a floating bridge. The colonel's command to cross the river did not specifically include a command to cut down the trees, but it was inherent to the command. Whether or not the colonel intended for the soldiers to cut down the trees is irrelevant. In fact, Brandom argues that even if the colonel were to dispute that he had ordered the soldiers to cut down the trees because he wanted them to camouflage his artillery, the fact would remain that by inference he had done so.[9] In the same way, the inferences which follow from a statement are not limited to the author's awareness of what those inferences may be. Further, if inferences develop from the statement which contradict the author's intentions, the author cannot appeal to those intentions as a reason to deny the inferences.[10] In response to Grice, Searle offers another example in which intention does not match meaning. A speaker may say something with the conviction that the statement means a certain thing, but with the hope that the listener will believe that it means something different. In this situation, Searle explains, meaning depends not only upon the intention of the speaker, but also upon the conventions or rules and circumstances surrounding that speech act.[11]

Based on these arguments, I conclude that the meaning of a linguistic construct is not limited to the author's intended meaning. In the face of this plurivocality, and even ambiguity, of the text, some factor must be available to determine meaning. Meaning cannot be determined by appealing to the author's intention, and the context of reading is not sufficient to do so either. Discernment of meaning comes from examination of the text itself.

MEANING IN ADDITION TO AUTHORIAL INTENT

The sixth premise of my argument in support of Ricoeur's textual autonomy states that "the meaning(s) of the linguistic construct, or text, other than those that the speaker or author wished to convey are also meaning(s) of the text." A text can mean something other than or in addition to what the author wanted it to mean. Hirsch presents the best-known modern argument against this claim when he asserts that the meaning of the text is the same as the intention of the author. Knapp and Michaels also present an argument that a text can be said to convey meaning only if it is related to the intention of an author. Support for Ricoeur's claim depends upon refutation of both of these arguments.

The Author Intends Meaning

Hirsch concedes that it is possible to read a text in multiple ways, but he claims that appropriate readings include only those that the author intended. He argues that we must accept author determined meaning because we need some criterion to determine singular textual meaning, and authorial intention is the only one we have.[12] Hirsch asserts that textual meaning is fixed and stable and includes elements such as unconscious components and implications. The significance of the text and the reader's response to it may change, but the meaning is fixed.[13] Hirsch appeals to Husserl's phenomenology to explain a difference between the meaning and significance of a text. For Hirsch, a text's meaning is fixed and stable, like an object. How that meaning is perceived by various readers is its significance, which changes according to the circumstances in which the reader encounters the text. This, for Hirsch, is analogous to Husserl's explanation that a single fixed object can have many different appearances, depending upon the perspective of the observer; the single physical object can be multiple intentional objects. Hirsch concludes from this that the single fixed meaning of a text provides a wide variety of significances, depending upon the reader's milieu. However, he maintains that any significance that a reader perceives in a text must arise from the text's single, stable meaning.[14] Ricoeur differs from Hirsch in two respects. First, Hirsch distinguishes between meaning and significance and Ricoeur does not. What Hirsch labels "meaning" is theoretical and can never be defined or verified. Because there is no such thing as a context-less reader, only significance is available. To use Husserl's terms, we can never discern the physical object because we only have intentional objects. Hirsch's readers are like Plato's cave-dwellers; they can only see the shadows on the wall but never the object behind them. It is impossible to make any assertion about the meaning of the text, as Hirsch defines it, because it is unapproachable. We can only examine the responses to this theoretical meaning, which Hirsch labels "significance." Ricoeur, however, claims that a text's meaning is what a reader perceives in the text. Second, Ricoeur asserts that a text is able to present multiple meanings, not the single meaning that Hirsch champions. There is no such thing as *the* meaning of a text.

The Text Exists Independently from the Author

For a text to mean something other than the author's intended meaning, it is necessary for the text to exist independently from the author. That is, it cannot be constrained by the author's context and world-view. Otherwise, Hirsch would be correct in his claim that textual meaning is equal to authorial intent. The independence of a text from its author, as well as from the circumstances of its writing and from its original audience, exists because of the relative permanence of the text. Depending upon the durability of the medium of inscription and the continued comprehensibility of the linguistic system which it employs, the text can exist indefinitely in contexts that the author cannot. Ricoeur agrees that the purpose for writing a text is for the author to share his intention with an audience.[15] He explains, however, that once the intention-as-discourse has been written, it becomes "an archive available for individual and collective memory."[16] He explains that functions of the shared language structure not only make the text intelligible for individuals other than the author, but they also function in the reader's understanding of the text. The referential nature of language reconnects the discourse to the world, but not always in ways that are congruent with the author's intention.

Ricoeur contrasts this with oral discourse, in which the speaker and listener share a setting and situation and have the opportunity for dialogue to negotiate a shared understanding which accords to the speaker's intention. The dialogue between speaker and listener includes not only the speaker's statement, but also the situation in which the statement has been made, to which both speaker and listener can refer in the dialogue.[17] The reference of the text is at hand and trumps appeals to the sense of the statement. Ricoeur points out that when discourse is lifted out of context by inscription, reference is available only through what is presented in the text itself.[18] He asserts that "the intended meaning of the text is not essentially the presumed intention of the author . . . but rather what the text means for whoever complies with its injunction. The text seeks to place us in its meaning."[19] Ricoeur explains that the task for the reader is not to identify the author's meaning, but the text's meaning. As he puts it, "textual meaning and psychological meaning have different destinies," because the text is freed from the socio-historical conditions of its production and is "recontextualized" in new settings each time it is read.[20] Ricoeur explains that "from the moment the text escapes from its author and from his situation, it also escapes from its original audience. Hence it can procure new readers for itself."[21] McLean goes so far as to argue that the concept of the Biblical canon "universalizes" the reader, based upon the conviction that the texts' audiences are not limited to the original readers but include everyone who can read them.[22] Van der Heiden explains that Ricoeur does not lament the loss of the context of the production of the text, but welcomes this distanciation as an opportunity for disclosure of additional meaning as the text is recontextualized in the reading event.[23]

As Grech puts it, "Reinterpretation . . . actuates possibilities which were hidden in the text even if not foreseen by the author himself."[24] Searle also explains that intentional acts occur in concert with unintentional acts. Some unintended acts are components of the intention, while others cannot be separated from the intentional action without self-description on the part of the agent. There is no distinction between the intended action and the unintended action with a self-referential description of the action on the part of the agent.[25] Although Hirsch explains in his later writings that authorial intentions may include future readings that the author could not foresee, he claims that they are "present-day exemplifications" of the author's intention, and not something different from that intention.[26] Hirsch's argument bears the marks of one who seeks to rescue a proposition that is not supported by evidence. First, he extends his definition of authorial intention to include meanings that the author did not foresee. This extension creates ambiguity about what he means by authorial intention; an author cannot intend something that he did not foresee. Second, he claims that all future apprehensions of meaning for a text must be related to the author's intention. But this is not the case if the author was unaware of the contexts for future readings of the text.

Knapp and Michaels provide a different but related argument for textual interpretation that is determined by authorial intent. In their example of successive stanzas of poetry that appear on the sand of a beach with each wave that washes over the area, they propose that the amazed observer has two options: he can either assume that there is some sort of an intentional agent at work composing these stanzas, or that the marks on the sand are pure coincidence with no agent behind their making. In the first case, the reader may be amazed at the process of writing and at the identity of the author, but the marks in the sand are a communication between an author and a reader. In the second case, Knapp and Michaels assert that there is no communication at all. If writing occurs in a way other than by an intentional agent, it is not writing at all. It is merely the "accidental likeness of language." Without the intention of an author behind it, a text is not a text at all and therefore can provide no meaning.[27] An action is a subset of a happening because it requires intention and commitment. Actions carry meaning, but happenings do not. They are merely chance occurrences. However, Knapp and Michaels' conclusion does not follow from their example. Suppose that we come upon this beach upon which lines of poetry can be found, and all theories about the authorship fail (i.e. there is no illusionist trickery, technical manipulation, occult or spiritual involvement, and so forth). We as observers decide that the marks in the sand appeared spontaneously from mindless (and intention-less) natural forces. This decision does not necessarily lead to the conclusion that the marks in the sand are not poetry; if the furrows on the beach are able to elicit from us a sense of understanding, then they are a text. Phenomenologically, if the marks create a possible world of meaning, then they are in fact a text. The manner by which a text is generated may influence the readers' appropriation of it, but it does not fully determine the world which the text presents.

Reference of the Text Is Not the Ostensive Reference of the Author

Hirsch responds to the thesis that a text can convey meaning other than the author's will by asking, "How can an author mean something he does not mean?"[28] But that is not the point. The question is, can a text mean something different from, or more than, what the author wanted it to when it is read in new contexts? A text is able to mean something other than what the author meant to express, as demonstrated in pp. 96–99. Even if the author successfully uses language to express his intended meaning, the resultant text presents more meaning than what the author wanted. This additional or different meaning may be more evident than the intended meaning in reading contexts that differ from the writing context. Ricoeur identifies a dialectic of meaning between "what the speaker means, that is, what he intends to say, and what the sentence means, that is, what the conjunction between the identification function and the predicative function yields." He explains that the meaning of the thing-which-is-said can be found only in that which is actually said (i.e. the text) and not through attempts to find out what the author wanted to say.[29]

Ricoeur explains that because spoken discourse happens within the world of its immediate situation, ostensive reference is always available; it can be designated by a physical gesture, by indicators such as verb tense, demonstrative pronouns, and adverbs, or through other descriptions that provide for singular identification.[30] Written discourse, in contrast, has no ostensive reference because it is not embedded in a particular situation. Instead, a written text refers to the world that it creates. Once discourse is written rather than spoken, the text's referent, or "world," is no longer limited to the speaker's appeal to ostensive reference. Indeed, it is not even limited to that which actually exists; the world of the text extends to fictional or theoretical referents.[31]

Ricoeur explains that because the "grounding of reference" that is present for oral discourse ceases to exist in written discourse, a text recreates "the conditions for ostensive reference" by assuming a shared universal context which writer and reader presume to share and which extends beyond a particular situation. Ricoeur notes that such references need not be descriptive, particularly when it comes to fictive texts which seek not to describe reality as such, but descriptions of what worlds may be.[32] While these texts do not need to conform to "the facts, empirical objects, and logical constraints of our established ways of thinking," they are restricted in meaning to their own virtual worlds.[33]

Hirsch supports his thesis by creating false distinctions; the only difference between the unconscious meaning of the author (which Hirsch counts as part of textual meaning) and a symptom (which he does not) is that unconscious meaning corresponds to the explicit authorial intention, while symptoms contradict it. Ricoeur points out that texts, like other forms of social action, detach from the author/actor as they bring about their own consequences beyond those which the author or actor intended. The text leaves its own social imprint independent from that which the author wanted. These unintended consequences are as real as those which the author planned.[34] Hirsch distinguishes between the text's meaning and its significance in order to separate intended meaning from unintended meaning. But this distinction is artificial because both are meanings of the text, whether intended by the author or not.

Finally, the weakness of Hirsch's claim for authorial intention to determine textual meaning is evident by his proposal to determine meaning by identifying the intrinsic genre of the text, which he defines as "that sense of the whole by means of which an interpreter can correctly understand any part in its determinacy."[35] He claims that the author's intention fixes the meaning of the text, but he argues that this meaning can be discovered only by finding the intrinsic genre of the text. The source of the meaning is different from the means to discern it. Hirsch attempts to control the damage by explaining that the author also uses the intrinsic genre to construct the work, but this only makes matters worse. Hirsch identifies intrinsic genre, not authorial intention, as the driving force for meaning that both the author and the interpreter use. As D'Souza points out, attempts to discern authorial intention turn necessarily to the text itself to identify that intention. The quest for authorial intention can only be conducted through the process of textual analysis.[36] Unlike Hirsch, Ricoeur does not depend upon the pretext of searching for authorial intention by examining the text. For him, the text itself is the object of study, not the author or situation of production behind the text. Stiver provides an appropriate stipulation for this assertion, however, by pointing out that critical consideration of the author and his context is an essential element of the explanatory element of Ricoeur's description of hermeneutics.[37]

READING CONTEXT

In order to support Ricoeur's claim that the meaning of a text is not limited to the meaning apparent when it was written, I argue for the seventh premise of my summary of Ricoeur's argument: "In the case of written discourse, different meanings of the text are apparent in different reading contexts." Support for this premise must come with an important proviso in order to separate Ricoeur's hermeneutics from approaches such as Fish's, typically referred to as "reader response," which claim that the meaning of the text is the effect that it has upon the reader as she is embedded in a particular linguistic community. This section therefore presents the case that a text presents different meaning in different reading contexts, but that the reading context does not determine the meaning.

The Text's Presence in Different Contexts

Ricoeur's argument for textual autonomy focuses upon the distinctions between oral and written discourse. In explaining the difference between spoken and written discourse, he notes that all discourse is addressed to an audience. The audience for spoken discourse consists of those present in the communication setting. In contrast, the audience for written discourse includes everyone who knows how to read and who has access to the text.[38] Oral discourse is temporary because it disappears as it occurs. It cannot exist apart from the circumstances of the utterance. It is embedded in an event which makes dialogue between speaker and listener available, and it is available only for those present in the event. When oral discourse is recorded, it is no longer oral but has now become inscribed. One may report about spoken discourse, but it is the report that is available, not the original discursive event. Written discourse, in contrast, is relatively permanent, exists beyond the event of its production, and is available for anyone with access to it. Ricoeur describes this as the text's "triple independence:" from its author, from its original context, and from its original audience.[39] He explains that when discourse is written, the meaning of that discourse is detached from the event of the discourse. What remains is not the event of discourse production, but the meaning which comes from that event. The process of inscription separates the discourse from the writer, and it becomes autonomous from its creator.[40] While a reader may choose to engage with a text as historical evidence in order to learn about the circumstances of its production, this is not the sole purpose for engaging with a text. Reading a text is an opportunity to create a dialectical relationship between the world of the text and the world of the reader. The text-world is not equivalent to the event of its production; it is the configuration of the world, either as a description of historical happenings or as a proposed or fictive world.

Because the text is able to exist independently from the author and the event of its production, it is present in new contexts and for new audiences. What remains to be demonstrated is that the text is able to have different meaning in these new contexts and for these new readers.

Reading as a Dialectical Event

In speaking of the event of a text's production, Ricoeur asserts that "the meaning of an important event exceeds, overcomes, transcends, the social conditions of its production and may be reenacted in new social contexts. Its importance is its durable relevance and, in some cases, its omnitemporal relevance."[41] The goal of interpretation therefore is not to recreate the original event, but "to generate a new event beginning from the text in which the initial event has been objectified."[42] Ricoeur identifies this event as a dialectic between the referential aspect of a text to the world it projects and the subjective aspect of reading in contingent circumstances. The meaning of the text is therefore both fixed, in that it is directed to the reference-world of the text, and contingent, based on the context of the reading of the text.[43] Following Gadamer, Brandom makes a similar claim. Because meaning develops out of the context in which a text is read, and because there is an "open-ended" number of contexts in which a text can be read, it follows that texts have the potential for a plethora of meanings that can arise from a single text.[44] Brandom explains that the context of the author is one context for reading a text, but that "all contexts define . . . equally valid perspectives from which to specify the conceptual content of a claim."[45]

Reading, according to Ricoeur, is an event which discerns the meaning of the text in a new setting. Because the contexts of reading events can vary greatly, a variety of results exist from readers' encounter with the text. While Ricoeur argues that the text itself provides the cues for meaning, he acknowledges that the text's meaning depends both upon the author, whose configuration of the text as an event monumentalizes it, and the reader, whose re-figuration of the text through the process of reading is a new event. As he puts it, "Libraries are full of unread books, whose configuration is, nonetheless, well laid out and yet they refigure nothing at all. . . . Without the reader who accompanies it, there is no configuring act at work in the text. Yet the illusion is endlessly reborn that the text is a structure in itself and for itself and that reading happens to the text as some extrinsic and contingent event."[46]

An alternative to Ricoeur's text-oriented interpretive strategy is one that places primary responsibility for meaning production upon the reader. Fish's earlier work represents the strongest form of this approach, which is typically referred to as reader-response theory. Although Ricoeur rejects theories of interpretation which give primary responsibility to the reader for determining the meaning of a text, he asserts that the reader is a necessary partner with the text in the process of discerning meaning. For Ricoeur, the reader's engagement with the text is not controlled by her preconceptions. The text's triple independence from the author, original audience, and circumstances is not a license for the reader to impose her perspective upon it, but presents an opportunity for the text to engage her in the setting of the reading event. The reader does not control the event of meaning discernment, but is a partner in dialectic with the text in order to do so.

For Fish, meaning is not a stable commodity that is housed in the text itself, waiting for the reader to tease it out. He maintains that meaning comes through the interaction of text and reader and that the reader has "joint responsibility for the production of meaning" together with the text. He claims that "the reader's response is not *to* the meaning; it *is* the meaning." A text means what it evokes in the reader.[47] According to Fish, the message of the text is constitutive of but not identical to its meaning. The reader must work through possibilities that the text offers in order to determine what it means through the event of reading. The reader is not a partner with the text; the text is a resource for the reader.[48] He claims that when the context changes, the resultant meaning changes as well. This indicates to him that the text itself offers no meaning per se, but is a set of possibilities upon which the readers project meanings that arise from their linguistic community rules and *Sitz im Leben*. As readers, we are only able to go where our conventions lead us.[49] For Fish, there is no empirical criteria by which a text can be understood definitively without its original context; when a text is "orphaned," or removed from its contextual cues, there are no constraints on its meaning.[50]

Ricoeur rejects Fish's reader-response theory of interpretation, pointing out that it would mean the reader configures the narrative, instead of re-figuring the configuration of the text. Reader response expects mimesis$_3$ (re-figuration) where there is no mimesis$_2$ (con-figuration). As Ricoeur puts it, "Reading then becomes a picnic where the author brings the words and the readers the meaning." The result for the reader, according to him, is frustration because of the lack of determinacy. Ricoeur also speaks against overly deterministic understandings of reading which allow for no sense of interplay between the reader and the text. Instead, Ricoeur advocates for an understanding of reading in which the meaning of the text is neither indeterminate nor fully prescribed. He seeks a dialectic in which the text "appears, by turns, both lacking and excessive in meaning. . . . A balance is sought between the signals provided by the text and the synthetic activity of reading." The re-figuration of the narrative through the act of reading is both consistent with and distinct from the configuration of the narrative created by the production of the text by the author.[51] Ricoeur acknowledges that the reader brings something to the picnic; she is bound not only to her historical situation but also to her preconceptions and to the conventions of her linguistic community. But in contrast to Fish, Ricoeur points out that the text brings a new world understanding which challenges, confirms, refutes, and alters the reader's prior commitments. Reading requires the reader to relinquish pride of position to the text and "to disassociate myself. . .from any attempt to impose the pre-eminence of the subject—the I-subject—on the whole process."[52] In addition, as Stiver explains, the reader provides elements necessary for the refiguration of the narrative that the text itself does not provide.[53] This relates directly to Chapter 2's description of appropriation; the purpose of reading is neither to project oneself into the text nor to read one's prior world-understanding into it. Rather, "interpretation is the process by which disclosure of new modes of being. . .gives to the subject a new capacity for knowing himself. If the reference of the text is the project of a world, then it is not the reader who primarily projects himself. The reader rather is enlarged in his capacity for self-projection by receiving a new mode of being from the text itself."[54]

Iser, like Fish, argues that the reader holds a primary role in the interpretative task, but he provides insights which move him more closely to Ricoeur's theory. Iser explains that meaning arises from the interaction between the cues that come from the text and the reader's comprehension of these cues, which is contingent upon the reader's context. "As text and reader merge into a single situation, the division between subject and object no longer applies, and it therefore follows that meaning is no longer an object to be defined, but is an effect to be experienced."[55] Iser considers the actualization of a text's work to occur between the artistic pole of the writer and the aesthetic pole of the reader; the text is an interaction between the two, and meaning arises from that interaction. The text, as received by the reader, sets limits within which the reader can construct possible meanings. Thus, while multiple meanings can arise from the act of reading, the text provides a spectrum of possible meanings. The structure of the text leads different readers to different meanings, which offer the potential for transformation for the reader. And yet, Iser asserts, readers are not free to construct whatever meanings they desire; the text provides parameters within which meanings can be determined.[56] He explains that because there is no corrective interaction between the author and the reader, the text is not able to control the reader's formulation of meaning from it. When the text is indeterminate the reader must "fill in the gaps" in order to constitute meaning. In the relationship between author (as represented by the text) and reader, the reader is in the privileged position, because she is the final arbiter of ambiguity.[57]

Stiver distinguishes Ricoeur's hermeneutics from reader-response, describing the role of the reader for Ricoeur as an "accomplice in the production of its [the text's] meaning."[58] Like Stiver, I note points of affinity and important distinctions between Fish and Ricoeur's approaches. They agree that the reader is involved in meaning-production and that the text cannot in itself present meaning. They both recognize the eventful nature of reading; Ricoeur emphasizes the event of text production but agrees with Fish about the event of reading. The most significant difference between Fish and Ricoeur is their description of the relationship between the text and the reader. For Ricoeur, the reader subordinates her preconceptions in order to encounter the world of the text.[59] The text has a challenge to offer to the reader, and the reader must attend to it. The semiotic system within which the text operates prevents it from meaning anything the reader wants, but the reader's experience of reading is what the text means. Fish claims that the reader's norms, and those of her community, orient her understanding of the text. Fish considers the linguistic code to be an unchanging system within which communication happens, and Ricoeur views it as a necessary but evolving framework for meaning production. For Fish, readers are free to impute their desired meaning upon the text. For Ricoeur, the structure of the text resists the reader's tendency to make it conform to her initial conceptions and interjects a new world understanding into her milieu.

The Mutual Influence of Text and Context

A Ricoeur-oriented theory of reading recognizes a productive interaction between the text and the linguistic constructs within which the text operates. The linguistic structure of the text provides constraints upon the possible meanings which the reader is able to discern. But at the same time, the text is able to change the structures which define it. Fish, in contrast, considers the meaning of the text to be wholly dependent upon the context in which it is encountered. He argues that there can be multiple readings of a text, each fully supported by the structure of the text and the institutions within which it operates. Discourse emerges from particular situations, and when it is set to writing it is present in other situations. In different contexts, different responses to the same text are equally normative. Fish explains that the norms by which a text can be understood are embedded in the reader's situation and background of understanding, in addition to the rules of the language community. Without this embeddedness, the text would provide "an infinite plurality of meanings." For Fish, the meaning of a text therefore depends upon the understandings of the discursive event. Difficulties in perceiving meaning arise when presumptions of shared contextual understandings are mistaken.[60]

   A key element of Fish's theory is the contextualization not only of the text, but of the reader. Fish explains that the reader must be a member of the language community from which the text comes, and she must have the "semantic competence" to be able to participate in the code system of that community. The linguistic structure constrains the reader's response by establishing boundaries of what the reader can "produce" from the text. Fish was confident that all "informed" (or fully competent) readers will share responses to the text within an acceptable range.[61] He maintains that textual meaning can only be discerned within an interpretive community which functions as a closed system.[62] Fish claims that meaning comes from the readers' community. As the community determines the text's meaning, there is agreement within the community because of the shared interpretive norms, and there is disagreement between different communities because they employ different norms.[63] Fish argues for reading that is mediated by the collective decision of a community of readers (i.e. language group) for how meaning is discerned from a text. It is the rules of the reader's linguistic community that determine the meaning of the text.[64] Disputes about the meaning of a text are resolved with a community by appeals to its reading-rules which ensure stability of meaning within that community for the text. According to Fish, these "disciplining rules" are not self-evident dicta that arise from the text itself, but develop from the prior assumptions of the community. Debates about meaning between communities, on the other hand, concern differences between their reading-rules. Fish asserts that there is a continuing social mix in which interpretive communities interact with and affect each other.[65]

For Fish, innovation in interpretation comes only as an interpretive community itself changes. He proposes that these changes occur as latent potentialities within the community are foregrounded and previously prominent commitments within the community are marginalized. Change also takes place when a previously unforeseen event intrudes upon the community and impels it to apply its code in a new way. People therefore are not free agents, but extensions of their community as they live out its code.[66] It follows from Fish's argument that the text is unable to produce a change in the community, which is trapped within its own rule structure. For Fish, the hapless reader is trapped in the prior categories of understanding of her community, with no resources at her disposal in a quest for meaning other than what she already has.

Ricoeur, on the other hand, asserts that the text is able to modify the community; the text changes the reader through her appropriation of it. Ricoeur highlights the innovations to the code itself through the impertinence of metaphor and poetics, which Chapters 2 and 5 address more fully. He contends that the work of explanation is the process for negotiating between interpretations of a text, or synthesizing new ones. The text is able to change the community, and the text provides parameters for debates between interpretive communities.[67] Fish's analysis fails to appreciate the guidance in interpretation which the text offers. The text does not provide singularity of meaning, but it provides parameters within which meaning can be ascertained. Further, the differences between interpretive communities ought not to be overstated. I agree with Fish that each community approaches the text with its own assumptions, priorities, and world-perspectives. For example, Biblical hermeneutics conducted by feminist, existentialist, and evangelical communities provide different meanings for the same texts. However, these communities are subsets of a larger linguistic community whose members share the competence to read the text. These communities are able to negotiate differences in interpretation by appealing to the parameters of the linguistic system within which they each operate. The result of these negotiations may be the refutation of some interpretations, the acceptance of multiple interpretations to each be valid, the synthesis of several interpretations into a new interpretation, or some other possibility.

More significantly, however, a Ricoeurian presentation of interpretation also recognizes that the text is able to challenge and change the language code and the tradition within which it operates. While Tracy asserts that the text is the field upon which the game of reading takes place,[68] Hall describes Ricoeur's understanding of tradition as a shared and "inherited" context that is not a static constraint upon the reader, but a dynamic structure which continues to change as a result of the interactions between texts and readers that occur within it. The hermeneutic work which occurs within the tradition is both a project of understanding the text as a voice from the tradition's past in light of the reader's world-understandings, and a challenge to the reader's conceptions that the text presents.[69] As Townsend explains Ricoeur's approach, "The text is never static. As structure, it is established and fixed, but as potential reading, it is subject to hermeneutical necessity. . . . Reading modifies the text and the text limits reading."[70] Iser also sees a greater potential than Fish for the text to challenge reader's conventions and norms even as it operates within them. The text is able to de-familiarize that which is familiar for the reader, to violate the linguistic norms in a way that can either altar or add to them, to emphasize that which had been latent, and to offer variations of perspective for the reader.[71] Iser, like Ricoeur and unlike Fish, explains that while the reader's linguistic community and code shape the reader's apprehension of the text, the text reshapes the community and code at the same time.[72]

To summarize this section, we can accept that different meanings of a text are apparent in different reading contexts for three reasons. First, the text exists in different contexts. Second, the perception of meaning in that text is a dialectic event that includes both the reader and the text, with the reader bringing her world understanding into the interaction. Third, the interaction provides at least for the possibility of the change both in the text's meaning and in the reader and her linguistic community.

MEANING FROM THE TEXT ITSELF

The final step to accept Ricoeur's argument for textual autonomy is to demonstrate that meaning comes from the text itself. As argued above, meaning comes neither from the author's intentions nor from the readers' preconceptions. Ricoeur argues that it is the text itself which provides meaning. After first demonstrating that this is the case, I describe how the explanatory mode of interpretation in Ricoeur's approach determines the meaning(s) of the text.

Meaning Is Found in the Text

Ricoeur agrees with Gadamer that interpretation of texts occurs only because of the tradition(s) which the writer and the reader share. "But the lingual experience exercises its mediating function only because the interlocutors fade away in the face of the things said that, as it were, direct the dialogue." That is, the text mediates between author and reader. "What enables us to communicate at a distance is thus the *matter of the text,* which belongs neither to its author nor to its reader."[73] Ricoeur explains that the speaker's intention and the meaning of the utterance coincide in oral discourse. But they do not coincide for written discourse because the text is not limited to the context or experience of the writer, and its meaning is not limited to the meaning intended by the writer. "What the text says now matters more than what the author meant to say."[74] The text is that which exists in both the context of writing and the context of reading. It is the feature of both contexts in which meaning resides.

Hall and Leavitt support Ricoeur on this point. As Hall puts it, "The text is a *structure* that guides interpretation and imposes its own limits on the scope of legitimate interpretation." While this structure permits multiple interpretations, it provides criteria by which the adequacy of a particular interpretation may be evaluated, with the proviso that such evaluations are never definitive.[75] Leavitt likewise cautions against readings of the text that do not conform to the parameters of the text itself.[76]

The Explanatory Mode Determines Meaning

A critical element of Ricoeur's hermeneutics is the relationship between the modes of understanding and explanation.[77] As he put it, explanation "is to bring out the structure. . .of the text; to interpret is to follow the path of thought opened up by the text."[78] Explanation is the process of validating or correcting the reader's initial guess about meaning by reconstituting the text as a whole after breaking it down into its constituent elements in order to reconstruct potential meanings that arise from their plurivocal possibilities.

This process can inform our sense of the text's meaning by ascertaining the probability or improbability of our initial guess. As Ricoeur puts it, "if it is true that there is always more than one way of construing a text, it is not true that all interpretations are equal." Ricoeur advocates a process of reading in which readers "imaginatively actualize the potential non-ostensive references of the text in a new situation, that of the reader." He argues that "understanding seeks to grasp the world-propositions opened up by the reference of the text. To understand a text is to follow its movement from sense to reference; from what it says, to what it talks about." This comprehension of a the world offered by the text takes place only through the use of explanatory strategies.[79]

Ricoeur advocates the use of structuralist analysis to inform textual interpretation, but he does not accept a structuralist ideology. He argues that structuralism by itself deadens the text by treating it as nothing more than an instantiation of the underlying code: "structuralism as ideology starts with the reversal in the relationship between code and message which makes the code essential and the message unessential." Instead, Ricoeur proposes that structural analysis can be employed to open the means for "existential interpretation" such that the text is recognized as discourse that cannot be simply reduced to its code. The text, understood in this way, becomes an event: the interaction between speaker and audience within a "world." Because the event occurs within a linguistic code, structuralist analysis of the code is an essential component for understanding the event. This analysis, however, is not the primary goal but a means toward a greater end.[80] Ricoeur speaks of "transcodage:" the transfer of a narrative from its original linguistic and cultural setting to a new one.[81] As Hettema explains, Ricoeur's hermeneutics move beyond the models offered by Nietzsche and the other "masters of suspicion"[82] on the one hand, and the phenomenological and existential models of Husserl and Heidegger on the other. A hermeneutic dedicated to ontological inquiry such as Heidegger's is unable to explore epistemological issues. But a critical hermeneutic such as Nietzsche's that is devoted to the archaeology of ur-concepts denies the role of the self in interpretation and understanding. Ricoeur, in contrast to both of these approaches, understands the symbols of language not as expressions of reality per se, but as vehicles for (self) reflection as they pass through the process of critical inquiry in order to form new configurations of reality.[83]

For Ricoeur, reading is only possible because of the linguistic conventions within which the text operates, and which it shares with the reader. These conventions include not only the *langue* or semiotic structure which the discourse employs, but also the cultural traditions and expectations that surround it. This structure and these traditions impose constraints on the allowable options for understanding the text. Ricoeur delimits the range of meanings for texts to the constraints imposed by the text itself and its context, as the text encounters the expectations of the reading community.[84] A text is not a free play of interpretation. Its structure constrains options for meaning, like guard-rails that keep the car from going over the cliff. Prince points out that while some questions asked of a text can have only one correct answer, others can have multiple answers, each of which can be fairly justified. This indicates, he argues, that the reading of a text depends not only upon the text but upon the reader. The linguistic structure of the text and its cultural setting are necessary informants for the reader, which guide and constrain the reader's options for understandings that come from the text. The reader, in order to ascertain the text's meaning, must be competent in his handling of these textual and cul-tural cues. However, Prince asserts, the reader must still choose from multiple semantic options as he determines a meaning from the text.[85] When textual and cultural cues, as identified by historical and literary analysis, leave room for more than one meaning, then the text in this case is polyvalent.

Explanatory hermeneutics, or critical inquiry, allow an interpreter to dis-cern inferences from the text that the author and original audience may have had. But the inferences that a reader can draw from the text are not limited to those which the author drew. Nor are they limited to the inferences that the reader had before reading the text. The text itself provides a statement; it is the context in which the text exists (both that of its production and those in which it is read) that provide the field from which inferences are drawn.

If the preceding arguments succeed and premises 5, 6, 7, and 8 can be accepted, then the final two premises of my summary of Ricoeur's argument are supported. A text is able to present meaning that is different from the author's desired meaning, and this meaning is determined by the linguistic constructs of the text itself. This supports the seventh premise of this project's overall argument: "The meaning of a text is not limited to the meaning that was apparent when it was written." For readers of Mark 13, the meaning of the text is not merely what the author wanted the text to say, or even what the original readers understood as they read it. The text is able to present different meaning for today's reader. The next chapter explains how metaphor is one way that a text presents meaning beyond the author's intention.

NOTES

1. Ricoeur, "Naming God" 220–23; cf. Ricoeur, *Interpretation Theory*, 25–30. Ricoeur explains discourse as an event, in contrast to the virtual and out-of-time existence of language. In this case he differentiates between discourse and language in the manner of Saussure's distinction of *parole* from *langue*. The inter-relationship between discourse and language means not only that language, which has only a virtual existence, can find actuality through its employment in discourse, but that

discourse can continue to exist through the enduring elements of language systems (cf. Ricoeur, *Interpretation Theory*, 8–9, Ricoeur, *Rule of Metaphor*, 69–70).
As an event, discourse (1) has a subject and an other that is addressed, (2) refers to
a world that it describes, (3) is the medium by which messages are exchanged, and
(4) produces meaning that endures at least potentially beyond the moment of its
production. For Ricoeur, the essence of the hermeneutic endeavor is to understand
the meaning that continues beyond the event of its production in discourse (Ricoeur,
"Hermeneutical Function," 77–8).

2. Cf. Ricoeur, "Creativity in Language," 127–30 and Vanhoozer, Biblical Narrative, 59–61 for a discussion of the difference between ordinary language and scientific
or artificial language.

3. Paul Ricoeur, "The Task of Hermeneutics," in *From Text to Action: Essays
in Hermeneutics, II*, trans. Kathleen Blamey and John B. Thompson (Evanston, IL:
Northwestern University Press, 1991), 54–5; Paul Ricoeur, "Creativity in Language:
Word, Polysemy, Metaphor," in *The Philosophy of Paul Ricoeur: An Anthology of
His Work*, eds. Charles E. Reagan and David Stewart (Boston: Beacon Press, 1978),
120–21.

4. Ricoeur, "Creativity in Language," 124–25.

5. Ricoeur, *Rule of Metaphor*, 94.

6. Wallace, *Second Naiveté*, 34–5.

7. Francesca M. Bosco, Monica Bucciarelli, and Bruno G. Bara, in "The Fundamental Context Categories in Understanding Communicative Intention," *Journal of
Pragmatics* 36.3 (2004): 467–83.

8. http://www.archives.gov/exhibits/american_originals/modern.html.

9. Robert B. Brandom, "Pretexts," in *Tales of the Mighty Dead: Historical Essays
in the Metaphysics of Intentionality* (Cambridge MA & London: Harvard University
Press, 2002), 102.

10. Cf. Austin Busch, "Questioning and Conviction: Double-Voiced Discourse in
Mark 3:22–30," *Journal of Biblical Literature* 125.3 (2006): 492–95.

11. John R. Searle, *Speech Acts: An Essay in the Philosophy of Language*
(Cambridge: Cambridge UP, 1969), 44–45.

12. Cf. Yoilah K. Yilpet, "Knowing the Biblical Author's Intention: The Problem
of Distanciation," *Africa Journal of Evangelical Theology* 19.2 (2000): 166–69.

13. E. D. Hirsch, *Validity in Interpretation* (New Haven: Yale University Press,
1967), 44. In his later writings, Hirsch broadens his explanation of what is included
in authorial intention to include future possibilities. Even though he maintains that a
text's meaning is fixed by the author's historical intention, Hirsch recognizes that an
author's future-oriented intention makes the author's actions less explicit. Unforeseen
elements of the reader's context in the future make the fulfillment of the author's
intentions variable. In fact, Hirsch recognizes that unforeseen future factors will affect
not only the fulfillment of intention, but will change of what that intention is. He concludes that the text's meaning, although fixed by the author's intention, is not limited
to the author's original context. Future applications of that meaning are an "extension" of that intention and are therefore the text's meaning. The application of a text,
Hirsch claims, is an element of its meaning (E. D. Hirsch, "Meaning and Significance

Reinterpreted," *Critical Inquiry* 11 (1984): 205–10). He argues that his insistence on a text's single meaning, based on author's intent at the event of its composition, does not "leave texts mired in the past and thus prey to pedantic antiquarianism" because readers in the future are able to "produce present-day exemplifications of meaning." These new exemplifications do not change the meaning of the text but are based on it. Hirsch recognizes that for this to be the case, the original meaning (i.e. the intention of the author) needs to be construed broadly enough to include elements that the author would not have foreseen in order for that meaning to continue (Hirsch, "Meaning and Significance," 216–17). Hirsch claims that authors are "provisional" when created intended meaning because they are looking to the future and must necessarily be tentative because of the unknowable elements of that future (Hirsch, "Meaning and Significance," 222–23).

14. Hirsch, "Meaning and Significance," 202–04.

15. Cf. H. Paul Grice, "Meaning," in *Studies in the Way of Words* (Cambridge, MA: Harvard University Press, 1989), 219.

16. Sutcliffe, in contrast, argues that the written text is a form of self-disclosure on the part of the author. As a result, the consciousness of the author remains present in the text (Peter A. Sutcliffe, *Is There an Author in This Text? Discovering the Otherness of the Text* (Eugene, Oregon: Wipf & Stock, 2014), 133).

17. Sutcliffe argues, however, that all communication is monologue. Oral discourse is not dialogue per se, but a series of monologues in which the participants anticipate meaning together (Sutcliffe, *Is There an Author*, 126, 189–91, 206).

18. Ricoeur, "What Is a Text," 107–09; cf. Joyce Ann Zimmerman, *Liturgy as Language of Faith: A Liturgical Methodology in the Mode of Paul Ricoeur's Textual Hermeneutics* (Lanham, MD: University Press of America, 1988), 66–8.

19. Ricoeur, "What Is a Text," 121.

20. Ricoeur, "Hermeneutical Function," 83.

21. Ricoeur, "Appropriation," 192.

22. McLean, *Biblical Interpretation*, 237–38.

23. Heiden, The Truth and Untruth, 79.

24. Grech, "Inner-Biblical Reinterpretation," 227.

25. John R. Searle, *Intentionality: An Essay in the Philosophy of Mind* (Cambridge: Cambridge UP, 1983), 101–02.

26. Hirsch, "Meaning and Significance," 205–17.

27. Steven Knapp and Walter Benn Michaels, "The Impossibility of Intentionless Meaning," in *Intention and Interpretation*, ed. Gary Iseminger. Arts and Their Philosophies (Philadelphia: Temple Univ Press, 1992), 54–56; cf. Sutcliffe, Is There an Author, 281.

28. Hirsch, *Validity in Interpretation*, 22.

29. Ricoeur, *Interpretation Theory*, 12–13.

30. Cf. Ricoeur, *Rule of Metaphor*, 75.

31. Ricoeur, "Hermeneutical Function," 84–5.

32. Ricoeur, *Interpretation Theory*, 34–7.

33. Ibid., 59–60.

34. Ricoeur, "Model of the Text," 153–54.

35. Hirsch, *Validity in Interpretation*, 86.
36. D'Souza, "Ricoeur's Narrative," 35–6.
37. Stiver, *Ricoeur and Theology*, 39–40.
38. Ricoeur, "Model of the Text," 149–50; cf. Ricoeur, *Interpretation Theory*, 31.
39. Ricoeur, "Naming God," 219; cf. Ricoeur, "Canon," 9.
40. Ricoeur, *Interpretation Theory*, 25–30.
41. Ricoeur, "Model of the Text," 155.
42. Ricoeur, *Interpretation Theory*, 75.
43. Ricoeur, *Time and Narrative* 3, 178–79.
44. Brandom, "Pretexts," 93.
45. Ibid., 106.
46. Ricoeur, *Time and Narrative* 3, 164.
47. Stanley Eugene Fish, Is There a Text in This Class?: The Authority of Interpretive Communities (Cambridge, MA: Harvard University Press, 1980), 2–3.
48. Ibid., 22–32.
49. Ibid., 322–33
50. Stanley Eugene Fish, *Doing What Comes Naturally*: Change, Rhetoric, and the Practice of Theory in Literary and Legal Studies (Durham, NC: Duke University Press, 1989), 37–48.
51. Ricoeur, *Time and Narrative* 3, 168–70.
52. Ricoeur, "Canon," 12.
53. Stiver, *Ricoeur and Theology*, 50–1.
54. Ricoeur, *Interpretation Theory*, 94.
55. Wolfgang Iser, *The Act of Reading: A Theory of Aesthetic Response* (Baltimore: Johns Hopkins University Press, 1978), 9–10.
56. Ibid., 21–7.
57. Ibid., 164–79.
58. Dan R. Stiver, *Theology after Ricoeur: New Directions in Hermeneutical Theology* (Louisville: Westminster John Knox, 2001), 117.
59. As Amherdt explains, Ricoeur cites Bultmann as a negative example of this subordination. Ricoeur rejects Bultmann's privileging of twentieth-century conceptions and excising aspects of the text which violate these conceptions. Instead, Ricoeur advocates a dialectic interaction between the reader's presuppositions and the world-understanding of the text, instead of a project by which the text is made to conform to the reader. According to Ricoeur, Bultmann applies his philosophical preconceptions to the text, instead of allowing the text to speak with its own voice. Amherdt asserts that this limits Bultmann's understanding of the kerygma to the individualistic level, and it prevents him from appreciating its message of hope (Amherdt, *L'herméneutique Philosophique*, 354–74).
60. Fish, Is There a Text, 305–11.
61. Ibid., 43–7.
62. Fish, *Doing What Comes Naturally*, 1–16.
63. Ibid., 141–42.
64. C. Jason White, in his quest to defend the authority of Biblical meaning, concedes that Hirsch's program of determining the author's intention is not possible,

argues that Christians are able to discern between "good" and "inadequate" readings by engaging in "essential practices" of the Christian community: prayer, memorization, baptism, eucharist, and mission. Although he does not explicitly refer to Fish, White employs his approach by defining the rules of the community that define the text's meaning (191–93).

65. Fish, Is There a Text, 4–17; Fish, *Doing What Comes Naturally*, 121–32.

66. Fish, *Doing What Comes Naturally*, 144–60.

67. In his more recent writings, Fish recognizes the flaws of reader-response theory and accepts authorial intention as the means by which meaning can be discerned. In "Intention Is All There Is," he argues that the purpose for interpretation is to determine the original intention of the author who wrote the text. He notes, however, that intentionalism is a theory and not a method. The hermeneut may pursue the goal of ascertaining the author's intention, but the pursuit of this goal does not offer a means by which that goal can be obtained. Fish concludes that the method by which the goal of determining the author's intention is simply "the empirical labor of trying to figure out what some purposive agent. . .meant by these signs" (1113–116). Fish proposes that linguistic system of the text provides the means for reading (1135–137). In proposing an interpretive theory similar to Hirsch's, Fish encounters the same problem that Hirsch did. Hirsch argues that meaning is determined by intention but proceeds to use genre analysis to determine meaning. Fish in similar fashion claims that the goal for reading is the identification of the author's intention, but that it is determined through an examination of the text as it occurs in a language system.

68. David Tracy, *Plurality and Ambiguity: Hermeneutics, Religion, Hope* (San Francisco: Harper & Row, 1987), 8–27.

69. W. David Hall, *Paul Ricoeur and the Poetic Imperative: The Creative Tension between Love and Justice* (Albany: SUNY, 2007), 50–2.

70. Dabney Townsend, "Metaphor, Hermeneutics, and Situations," in *The Philosophy of Paul Ricoeur*, ed. Lewis E. Hahn. The Library of Living Philosophers (Chicago: Open Court Press, 1995), 195.

71. Iser, *The Act of Reading*, 53–101.

72. Holland's description of reading as "transactive criticism" is similar to Iser's proposal. Holland rejects a "text-active" understanding of reading, in which text informs the passive reader, because it fails to recognize the importance of elements of the reader's personal and social background which influence her apprehension of meaning. Holland also found flaws in a "biactive" theory of reading; while it recognizes the role of the reader's response to the text in meaning production, it does so in a "stop-motion" fashion. The reader is supposed to read a line of the text, pause to make a decision about it, and then move on. In "transactive" reading, Holland explains, the reader engages in the task of reading and of deciding at the same time. In reading, he writes, "I am engaged in a feedback loop no part of which is independent from the other parts" (Norman N. Holland, "Re-Covering 'the Purloined Letter': Reading as a Personal Transaction," in The Reader in the Text: Essays on Audience and Interpretation, ed. Susan R. Suleiman and Inge Crosman (Princeton: Princeton UP, 1980), 362–67). Like Iser, and unlike Fish, Holland argues that an encounter with the text can change the reader.

73. Ricoeur, "The Task of Hermeneutics," 73–4.

74. Ricoeur, "Model of the Text," 147–48.

75. Hall, *Paul Ricoeur*, 5.

76. Robert F. Leavitt, "Raymond Brown and Paul Ricoeur on the Surplus of Meaning," in *Life in Abundance: Studies of John's Gospel in Tribute to Raymond E. Brown*, eds. Raymond Edward Brown and John R. Donahue (Collegeville: Liturgical Press, 2005), 207–09.

77. Ricoeur, "What Is a Text," 110–17.

78. Ibid., 121–22.

79. Ricoeur, *Interpretation Theory*, 71–88.

80. Ricoeur, "Biblical Hermeneutics," 64–6.

81. Ibid., 58–60.

82. Cf. Ricoeur, *Freud and Philosophy*, 32–5.

83. Hettema, *Reading for Good*, 23–4.

84. Leavitt, "Raymond Brown," 214.

85. Gerald Prince, "Notes on the Text as Reader," in *The Reader in the Text: Essays on Audience and Interpretation*, eds. Susan R. Suleiman and Inge Crosman (Princeton: Princeton UP, 1980), 225–29.

Chapter 5

Ricoeur's Description of Metaphor

The previous chapter demonstrates that the meaning of a text can be something other than or different from the author's intention. Therefore, while the first section of Chapter 3 concludes that the author of Mark 13 intended for the discourse to be a prediction of literal historical events, this is not the only meaning available for today's reader. In addition to the literal meaning intended by the author, today's reader is also able to appropriate Mark 13 metaphorically. To do so, I provide a Ricoeurian description of metaphor and discuss how metaphor expresses truth. The following chapter explains how Mark 13 functions as this sort of metaphor.

As Ricoeur describes it, metaphor is a non-conventional discursive act that makes creativity possible in language. It offers multiplicity of meaning through the violation of pre-existing conceptualizations and categories of language and world. It does so by equating concepts that are not normally associated with each other, and in the process it creates an evocative dialectic tension, either by applying a literally false predicate to a subject or by giving the same name to two or more different things. When metaphor forms this relationship between two ideas or subjects, it has the capacity to manifest new truth. It does so through the use of conventional or literal reference and of extended or innovative orders of reference. Ricoeur's description of metaphor depends upon an explanation that multiple but not infinite possibilities for meaning do not necessarily create ambiguity. He also claims that metaphor creates new truth which had previously been unrecognizable or non-existent. This chapter elaborates upon and supports this description of metaphor by drawing upon Ricoeur's work.

REJECTION OF METAPHOR AS A RHETORICAL ORNAMENT

Ricoeur quotes Aristotle's definition of a metaphor thus: "Metaphor consists in giving the thing a name that belongs to something else; the transference being either from genus to species, or from species to genus, or from species to species, or on grounds of analogy."[1] However, Ricoeur points out that Aristotle considers metaphor to be the borrowing of a term to fill a semantic void by removing the term from its original meaning in order for it to substitute for the missing word.[2] Ricoeur rejects the classical rhetorical understanding of metaphor as a figure which can be reduced to its original terms. Instead, metaphor on the sentence level presents through predication a kinship of concepts which normally are not brought together, and which may in fact be considered to be absurd. In so doing, metaphor creates new truth: "A metaphor, in short, tells us something new about reality."[3]

Ricoeur rejects substitutionary descriptions of metaphor. Such descriptions consider metaphor as the presentation of "one idea under the sign of another," or as a "borrowed idea" to express an "original idea" and "the borrowed idea." Ricoeur explains that each of these descriptions depends upon the notion of an appropriate, correct, or "literal" meaning for a word, from which the metaphor borrows to form a different meaning. Such descriptions are a "return to a non-contextual theory of idea:" that is, the notion that words carry intrinsic and definitive meaning independent of their context. Instead, Ricoeur prefers Richards' concept of metaphor as a tenor and vehicle, because it describes metaphor as a creative tension between two ideas without privileging one over the other.[4]

Ricoeur distinguishes metaphor from allegory, which he describes as a rhetorical ornamentation which substitutes the name for something with another term which is "more pleasant" or better suits the speaker or author's needs. The use of allegory is a process of substitution on the part of the speaker or writer and restitution on the part of the listener or reader; no meaning is added through this strategy. Ricoeur argues that metaphor, in contrast, can be used "to break through previous categorization and to establish new logical boundaries on the ruins of the preceding ones."[5] It is the source of innovative language use which produces new truth and challenges the listener/reader to understand self and world in new ways. To understand Ricoeur's point, consider 1 Peter 5:13: "Your sister church in Babylon . . . sends you greetings." This is uniformly understood to be a reference not to a Christian community in Mesopotamia, but to one in Rome.[6] An understanding of metaphor-as-ornamentation, or as a sort of allegory, would lead us to believe that the author substituted "Rome" with "Babylon" for his own purposes; in this case perhaps to obscure the identity of the Christian community in order to avoid persecution. The well-informed reader would replace the term "Babylon" with the word "Rome." But metaphor is not like a cereal-box decoder ring: as long as the speaker/author and listener/reader share the same code book, metaphor is a transparent lens through which meaning can pass. According to Ricoeur's sense of metaphor, the use of metaphor creates new truth. In this example, the use of the term "Babylon" opens connotations and possibilities for meaning which would not be available otherwise. Had the author of 1 Peter written "Your sister church in Gobbledegook sends you greetings," the substituted term would offer no extended meaning; it serves as a mere placeholder for the "real" term. "Babylon," however, offers a variety of associated meanings which the author wished to be associated with Rome, such as the capital of an oppressive empire and persecutor of God's people. As the readers of 1 Peter restore the term "Rome" to the discourse, associations of the term "Babylon" challenge them to understand "Rome" in new and different ways.

Ricoeur offers three objections to the conception of metaphor as a deviation of a linguistic figure. First, such a concept is based on the assumption that there is a fixed standard for the figure from which a metaphor deviates, but such a "rhetoric degree zero" cannot be identified. There is no primitive, original, or formal meaning for a term that metaphor subverts. Second, this definition relies upon two metaphors itself: a spatial metaphor of "deviation" and "figure" as a metaphor of embodiment. It is not clear how these two metaphors operate together and clarify each other, if non-metaphorical discourse is asserted to be the norm which metaphoric discourse violates. Third, a concept of metaphor as deviation needs to explain the meta-linguistic rules or process by which this deviation occurs, and how the deviation can be inverted or reversed to reveal the point of origination. Instead, Ricoeur argues that metaphor is a violation of the linguistic code which changes the code in the process of violating it. A purely semiotic approach does not promote comprehension of the reference or meaning of the text. He proposes instead that metaphor ought to be recognized as a source of something new, rather than a mere rearrangement of the old.[7] As Dunn expresses it, "If we follow Ricoeur . . . metaphor is not a synonym or alternative for another linguistic mode of description. Metaphor says what cannot be said otherwise. . . . The metaphor not only expresses the hope, as though for something else. The metaphor *is* the hope. One can still ask what the metaphor refers to, but the appropriate correlative question is not, What does this *mean*?, but What does this *evoke*?"[8]

Taylor explains that Ricoeur's consideration of metaphor contrasts with the more common view of metaphor as the substitution of a "proper" or literal term with a deviated or substitute term, in which case the original term can be restored with no loss of meaning. Instead, Ricoeur argues that the "literal" term is nothing more than the usual or customary designation. As Taylor explains, even the "literal" term does not carry meaning because of some fundamental irreducible association of the term with the thing; all meanings arise from relational associations of terms with their predications in sentences. Associations between terms and things develop from categories of order which metaphors create by identifying A with X.[9] All language use begins metaphorically because there is no inherent connection between the term and its referent. It is only when metaphor is used pervasively that it becomes a commonality and the notion of a "literal" meaning exists. There is no original, non-figurative expression which can be used to replace the metaphor. Those expressions which appear to be non-figurative are merely terms whose association to a particular concept have become so banal through long usage as to become conventional, such as a computer "mouse" or the "roof" of the mouth. The difference is not between original and substituted expressions, but between conventional and innovative associations of meaning. In the process of forming a new association of words and concepts, metaphor creates meaning that cannot be translated with an equivalent or less innovative expression, because the meaning of the metaphor is lost through such a process of reduction.[10] Biblical scholars who present figurative interpretations for Mark 13 tend not to recognize metaphor in this way. Consider, for example, Wright's contention that the Olivet Discourse is a description of the restoration of Israel, and that its language, while colorfully evocative, can be explicated fully through non-figurative discourse (cf. pp. 7–8). Kümmel betrays his failure to distinguish metaphor from substitutionary tropes like allegory when he refers to the "metaphorical features" of the parable of the householder (vv. 34–7) in one sentence, but in the next sentence describes them as "these allegorizing features."[11]

To be understood properly, metaphor must be distinguished not only from allegory but also from simile. Simile, which considers two objects or concepts to be similar to each other, differs from metaphor, which equates the two with each other. Levinson[12] and M. Black[13] both concede that some metaphors are compressed similes that suppress the copula; "my love is like a rose" becomes "my love is a rose." But they also explain that other metaphors create an interaction between the elements of the statement and that the elements change in the process. In these instances, metaphor is more evocative than the literal comparison of a simile. Ricoeur points out that if the missing literal term could be inserted in place of the figurative term, the sentence would be a simile.[14] And if the metaphor is used only to fill a gap in the lexicon, it merely adds a new definition to a term and nothing more. Instead, Ricoeur argues that metaphor establishes a new relationship between two concepts by having them share the same term or by identifying a shared predication. In so doing, metaphor evokes new understandings of both.[15]

Metaphor can also be confused with the non-literal linguistic strategy of irony. Following Beardsley, Ricoeur points out that metaphor and irony are examples of strategies which "suggest something other than what is stated," as the speaker says the opposite of what is meant. Each of these strategies can be recognized through factors in the discourse which indicate that the primary meaning is logically absurd or empty. Such factors include "self-contradictory attributions," redundancies, and tautologies, and incompatibilities.[16] Irony depends on the readers' understanding of what is normal. The use of irony assumes that the readers will understand that the literal cannot be the intended meaning, because it is ridiculous or impossible. We can accept an ironic understanding of a text when we learn that there is an original irony which is lost on us because we no longer intuit the ridiculousness of the literal, or when the idiom that is reversed is no longer in use. The interpreter must employ textual and historical criticism in order to recognize the presence of irony and recognize that the literal meaning is not the real meaning. Hayden White[17] identifies irony, together with metonymy and synecdoche, as types of metaphor. He describes irony as a metaphor which negates the literal level of meaning. While Ricoeur argues that all metaphor depends upon some level of dissonance on the literal level, White explains that irony rises beyond dissonance to absurdity. "My love is a daisy," "man is a wolf," and "the butterfly of time," are all literally false. This literal falsity ought to jar the reader into seeking for a deeper meaning to the statement. "Man is a wolf" evokes a quest for understanding that is much more profound than that which is comes from the more banal commonality "Man is a vertebrate." Irony, however, is not meant to evoke a deeper (i.e. secondary, or polysemous) meaning. It negates the literal meaning. The intended meaning is the opposite of, or inconsistent with, the stated sense of the utterance. Irony depends upon the reader or listener being able to recognize the falsity of the statement. If one's lover has just acted in an obviously crass or brutal manner, the utterance "my love is a daisy" is ironic; the listener is presumed to realize that the lover bears none of the qualities of a daisy. In saying this, the speaker can be understood not to be insisting, despite appearances to the contrary, that the lover really is like a daisy and that you have to realize that this was an uncharacteristic moment. Rather, the meaning in this example lies directly in the negation. It is the contradiction between the event and the verbal response that brings forth meaning. In this instance, the intent may be something like: "Lovers ought to be daisies. I wish my lover was a daisy. But you've just seen how he isn't. I'm bothered by his failure to meet my expectation of a lover."

METAPHOR AS A TRANSGRESSION OF CODE AND CATEGORY

For Ricoeur, metaphor provides innovation of meaning by violating preexisting linguistic structures. He describes the metaphorical statement as one that perceives similarity "*despite* difference, *in spite of* contradiction." It creates a tension of resemblance and difference between two elements at the same time; the literal contradiction highlights the contradiction while the copula focuses attention upon the sameness. "Through this specific trait, enigma lives on in the heart of metaphor. In metaphor, 'the same' operates *in spite of* 'the different.'"[18] This "semantic impertinence" does not disintegrate the metaphor into "a self-destructive self-contradictory statement," but challenges the reader to recognize a "new pertinence." As Ricoeur puts it, "Things that until that moment were 'far apart' suddenly appear as 'closely related.'"[19] For Ricoeur metaphor allows reality to "seem" different from how it would otherwise be understood. It replaces one "mask" or indirect perception of reality with another.[20] Metaphor provides a shocking challenge to prior conventions. It challenges the reader to accept the dialectic and the creative tension that it provides, rather than dismiss the text as false or twist it to make it conform to the "is" of history. Ricoeur explains that the failure of a metaphor's literal meaning creates the possibility for a new "referential design" to arise from the metaphorical meaning.[21] Metaphor is a lexical violation that assigns a previously non-existent relationship between a word and a meaning; that is, a sense gains a new referent. In doing so, the metaphor claims a relationship between the new referent and the previous referents associated with the word. Ricoeur thus describes metaphor as a relationship between ideas. Metaphor, unlike other tropes, can create relationships not only through nouns but also with adjectives, participles, verbs, and adverbs. The metaphor does not merely change the designation of a word; it connects two previously disparate concepts with each other.[22]

Ricoeur explains that "metaphor names an object with the help of the most typical representative of one of its attributes." It provides a new name for the object, but not in the sense of denomination, that is, by assigning an arbitrary term to the object. Metaphor classifies two objects or concepts together through predicative association and gives them the same name because of that classification.[23] Building on the work of Konrad, he identifies four factors which contribute to the formation of a metaphor. First, particular traits of the conventional designation are overlooked or "forgotten" as the metaphor extends meaning to a new designation. Second, the word loses its ostensive reference to a particular object or concept and becomes generalized. Third, this generalization is concretized as it designates representatives of the attribute. Finally, the metaphor establishes a new classification of hitherto-unrelated concepts brought together because of the shared trait that the metaphor identifies.[24] Ricoeur explains that metaphor is a category mistake in which resemblances are revealed which are otherwise hidden because of classification differences. Metaphor creates a new genus by identifying new similarities.[25] It associates a subject with a predicate that does not pertain to it, thereby providing new meaning for the subject which cannot be reduced through the substitution of a different term for the subject.[26] Ricoeur points out that the only difference between literal and metaphoric application of predicates is one of convention; literal is not privileged over metaphoric. Each schema classifies the world in a different way. Ricoeur stipulates that metaphoric designations must be fitting and satisfying, even while they are innovative and surprising. Metaphor remakes reality, but it must do so in a way that makes sense, at least on its own terms.[27]

Because metaphor occurs within a pre-existing linguistic system of genus and species, it violates the rules and interrelationships of the system within which it exists. Ricoeur points out that this transgression creates meaning because of the dis-ordering and re-ordering of the language network. In fact, Ricoeur argues, it is through the creation and use of metaphor that language systems are created, grow, and change.[28] The impertinence of metaphor, when present at the level of narrative, challenges the barriers of its own linguistic structure to the point that the narrative pattern breaks down and the plot appears to become inconsistent. "The parabolic [i.e. metaphoric] message proceeds from this *tension* between a form which circumscribes it and a process which transgresses the narrative boundaries and points to an 'other,' to a 'beyond.'"[29] For religious texts, this transgression allows the reference of the narrative which lies at the fringes of human experience and beyond to make its presence known by intruding into a pattern of discourse which cannot contain it.

Lakoff and Turner, however, argue against the notion that metaphors violate linguistic codes. Instead, they point out that metaphors tend to operate with a sense of coherency. New metaphors conform to the general similarities which exist in the culture's previous metaphors.[30] Lakoff and Johnson also point out that the use of metaphor in a culture expresses the values of that culture, as those values relate to particular issues or practices. They provide the example that the metaphoric use of "up" and "down" functions in English to express positive and negative values respectively. New metaphors necessarily conform to these cultural fundamentals in order to be coherent.[31] Such a restriction of metaphor conflicts with Ricoeur's sense that metaphor-production is a freely operating process that violates linguistic and cognitive codes. To limit metaphor use to those practices which cohere to existing patterns would prevent it from performing its most evocative and powerful function. In response to Lakoff and his associates, I allow that metaphoric innovation depends upon cultural conventions to the extent that these conventions are necessary for the metaphor to be recognized. However, metaphor is not bound to these conventions and extends or adapts them to allow new meanings and new conceptual relationships to emerge.

Ricoeur's presentation of metaphoric innovation depends upon the possibility that linguistic impertinence is productive. As McDowell explains, the communal aspect of language requires that all language-users within that community follow the rules of the language code. Violations of that code are "wrong" in that they seek to assert personal understandings that are "out of step" with fellow language-users. If someone uses a linguistic sign differently from everyone else in that language community, it is incomprehensible. To be understood, language use must be shared.[32] McDowell's point raises the Humpty Dumpty dilemma. In Lewis Carroll's *Through the Looking Glass*, Humpty Dumpty tells Alice, "When I use a word . . . it means just what I choose it to mean—neither more nor less." Language users, in order to be intelligible to others, must use words in the same way that the others do. Anyone who chooses to assign his own meanings to words invents a private language that no one else shares. This problem is exacerbated if we accept Ricoeur's proposal that textual meaning is independent from authorial intention. If Humpty Dumpty assigns the meaning "a nice knock-down argument" to the word "glory," that meaning only exists if we give Humpty the ability to assign his intention to the words that he uses. But if we follow Ricoeur and agree that the text provides its own meaning regardless of the author's intention, then "glory" can only mean what it means for the common language community. Humpty can only use words the same way that everyone else does, because his intentional meaning is moot. Humpty's violation of linguistic conventions renders his discourse unintelligible. There is no room for him, or anyone else, to provide innovations of meaning.

With Ricoeur, however, I defend linguistic innovation against McDowell's insistence upon the necessity of following rules by considering situations in which the violation of the rule does not render a statement to be unintelligible. Ricoeur credits the reader with the capacity for imagination; when confronted with a text that is absurd according to established language rules, she will seek to determine how meaning arises from that text nonetheless. Language rules are not a straitjacket for meaning: they are foundations upon which meaning-apprehension builds. When the foundational rules appear not to apply as they ought, the reader adapts or adds to those rules because of her insatiable desire for meaning. Linguistic impertinence cues the reader to the presence of metaphoric innovation. If the text is absurd or unintelligible when read with conventional language rules, the reader seeks to understand how those rules were violated and how those violations, as innovations, can operate within the language code. Discourse as it occurs in the common usage is open to innovation, violation, and conflict.

THE DIALECTICAL NATURE OF METAPHOR

Metaphor is a dialectic in which two unlike elements are brought together in such a way that they are equated with each other and held in contrast with each other. Because Ricoeur argues that metaphor functions within a sentence, he explains that the "place" of the metaphor is neither the term nor the predicate; metaphor occurs because the copula of the sentence creates the dialectic tension that something "is" and "is not" something else.[33] For Ricoeur, this dialectic is essential to metaphor and what it offers. He explains the metaphor is the process of holding two different thoughts together in such a way as to create a new thought. Metaphor therefore is not the "transfer" of meaning of a term from one referent to another; it is a "transaction" between words which creates something new.[34] Brabant points out that good metaphors bring together elements that are dissimilar, yet correspond sufficiently for the production of meaning to be possible.[35] Ricoeur welcomes, rather than bemoans, the tension between "is" and "is not" of metaphor, that is, that two things which are not the same are presented as though they are. For Ricoeur, this is the operating feature of language. "My inclination is to see the universe of discourse as a universe kept in motion by an interplay of attractions and repulsions that ceaselessly promote the interaction and intersection of domains . . .; and still this interplay never comes to rest in an absolute knowledge that would subsume the tensions."[36] Using the example "Man is a wolf," Ricoeur explains that metaphor connects the commonplace associations of one term to the second term. In this case, the metaphor invites the reader to view man with wolf-like associations: "The wolf-metaphor . . . *organizes* our view of man." However, the connotations associated with man through this metaphor are not limited simply to those associated with wolves prior to the introduction of the metaphor. The metaphor forms new "configurations of implications" for both "man" and "wolf" which neither previously had. "The wolf appears more human at the same moment that by calling the man a wolf places the man in a special light." New meaning for both terms emerges through the construction of the metaphor.[37] Ricoeur explains that understanding of metaphor consists of seeking the "rationale" for the metaphor. While this rationale may be a resemblance between the two ideas, it is not limited to resemblance alone. Metaphor may be created and understood through "common attitudes" toward the two ideas, through "apprehending certain aspects of one thing through the co-presence of the other," and even (or especially) the association of two dissimilar ideas.[38]

Ricoeur refers to the "split reference" of metaphorical expressions. Metaphor does away with the ordinary descriptive reference of language in order to create an indirect or "second-order" reference, which is "built on the ruins of the direct reference." He explains that metaphorical reference is "second-order" only because it follows from primary direct reference, but that it is an expression of reality at a more profound level than is possible through ordinary descriptive means. Ricoeur emphasizes, however, that metaphoric description exists only through the "abolition" of literal reference because of its "incompatibility or absurdity." Through the suspension of this literal or first-order of reference, the metaphorical or second-order of reference becomes apparent and possible.[39] According to Fodor, Ricoeur does not claim that second-order reference replaces first-order reference. Rather, both the literal or first order of meaning and the multiple metaphoric or second orders of meaning operate simultaneously. The "oscillation" between these meanings forms a creative tension between competing messages, which drives the reader to new levels of world- and self-understanding.[40]

The "is/is not" tension of a metaphor does not destroy the possibility for meaning but evokes new meanings which were not previously present. The dialectic occurs between the literal and extended meaning (i.e. first order and second order of reference); metaphoric meaning does not exclude but interacts with literal meaning. Metaphorical meaning is in addition to, and not in place of, literal meaning. The absurdity of naming an "is" where there is an "is not" urges the reader to a second-order of meaning which explores the possibilities of this tension. However, not all statements that are absurd on the literal level evoke explorations for second-level meanings. The dialectic of the "is" and the "is not" is broken when one element overpowers the other. "Heinz Field is Pittsburgh's holy shrine" is a positive example: it is a sports venue and not a religious site. But the "is" and "is not" evoke the metaphoric meaning that football fans in Pittsburgh display near-religious fervor about the facility and the teams that play there. However, some absurd-on-the-literal-level statements offer no meaning on the metaphoric level: the "is not" exceeds the ability of the "is" to evoke meaning. "The United States government has a balanced budget" is false, and has been since 2001. To the despair of fiscal conservatives, there is no space for metaphorical meaning to lift its head above the weight of this "is not." This statement can be identified as a simple falsehood, redeemable only through something like irony or sarcasm: the imputation of an opposite meaning to the text on the part of the author for rhetorical effect.

THE CREATIVE NATURE OF METAPHOR

The creative imagination is a key element of Ricoeur's understanding of metaphor. For him, imagination is not mere escapism or seduction, but develops out of a bracketing of the literal in order to release new truth through metaphor.[41] Imagination is an innovation of reference, not an interplay within the linguistic structure. Language projects new truth about reality.[42] As Stiver explains, the imprecision of metaphor does not lead to chaos or unintelligibility, but offers new means of understanding.[43] Ricoeur understands discourse, particularly poetic discourse, to be polysemous: a communication act offers more than one meaning. He claims that metaphor is particularly well suited for this purpose.[44] As Ricoeur puts it, "a word receives metaphorical meaning in specific contexts within which they are opposed to other words taken literally; this shift in meaning results mainly from a clash between literal meanings, which excludes a literal use of the word in question, and gives clues for the finding of a new meaning which is able to fit in the context of the sentence and to make sense in this context."[45] Citing Ricoeur, Klemm points out that "in metaphorical language the literal level of meaning abolishes itself in a self-destruction and because of this self-destruction of sense, the literal reference also founders." This destruction of the literal meaning allows metaphorical meaning to emerge with a new network of reference. That which is nonsense on the literal level becomes new sense on the metaphoric.[46]

Because of its dynamic nature, Ricoeur asserts that metaphor is the most appropriate way to express reality. He explains that reality constantly changes and cannot be described properly in a static linguistic system. Language therefore requires the innovative function of metaphor, which changes not only itself but its "home" of language.[47] As Ricoeur puts it, "Metaphor is living not only to the extent that it vivifies a constituted language. Metaphor is living by virtue of the fact that it introduces the spark of imagination into a 'thinking more' at the conceptual level."[48] A metaphor-producing author defies the conventions of language use and reconfigures them in a new way so that a different sort of meaning is produced. In fact, as Stiver explains, metaphor does not simply provide a new way to describe reality; it creates a new reality because from a phenomenological perspective there is no difference between description and an individual's world.[49] Linguistic structures, like other tools, can be used for something other than their conventional purposes. When this occurs, the action of production is to be evaluated not by the conventions but by the newly reconfigured structure of the text itself. This evaluation considers both conventional uses and possibilities for innovations within the system. We are not mere residents of language; we are creators and adaptors of it as well. We are competent to rearrange and alter our linguistic dwellings. This is true not only for the author, who produces linguistic innovation, but also for the reader, who is able to recognize the innovation for what it is.

The innovative meaning of a metaphor is not limited to the author's intention, any more than meaning of the text is limited to the author's intention (cf. pp. 95–99). In the case of Mark 13, the text is able to offer innovative metaphor even though the author did not intend it. As I argue in Chapter 3, the author intended the discourse to be a literal description of future events. When future reality unfolded in such a way that the discourse fails to offer a reasonable configuration of it, the discourse becomes metaphoric in the sense that its first-order meaning is absurd for the twenty-first century reader. That which was not intended to be metaphor becomes so. The text offers a novel and creative configuration of the world. The failure of the first-order meaning of the text to conform to reality creates second-order or metaphoric meaning. The possibility for the second-order meaning to be a configuration of the world which is valid depends upon the correspondence of that meaning with actual world situations. Chapter 6 supports and elaborates upon this assertion.

Ricoeur explains that metaphor is the process through which participants in a language system connect signs to new ideas. I take it as a truism that new ideas constantly arise: this is what makes life dynamic and academic research possible. Whether the idea is a new object or a new concept, it needs a linguistic designation in order for people to talk about it. It is through metaphor that the meanings of existing signs are extended to the new ideas. The newly-minted metaphor is striking and evocative, but as its usage becomes ubiquitous, the language system acquires a new convention.[50] Ricoeur argues that because the event which produces a text cannot be re-created, the semantic innovation of a metaphor in that text cannot be identified by analyzing it in terms of the event which produced it. Attempts to do so reduce metaphor to substitution: offering a literal explication of what the metaphor "means." Ricoeur explains that the metaphor can be read only in terms of the eventfulness of the reading of the text: "one must adopt the point of view of the hearer or reader and treat the novelty of an emerging meaning as his work within the very act of hearing or reading." However, he notes that as we consider the diachronic nature of metaphor, we recognize that an "authentic" metaphor exists only when the meaning and event coincide. A metaphor may be striking and innovative at the time of the text's production. But by the time a reader examines the text (two millennia later in the case of this project) the metaphor may have moved through its life cycle to the point that it is now "dead," or has become an element of common parlance. The surprising and evocative nature of the metaphor is gone forever.[51] As the following chapter suggests, however, the "life cycle" of a metaphor can be reversed when an expression that is ubiquitous in its original setting becomes striking or evocative in new circumstances.

In contrast to M. Black,[52] Davidson,[53] and Searle,[54] Ricoeur argues that the creative work of metaphor is rule-governed. As he puts it, "Innovation remains a form of behavior governed by rules. The labor of imagination is not born from nothing."[55] Ricoeur argues against the Romanticist concept that creativity is a product of genius. Instead, metaphor arises out of existing linguistic conventions and therefore is grounded in those rules. He defines imagination as a "rule-governed form of invention," in which reality can be re-described according to conventional patterns. Reading is not a "closed" or fixed endeavor of rehearsing fixed significations, but one in which the dynamics of de-contextualizing and re-contextualizing reveal meaning in novel contexts. He asserts, however, that there is no process or procedure for the creative process which imagination expresses.[56] Stiver points out that metaphor creates a holistic yet fluid and integrative presentation of truth.[57] Lakoff and Turner's catalogue of the use of metaphor in American English supports Ricoeur's contention; their work reveals an overall cultural coherence and strategy which governs the creation and use of metaphor.[58] However, they recognize that metaphors not only express a society's understanding of reality, but that new metaphors can reshape that understanding. New metaphors are able "to create a new reality rather than simply to give us a way of conceptualizing a preexisting reality."[59]

MULTIPLICITY BUT NOT AMBIGUITY OF MEANING

Ricoeur contends that metaphor creates multiple possibilities for meaning; he characterizes this attribute of metaphor as polysemic. While this is a notable characteristic of metaphor in particular, he claims that polysemy exists in all ordinary language use. While making this claim, Ricoeur explains that multiplicity of meaning is different from ambiguity of meaning.

In describing the polysemic nature of ordinary language use, Ricoeur distinguishes it from scientific or artificial language use, which introduces technical terms in order to eliminate multiple possibilities for meaning. He explains that polysemic potentiality within ordinary language use is reduced through the linguistic and socio-cultural context within which the discourse exists. Poetic language (which can be understood as metaphor writ large[60]), in contrast, uses the polysemous nature of language to create new truth. That which is an unfortunate but necessary element of ordinary language, and which is eliminated in scientific language, is put to work to produce new truth.[61]

When metaphor is considered synchronically, as is typically the case in semiotic approaches whose genealogies arise from Saussure, the word is assumed to be the carrier of concrete meaning which exists independently from its context in the sentence or larger discourse. The word is not only the name for an object or concept; it is the sense of the term as it operates within the overall linguistic structure. Ricoeur advocates a diachronic approach to linguistics as well. Using this approach, he demonstrates that the one-to-one relationship between word and sense exists only in artificial or technical language.[62] In common parlance, more than one word can associate to one sense; hence synonyms. Conversely, one word can be associated to several senses; hence polysemy. Ricoeur differentiates polysemy from homonymy, which is also the case of a single term expressing different meanings, because no family of associations exist between the two meanings.[63] Polysemy, in contrast, is a healthy feature of language which provides economy and flexibility of expression. It develops historically, or diachronically, as new contexts require linguistic innovation to provide terms for new concepts. Ricoeur explains that such developments tend to occur suddenly, with surprise and perhaps shock, rather than as an evolution of language use. Word use is therefore not "closed," as a strictly synchronic analysis would suggest; it is dynamic and fluid.[64] Ricoeur explains that metaphor straddles the dichotomy of synchronicity and diachronicity. It exists both within a structure and as an element of history. At the present moment within a linguistic system, metaphor signifies several things. But it is the means by which associations between words and things develop within that language. Ricoeur proposed that metaphor ought therefore to be considered from "a panchronistic point of view," using the expression's origins to identify polysemy.[65]

Ricoeur points out that metaphor creates a "surplus of signification" as it offers two or more meanings at the same time. It cannot be reduced by replacing the secondary signification with the primary signification, as is the case for allegory, because in the process of associating two concepts with each other, new and irreducible meaning is created.[66] Following Henle, Ricoeur explains that the meaning which metaphor creates cannot be replicated fully through literal paraphrase, because it is not a case of substituting words as they are used literally with other words as they are used metaphorically. Paraphrase of metaphor can never be fully complete: "it is endless precisely because it can always spring back to life."[67] As Ricoeur explains, "*true metaphors are untranslatable*. Only metaphors of substitution are capable of a translation which restores the proper meaning. Tension metaphors are untranslatable because they create meaning. To say that they are untranslatable does not mean that they cannot be paraphrased, but the paraphrase is infinite and does not exhaust the innovation in meaning."[68] Metaphor continues to offer new meanings, even beyond those which the author envisaged. As the metaphor operates in new contexts, it continues to evoke new meanings. And it is able to do so because it is not defined by the linguistic code in which it operates. By violating that code and relying instead upon the context in which it operates, metaphor produces new meanings through each event in which it operates; the event of reading the text in which the metaphor resides for different readers in different world situations.

Ricoeur defends his argument for the polysemous nature of metaphor against the charge that multiplicity of meaning leads to a breakdown of communication by distinguishing between polysemy on the one hand and ambiguity, equivocity, and misunderstanding on the other. The appropriateness of *multiple* meanings does not imply that *all* possible interpretations are appropriate. Ricoeur defines ambiguity as "the character of the discourse itself as opened to several interpretations;" such a trait is acceptable and even valuable in the case of poetics. Equivocity refers to "interpretation hesitating between these [different possible] interpretations." Misunderstanding is the break-down of communication which may result from ambiguity and equivocity.[69] Stiver explains that metaphor's multiplicity of meaning does not fall into chaos because the rules of discourse provide a "directed" rather than "precise" meaning. The text establishes parameters within which meanings may be found, in what he terms "limited infinity."[70] As a visual analogy, consider mathematical fractals, in which a structure in a limited space has theoretically infinite features.[71] Ricoeur points out that a word has a range of possible "connotations" or meanings by itself; setting it within a larger linguistic context sometimes limits the possible connotations to the word's implicit meaning. Other contexts, however, open up a range of possible meanings: "play on words, implication, metaphor and irony are some particular cases of this polysemy." However, Ricoeur is careful to point out that polysemy is not ambiguity: "we are confronted with ambiguity only when one meaning alone of two possible meanings is required, and the context does not provide us with grounds for deciding between them." Polysemy, on the other hand, means several things all at the same time, and the reader does not need to choose between the possible meanings.[72]

HOW METAPHOR EXPRESSES TRUTH

A defense of Ricoeur's definition of metaphor depends upon the success of showing how the dialectic of metaphor does not collapse into absurdity (i.e. a language act which has no meaning). It is not enough to argue that metaphor presents meaning in addition to literal meaning; that extended meaning must be a description of the world, or of possibilities for the world, which the reader is able to appropriate. The metaphor must present a configuration of the world which confirms, challenges, clarifies, or reorients the reader's world-understanding, even if she ultimately rejects that configuration. While a metaphor's world-configuration may be false, it is possible for that configuration to be true as well. This section argues for that possibility.

As I explain in pp. 33–36, expressions of truth are not limited to descriptions of historical events, or adequation. Metaphor, as a type of fictive discourse, seeks to present truth as manifestation. It manifests truth that had been concealed by conventional conceptual frameworks. Ricoeur explains that metaphor is a form of poetic discourse which does not depend upon "direct description," but "redescribes reality by the roundabout route of heuristic fiction."[73] Descriptions of reality, or truthful statements, are not limited to straightforward propositional statements but include strategies which employ indirect expositions of that which is not explicable directly.

Ricoeur outlines the difficulty in accepting metaphor as truth by pointing out that "linguistic analysis is so heavily determined by the . . . principles of

verification and falsification that it is very difficult . . . to conceive of a concept of truth that would not be taken for granted and defined a priori as adequation. The idea . . . that truth may mean not adequation but manifestation
seems to be alien to the main thesis of linguistic analysis."[74] More recently,
however, Stiver notes a change in scholarship in the last several decades away
from the sense that figurative discourse must be translated into literal description in order to express truth to the understanding that such discourse, and
metaphor in particular, is not able to be reduced to literal language. Indeed,
Stiver claims, metaphor is at times a better way to express truth.[75] According
to Amherdt, Ricoeur proposes that metaphor is true when the primary reference of a world object is supplanted by the secondary reference which reveals
a new and true dimension of reality. In this way, Ricoeur moves beyond
conceptions of truth as adequation, based on the proper naming of objects or
on accord with historical circumstances. Truth also includes existential truth,
which relates to human identity and life activity, and eschatological truth,
which expresses hope for future possibilities. Religious texts, according to
Amherdt, function as metaphorical and poetic texts by presenting truth in
these ways.[76] Stiver also supports Ricoeur's notion of metaphorical truth when
he relies upon Aquinas' description of a third way for religious language,
between univocal and equivocal, to make a claim for how it is able to make
truth statements as metaphor. While these statements are imprecise, they are
still capable of stating the truth. The inexactitude of religious discourse is a
function of its subject matter, which is liminal and contains an inherent element of mystery. Nonetheless, Stiver argues, it is not an entirely unknowable
field of inquiry. Metaphor is able to present real meaning without making a
false claim of full explication. It is an appropriate discursive strategy to make
statements about God which can be affirmed and rejected at the same time,
with its inherent tension between the "is" and the "is not."[77]

Ricoeur claims that metaphorical truth arises out of the tensions in the
discourse, whether they exist internally in the text, between literal and figurative interpretations of the text, or between the sameness and difference of the
elements brought together in the metaphor. Ricoeur emphasizes the "existential function" of the metaphor's copula over its "relational function" for its
capacity to express truth.[78] Metaphor produces truth when the balance of "is/
is not" is maintained. Metaphor's capacity for truth depends upon the literal
falsity of the metaphorical statement. When the first-order of reference of
the statement fails (i.e. is recognized to be false), the second-order of reference becomes evident. The reference, or "about what," of the text is a world,
or worlds, toward which the reader can be oriented. Negative metaphors,
such as "no man is an island" are not counter examples because in order to
conceive of how a man is not an island, one must first have a sense of how
a man could be an island. In response to this particular example, Davidson

explains that "the negation of a metaphor seems always to be a potential metaphor."[79] Taylor describes the process by which metaphor can reveal truth through the example of the parable of the Good Samaritan (Luke 10:25–37). "The parable as metaphor disorients by presenting a clash with known reality: the juxtaposition of Samaritan and neighbor." In so doing, the metaphor reveals a new reality that Samaritans are not enemies but neighbors.[80] In this instance, the metaphor's tension comes not from elements internal to the text, but from the text's description of reality and the reader's perception of reality. As the following chapter explains, this is the primary metaphorical tension present as today's reader engages with Mark 13.

According to Ricoeur, metaphor suspends the historical world in order to develop a new one. He acknowledges that it is meaningless for a text to present a "world" which cannot be inhabited, but he contrasts this objection with his assertion that the text can create a virtual world, or promised reality, which the reader can enter, much like the virtual worlds that online gamers inhabit while gazing at a glowing screen in their parents' basements. The text evokes a "mood, or 'state of soul'" in its readers, which extends beyond the text and offers the readers a new way to understand themselves and their lived worlds. Metaphor provides the clue for how the virtual world of the text affects the reader's sense of the lived world. Just as metaphor (on the sentence level) identifies similarities which previously were not there, similarities between the text-world and the lived-world create a new world for the reader to live into.[81] Metaphor's new understandings allow the reader to apprehend the world or self in a way that was previously not possible within the structures of previous linguistic and conceptual categories and frameworks. By equating two different concepts, metaphor creates new thought as a configuration which makes previously unrecognizable implications apparent. Ricoeur considers metaphor to be an intentional denial of the statement's nature as simply fictional in order to see reality in a way that would otherwise not be evident. Metaphor continues therefore to be fictional, i.e. not a true presentation of reality, but at the same time it expresses truth by introducing a new reality.[82] In the case of Mark 13, metaphor brings a new reality into existence, even if its fulfillment lies in the future.

NOTES

1. Ricoeur, *Rule of Metaphor*, 12–13.
2. Ibid., 18–19.
3. Ricoeur, *Interpretation Theory*, 46–53.
4. Ricoeur, *Rule of Metaphor*, 80–1.
5. Ricoeur, "Creativity in Language," 130–31.

6. Cf. e.g. Edward Gordon Selwyn, *The First Epistle of St. Peter*, second edition (Grand Rapids: Baker Book House, 1981), pp. 243–44.

7. Ricoeur, *Rule of Metaphor*, 136–59.

8. Dunn, "Jesus and the Kingdom," 35.

9. Taylor, "Editor's Introduction," xxiii–xxiv.

10. Ricoeur, *Rule of Metaphor* 138–43.

11. Kümmel,. *Promise and Fulfilment*, 55.

12. Stephen C. Levinson, *Pragmatics* (Cambridge & New York: Cambridge University Press, 1983), 148.

13. Max Black, "More About Metaphor," in *Metaphor and Thought*, ed. Andrew Ortony (Cambridge: Cambridge University Press, 1979), 31–2.

14. Ricoeur, *Rule of Metaphor*, 118–20.

15. Ibid., 85–7.

16. Ibid., 94–5.

17. Hayden V. White, *Metahistory: The Historical Imagination in Nineteenth-Century Europe* (Baltimore: Johns Hopkins University Press, 1973), 31–38.

18. Ricoeur, *Rule of Metaphor*, 196.

19. Ibid., 194.

20. Ibid., 253.

21. Ibid., 230.

22. Ibid., 57–9.

23. Ibid., 108–09.

24. Ibid., 106–7.

25. Ibid., 197–98.

26. Ibid., 151–54.

27. Ibid., 236–37.

28. Ibid., 21–3.

29. Ricoeur, "Biblical Hermeneutics," 99.

30. George Lakoff and Mark Turner, *More Than Cool Reason: A Field Guide to Poetic Metaphor* (Chicago: University of Chicago Press, 1989), 86–7.

31. George Lakoff and Mark Johnson, *Metaphors We Live By* (Chicago: University of Chicago Press, 1980), 14–24; cf. Lakoff and Turner, Cool Reason, 49–52.

32. John Henry McDowell, "Wittgenstein on Following a Rule," in *Mind, Value, and Reality* (Cambridge, MA: Harvard University Press, 1998), 225–27.

33. Ricoeur, *Rule of Metaphor*, 7.

34. Ibid., 80.

35. Brabant, "Ricoeur's Hermeneutical Ontology," 458–59.

36. Ricoeur, *Rule of Metaphor*, 302.

37. Ibid., 87–8.

38. Ibid., 81–2.

39. Paul Ricoeur, "The Metaphorical Process as Cognition, Imagination, and Feeling," in *On Metaphor*, ed. Sheldon Sacks (Chicago: University of Chicago Press, 1979), 152–54.

40. Fodor, *Christian Hermeneutics*, 154–55.

41. Ricoeur's understanding of metaphor contrasts with White, for whom metaphor is an escape from the privations of life and the horrors of too much knowledge. It is an attempt to forget by embracing the metaphor as truth in order to escape reality (339). Ricoeur, however, considers metaphor to be a means by which the significance of the lived world can be recognized and faced in a new way. It is a way to escape from the forgetfulness of conventional knowing so that one can discern the world.

42. Evans, *Paul Ricoeur's Hermeneutics*, 97, 119–20, 123–24.

43. Stiver, *Ricoeur and Theology*, 73.

44. Ricoeur, "Creativity in Language," 120–21.

45. Ricoeur, "Metaphor and the Main Problem," 138.

46. Ricoeur, *Hermeneutical Theory*, 97–8.

47. Ricoeur, *Rule of Metaphor* 42–3.

48. Ibid., 303.

49. Stiver, *Ricoeur and Theology*, 71.

50. Ricoeur, *Rule of Metaphor* 62–3.

51. Ibid., 98–9.

52. M. Black, "More About Metaphor," 23–5.

53. Donald, Davidson, "Metaphor and Religion: The Test Case of Christian Texts," in *On Metaphor*, ed. Sheldon Sacks (Chicago: University of Chicago Press, 1979), 29.

54. Searle, Intentionality, 148–49.

55. Ricoeur, *Time and Narrative* 1, 69.

56. Paul Ricoeur, "The Bible and Imagination," trans. David Pellauer, in *Figuring the Sacred: Religion, Narrative, and Imagination*, ed. Mark I. Wallace (Minneapolis: Augsburg Fortress, 1995), 144–45.

57. Stiver, *Ricoeur and Theology*, 74.

58. Lakoff and Turner, *Cool Reason*, 60.

59. Ibid., 143–46.

60. Elsewhere Ricoeur echoes Beardsley's description of metaphor as a "poem in miniature" (cf. e.g. *Interpretation Theory* 46, *Rule of Metaphor* 94). Conversely, therefore, poems are extended metaphors.

61. Ricoeur, "Creativity in Language," 127–30; cf. Vanhoozer, *Biblical Narrative*, 59–61.

62. As Stiver notes, however, recent research into the use of scientific language shows that even it does not have the one-to-one correspondence between sign and meaning that it is claimed to have (Stiver, *Ricoeur and Theology*, 74).

63. Consider the word "bank," which has the two unrelated meanings of a repository for money and the edge of a river.

64. Ricoeur, *Rule of Metaphor*, 110–17.

65. Ibid., 122–23.

66. Ricoeur, *Interpretation Theory*, 55–7; cf. Stiver, *Ricoeur and Theology*, 68.

67. Ricoeur, *Rule of Metaphor* 188; cf. Ibid., 290–91; Paul Ricoeur, *The Symbolism of Evil*, trans. Emerson Buchanan (New York: Harper & Row, 1967), 351.

68. Ricoeur, "Biblical Hermeneutics," 80.

69. Ricoeur, "Creativity in Language," 126–27.

70. Stiver, *Ricoeur and Theology*, 81–2.

71. Cf. McLean, *Biblical Interpretation*, 277.

72. Ricoeur, *Rule of Metaphor*, 91; cf. Ibid., 123–24.

73. Ibid., 247.

74. Ricoeur, "Creativity in Language," 132–33.

75. Stiver, *Life Together*, 275.

76. Amherdt, *L'herméneutique Philosophique*, 162–65.

77. Dan R. Stiver, *The Philosophy of Religious Language: Sign, Symbol, and Story* (Oxford, Cambridge MA: Blackwell, 1996), 130–33.

78. Ricoeur, *Rule of Metaphor*, 247–49.

79. Davidson, "Metaphor and Religion," 40.

80. George H. Taylor, "Derrick Bell's Narratives as Parables," *New York University Review of Law and Social Change* 31 (2007): 239.

81. Ricoeur, *Rule of Metaphor*, 229–30.

82. Ibid., 252.

Chapter 6

Mark 13 As Metaphor

The apparent meaning of Mark 13 when it was written was a literal prediction that certain events would take place within the next three to four decades. Because some of these events never took place, it is evident that the predictions are false. Therefore today's reader is only able to appropriate Mark 13 as a false text, provided that the only meaning available to her is the meaning that was apparent when the text was written. However, a text is able to present different meaning from and in addition to what was apparent when it was written. It is therefore possible for Mark 13 to present meaning today that was latent at the time of its writing. I argue that today's reader is able to read Mark 13 as a metaphor in the manner described by Ricoeur. When read in this way, she may appropriate it as a true text. It is worth reiterating at this point that the goal of this project is not to prove that Mark 13 is a true text and that it must be read metaphorically. My argument is that the reader is able to do so, not that she must.

THE DOUBLE DISSONANCE OF MARK 13

The first section of Chapter 3 argues that the Olivet discourse of Mark 13 originally presented a prediction of the eschaton as it was understood by theological and cosmological conventions of the time. It is likely that this was the author's intention. However, the text's meaning is not limited to the author's intention or to the way that it was originally understood. The meaning of the text is able to be more than the author himself understood it to be.[1] The text can be ironic, subversive, and/or metaphoric, even if the author did not intend it to be so. Ricoeur provides a way to identify metaphorical meaning that neither requires nor contradicts conventional reading. To the contrary; Ricoeur describes literal, or first-order, meaning as a requirement for metaphorical, or second-order, meaning (cf. pp. 123–124). The world which Mark 13 presents to today's reader, as she reads it literally or conventionally, is not a historically true description of the real world. In order for the reader to appropriate the text as true, she must do so by seeking non-literal meaning.

Ricoeur describes the metaphorical statement as that which perceives similarity *"despite* difference, *in spite of* contradiction."[2] Metaphor exists when there is a creative dissonance between two elements of a statement, or between the world-configuration of the text and the experienced world of the reader. This dissonance is creative when it is not a simple contradiction that can be refuted easily because there is no way to associate the two features with each other. Conversely, it is creative only when the commonality between the two features is not readily apparent through the use of previously existing conceptual frameworks. The metaphor creates new associations where there had been none. In the case of the discourse of Mark 13, today's reader recognizes a clash between difference and sameness: the text claims a similarity between its world description and reality, but the reader recognizes that they are different. This is not an enigma that the original audience was able to perceive, but it is a tension that is obvious today. The Jewish War did not culminate in the parousia. The difference between experienced history and portrayed history is apparent, but the text draws them together. It challenges the reader to find similarity between history as it is configured by the text and history as it has been experienced.

Mark 13, as it is read today, provides two types of creative dissonance. In both cases, the text presents metaphorical impertinence which was not discernible at the time of the text's writing; that which was latent is now apparent. First, vv. 30 and 32 stand in tension with each other. It is no longer possible to argue that v. 30 presents the claim that Jesus can predict the broad time frame for when events will take place, and that v. 32 qualifies this claim by explaining that Jesus' predictive ability is imprecise. The claim of v. 30 for Jesus' ability to predict future events, even within broad time parameters, is now recognized to be false, at least in this case. "All these things" (ταῦτα πάντα) did not happen within a generation. V. 32 is now not merely a qualifying statement ("Jesus can predict that these things will happen within the next few decades, but he cannot identify the very day and hour") but stands in contrast with v. 30; Jesus is not able to predict when these events will take place at all. This is a creative dissonance: the text claims that Jesus can predict when these things will take place, but it also states that he is unable to do so. As originally read, v. 32 limited a too-precise anticipation of the expected events. It claims that Jesus is only able to know that they will happen within a generation. Once the generation has passed, however, the most salient feature of this verse is no longer the precision of "day or hour" (τῆς ἡμέρας ἐκείνης ἢ τῆς ὥρας) but Jesus' ignorance of when events will take place. This is at odds with v. 30's description of Jesus being able to predict, albeit relatively broadly, when events will happen. The presence of these two logia in the same discourse, separated only by another logion which emphasizes the permanence of Jesus' words, suggests that they must be read together.[3] This close association of the logia highlights the dissonance between them and challenges the reader to seek ways to discern meaning in their association with each other.

Second, there exists a dissonance between the configured world of the text and the lived world of the reader. This dissonance functions as metaphor because as McCarthy puts it, Ricoeur understands metaphor to be "a space for imagination and action distanced, but not separated, from the situation of the original autograph or the sense of the inscription."[4] The events described by Mark 13 are a split reference, as metaphor: the literal events as understood in the writing-conditions, and the metaphorical meanings that are recognized in the reading-conditions. The metaphor of Mark 13 is the difference of history as portrayed by the text and history as understood by today's reader. The text describes a world in which celestial objects collapse, an other-worldly being appears, and the faithful are gathered together. The world experienced by today's reader is one in which none of these events takes place. Mark 13, as encountered in today's reading-conditions, violates convention by claiming events will happen in a time period when they did not. The failure of the prediction does not necessarily lead only to a conclusion that the text is a false world configuration, but enables the reader to re-evaluate prior world understanding. In order for Mark 13 to be appropriated as a true text, its world-description must be able to evoke possibilities for understanding the world. The "is not" must not overpower the "is." The events predicted in Mark 13 are both typical of and distinct from ordinary experience.

As Chapter 5 explains, metaphor exists only if the "is not" of the statement is not too strong to allow second-level meaning to arise. I contend that the "is not" which arises from the disjuncture of the text's world description with real-world situations does not lead simply to the conclusion that it is "wrong," or even ironic. It interacts with the "is" that the text presents in order to form a contradiction from which metaphor arises. There is a disjuncture between the world which the discourse describes and the world of historical events, but this disjuncture does not mean that the discourse is necessarily false or that the world that it presents has nothing to offer the reader. Despite the discourse's failure to describe or predict historical events accurately, its "is" and "is not" challenges the reader who is open to the text to explore the dialectic in order to discern a new configuration of the lived world. As Allison puts it, "Once one gets around the scandal of a missed date . . . one can get used to it." He explains that for some interpreters, Jesus' eschatology directs the reader's attention to the overarching importance of his message. That which is described as final is to be understood as critically important.[5]

If we accept the argument in Chapter 3 that v. 30's temporal placement of events that will occur in a generation is inclusive (i.e. that "all these things" includes the collapse of celestial objects and/or beings, the appearance of the glorified Son of Man, and the in-gathering and vindication of the elect), and that these things have not happened historically and literally, then on a literal level the text is false. It predicts that which did not happen within the predicted time. But the failure of the text to present truth is accurate only on the first order of meaning; i.e. at the literal level. If we contend with Allison that the author intended a literal meaning (e.g. that the collapse of the stars actually meant that the Big Dipper would fall into the Black Sea), and if we assert with Hirsch that the only meaning a text has is the meaning that the author intended it to have, the matter is settled. The text means one thing, and that one thing is wrong. Just as it is inaccurate to say that the US government has a budget surplus, it is inaccurate to say that the text's predictions have been fulfilled. However, if we accept Ricoeur's contention that a text's meaning is not limited to the author's intention, the text continues to be evocative. Because the text has been liberated from the constraints of its environment of production (the author's work, the audience's response, and the *Sitz im Leben* in which it was written) by virtue of its temporal durability, the meanings of the discourse extend beyond what the author intended. The Olivet discourse is able to offer metaphorical or second-order meanings which may be true, even if its author intended only literal, first-order meanings which is false. These possibilities of meaning are not infinite. And rigorous employment of the explanatory mode of interpretation (typically identified as exegesis in Biblical studies) distinguishes meanings that are inconsistent with the text from those that are consistent with what it presents. Once the reader has done the work of explanation, she can recognize the meanings that arise appropriately from the text. This is the polysemous meaning which Ricoeur argues that texts present.

THE INTEGRATION OF LITERAL AND FIGURATIVE MEANING

As Ricoeur describes it,[6] a text presents metaphorical meaning, or a second level of reference, only when the first level of reference, or the literal meaning, is false. Metaphorical meaning depends upon a literal meaning. When the reader understands that literal meaning to be false or absurd, figurative meaning becomes possible. Reading the Olivet discourse metaphorically does not exclude but actually depends upon a literal understanding of it. That is, a claim that Mark 13 can be read metaphorically does not contradict but develops from literal readings. When the reader recognizes the literal meaning to be false, she has the opportunity to explore metaphorical meanings. The Olivet discourse employs metaphor in order not to be constrained by conventions as it expresses a limit experience. With the exception of Bultmann, commentators who argue for figurative meaning claim that literal meaning is impossible or unwarranted. Unlike Bultmann and the others, a Ricoeurian reading of Mark 13 brings the two together instead of replacing the one with the other.

At this point it is helpful to recall Frei's argument for the literal meaning of the text and its historicity or "history-like" quality, in contrast to figurative meaning. The text can be considered in three ways: T^h, or the text as a configuration of actual historical events, T^l, or the literal, first-order meaning of the text, and T^f, or the figurative, second-order meaning of the text. When T^h and T^l do not correspond (i.e. when the configuration of the text is not consistent with the historical events it purportedly describes), the reader may turn to T^f as a way to provide comprehensibility for the text. Frei argues, however, that she should seek to appropriate only T^l, even when it is non-historical. The literal meaning, or T^l, of Mark 13 (a cosmic and spiritual upheaval to happen at some point in the first century) does not accord with T^h. Our reader has four choices. First, she may conclude that T^l therefore is to be rejected, and that any possible world which it presents is false. Second, she may accept Frei's argument and decide that while T^l does not match T^h, it offers options for the reader's attempts to understand self and world. Third, she may propose that the rupture between T^h and T^l necessitates T^f, a different way of reading the text in a figurative fashion, so that it can provide potential meaning. Fourth, she may pursue a Ricoeur-oriented reading and claim that the choice between T^l and T^f is a false one. The interaction between the literal and figurative meanings is the impetus for creative possibility. As the reader holds the literal and figurative meanings together, she is able to discern new ways of understanding self and world.

Allison's interpretation of Mark 13 is similar to the Ricoeur-oriented option. He explains that a literal reading of passages such as Mark 13 does not preclude symbolic or metaphoric reading. Indeed, he asserts, even though the predictions of this discourse are literal, the primary message of the text is not a rearrangement of the physical universe but the re-creation of a profoundly evil world. The physical aspects of this transformation indicate not only the pervasiveness of evil but also the extraordinary steps God must take to rectify it.[7] Allison asserts that we need not be forced into a choice between "flat-footed literalism and metaphor." That which is understood to be a literal occurrence can also be imbued with evocative symbolic meaning. The transformation of the physical world can therefore be both a literal happening and an indication of God's redemptive action.[8] He concludes that

"Jesus the millenarian prophet, like all millenarian prophets, was wrong: reality has taken no notice of his imagination." The promise of a world transformed, in which evil and suffering are obliterated and the faithful are vindicated, has not taken place. The best Allison can offer is that, despite the failure of Jesus' predictions as portrayed by Mark, "his dream is the only one worth dreaming."[9] This comment is not merely a poetic way to say that Jesus offers us nothing more than wishful thinking in a brutal and painful world, but that he points us to something more. Despite the failure of the Olivet discourse to correspond with reality, its claim for God's ultimate victory over death and evil challenges today's reader to apprehend the world in a new way.

REVERSAL OF THE METAPHOR'S LIFE CYCLE

As outlined on p. 126, Ricoeur describes the process by which metaphors change diachronically from being surprising transgressions of conceptual frameworks and become part of those frameworks, which have been altered by the inclusion of the metaphor. I claim that this process is reversed in the case of Mark 13. The text began as one which conformed to the conventions of the time, but as conventions changed and as history proved not to conform to the predictions of the text, the discourse became provocative.

Ricoeur explains that metaphors begin as a function of discourse rather than as an element of a linguistic system. At this point the metaphor offers a challenge to existing patterns of thought prescribed by language and presents new meaning. As the metaphor's challenge and possibility is received and accepted by the linguistic community, it becomes part of the language system which it had challenged, and the system itself is different as a result. Once the new or extended meanings presented by the metaphor are accepted, the polysemy of the terms of the metaphor is extended. By the final stages of the life of a metaphor, it has become "dead": it loses its evocative nature as it becomes part of common parlance.[10] For example, when automobiles first appeared in the United States, the word "hood" was used metaphorically to describe the cover of the engine compartment. In Great Britain, "bonnet" was used in a similar metaphoric fashion. A word typically associated with the cover for a person's head was used to describe the cover for an important component of the vehicle. In time, the evocative nature of this metaphor was lost, and this designation has become merely another meaning for the word. The metaphor died, and the polysemy of the word grew as a result.[11] The metaphor's life cycle begins with a surprising transgression of conceptual categories and ends when the metaphor "dies" or becomes "domesticated," as Stiver puts it[12] and becomes a convention itself.

Ricoeur describes this process in his analysis of New Testament parables, which he understands as metaphors. While he acknowledges that other scholars reduce the parable to simile or allegory in which literal terms are substituted with figurative ones, Ricoeur argues that the parable does not offer literal thought cloaked in figurative terms. Instead, the parable as a metaphor creates a tension which "twists" the meaning of the words through which it is conveyed. Like other metaphors, the parable exists as parable only as long as its innovative tension continues. Once the parable is common and accepted, it no longer operates as a metaphor, just as a more conventional metaphor frequently becomes an extension of the word's meaning.[13] Apocalyptic discourse operates in a similar way. Apocalyptic texts, like other metaphors, cannot be reduced to literal expressions (although incomplete paraphrase is possible) because they create meaning through their surprising and innovative re-descriptions of reality. Once this new reality-description becomes commonplace the text loses its metaphoric aspect because the tension is gone.

In the case of Mark 13, the pattern is reversed. A linguistic construction which was conventional and comprehensible at the literal level when it was produced now violates conventions and is incompatible in the context of a later reader. It makes claims that events will happen when they did not, and it provides conflicting descriptions of Jesus' predictive abilities. We are able to recognize a metaphor today where none was present in the original context; the conventional has become provocative. The predicted events and the expectation for when these events would occur were logically possible at the time when Mark's gospel was written, and they were consistent with conventional expectations of the time. However, it is impossible for today's reader to accept that a cosmos-shattering event occurred within the span of a generation of Jesus' career. But if a linguistic expression which may not have functioned metaphorically during the event of its production is a metaphor in the event of its reading in a different context, the text is able to open an evocative possibility of what the world may be, may become, or may have been.[14]

APOCALYPTICISM AND MARK 13 AS POLYSEMOUS METAPHOR

As commentators propose figurative possibilities for meaning in the Olivet discourse, it is not the case that one must select a particular understanding of the text to the exclusion of others. Ricoeur's presentation of the multiplicity of meaning which metaphor creates (cf. pp. 127–129) demonstrates that it is a false dichotomy to choose between *either* one meaning *or* another; metaphor makes possible the choice of *both* one reading *and* a second. Indeed, the polysemous nature of metaphor creates more meaning than can be explicated.

All meaning-possibilities must be based upon the text itself, but they may offer multiple ways for it to be appropriated. Just as Ricoeur asserts that interpretation of the Song of Songs must not be limited to a singular meaning,[15] we may also read Mark 13 in multiple ways: as a prediction of future events, as a recasting of the present situation with references to past crises, as a summons to a new way of being in the world, and so forth. Ricoeur encourages us not to narrow our options to a single meaning for metaphoric texts, but to consider the meanings which emerge as the different possibilities are held together. For Ricoeur, the primary meaning of a statement creates multiple meanings which develop from it.[16] Thus, while the symbolism of Mark 13 may initially focus upon historical events of the first century and spiritual aspects of those events, the discourse is not a simple sign that points only to those events. As understood through this primary designation, the Olivet discourse offers meaning beyond what the author and original audience conceived. Diaz notes that apocalyptic texts in particular employ images which convey multiple designations. With an argument based on Ricoeur, she explains that because of the infinitely evocative nature of metaphor, the referents of the images in apocalyptic are often in tension with each other. Diaz cites the conflicting portrayals of a city in Revelation as corrupt Babylon and as glorious New Jerusalem to provide an example of this.[17]

The plurality of symbolic designation in Mark 13 extends in a similar way. Beasley-Murray acknowledges that discursive analyses of symbolic descriptions of the parousia cannot capture their full meaning. "If the parousia represents the climactic intervention of God in Christ, let us acknowledge with candor that the representations of the event do not permit us to describe it."[18] As Chapter 1 outlines, scholars offer many suggestions for the literal or figurative meaning of the Olivet discourse. A Ricoeurian appreciation for the superabundance of meaning would lead us to recognize multiple meanings in the text, so far as they can be supported by analysis of the text itself. The reader can appropriate the Olivet discourse by recognizing the evocative nature of metaphor and by integrating conventional and figurative understandings of the text. Is the coming of the Son of Man a literal historical event which did not happen when it was predicted to take place? Or is it a figurative expression of something that has happened (such as the restoration of Israel, following Wright, or the existential decision for faith, following Bultmann)? I argue instead that the question which the metaphor raises is not one of "either/or" but of "both/and." Mark 13 both predicts literal historical events and provides several figurative configurations. The Ricoeur-oriented reader does not seek to resolve the tension but explores the insights that emerge from it. The holding-together of different interpretive options challenges the reader's previously-held conceptions of each possibility in order to reformulate them in light of their rivals.

The presence in the discourse of images and symbols that come from Daniel, Isaiah, Joel, and other Old Testament texts demonstrates this point. For example, Daniel's presentation of the abomination of desolation most likely operated originally as a sign for Antiochus Epiphanes and his profanation of the temple. This expression is mediated through the original Antiochus reference and evokes meaning(s) beyond this initial referent. The presence of a commonly-understood expression directs the original readers' attention to meanings other than and subsequent to the Antiochus referent. But the symbol does not come to a dead end with Mark's re-use of it. Given the polysemous nature of symbols, our understanding of the abomination of desolation need not be limited to a single person or situation, whether it is Antiochus, Caligula, Eleazar, Vespasian, the high priest, or any of a number of other possibilities outlined on pp. 71–74. The power of symbolic discourse is that the text is able to refer to all of these possible referents, and others, with the term "abomination of desolation." The polysemy of metaphor creates an evocative tension for some readers when its referents are in conflict with each other.

This strategy requires a demonstration that the text does indeed present this tension. Metaphor cannot mean anything we want; its meanings are multiple but not boundless. Ricoeur's description of metaphoric tension assumes the prior work of explanation, or critical exegetical analysis, to conform our conception of the text's meaning with what the text actually presents. It is only as our interpretive work passes through the explanatory mode of critical analysis that we can move to Ricoeur's possibilities for the creative tension of conflicting interpretations. Mark 13 draws together both the real-world experiences of its original readers (i.e. deception, calamity, and persecution) and their perception of the world which includes a conflict between spiritual powers. But it does so in a way that presents a consummating event in the future that draws them together. The perspective of today's reader allows her to recognize that the future event did not happen as the text presents it. Thus, while it was not present in the initial production-event of the text, the text now presents a tension for today's reader to confront. That which may be dismissed as nonsense becomes an opportunity for new sense to be discerned.

Ricoeur's treatment of metaphor is particularly compelling as it relates to apocalyptic texts. As Diaz puts it, "When we consider with Ricoeur that the power of a religious text [as metaphor] comes from the ordinary mixed with the extraordinary, or images of abundance, here [in apocalyptic literature] we have a prime example of how the two work together." She goes on to describe how the seven letters of Revelation 2–3 use cosmic imagery to address the issues of everyday life in order to impress upon the readers that the issues they face extend beyond the apparently mundane context and are direct expressions of universal realities which are seldom recognized.

She cautions against attempts to resolve the tension that this juxtaposition of the ordinary and extraordinary creates by treating apocalyptic images as mere "exotic symbolism" and considering the ordinary to be the only matter which the text addresses.[19]

My review in Chapter 1 reveals that many scholars succumb to this temptation in one way or another when addressing Mark 13. The fantastic images of the discourse, particularly vv. 24–7, are either domesticated into mere ciphers for literal historical events (yet to occur when the text was written) or elevated as descriptions that are disconnected from history. Both options separate the ordinary from the extraordinary, either by denying the extraordinary aspect or by escaping from the ordinary. The text, however, brings the two together; it presents a world configuration which challenges the reader on the one hand to recognize a more profound, universal, and cosmic dimension to their life situation, while on the other hand connecting their spiritual hopes and aspirations to their lived reality. Apocalyptic seeks to integrate idealistic spiritual aspirations with the messiness of life in a world which can be confusing, confounding, and ominous. We lose that appeal when we seek either to explain away the fantastic or to ignore the everyday.

When the apocalyptic image is treated as an allegory for a real-world figure (e.g. the abomination of desolation is Antiochus Epiphanes' desecration of the temple), the text no longer challenges the reader to a new understanding of the world. It becomes simply a fanciful way to describe what everyone already sees and understands. The re-use of the image in a new setting (such as Daniel's image of the abomination in Mark 13:14) requires that the new expression be evaluated in light of the original. When treated as allegory or simile, the Markan abomination is simply a repetition of the Danielic abomination, which has already been domesticated into a rhetorical ornament referring to Antiochus. But if the tension created by the identification of the abomination with Antiochus continues to generate innovative meaning, its repetition in Mark is no mere substitution of A = X. The reader may now consider what it means to refer to an event or person as an abomination of desolation. Once an apocalyptic text is considered to be nothing more than a fanciful way to describe world events without offering innovative meanings which challenge the reader to understand the world in new ways, its provocative nature is lost. Like the parables, apocalyptic texts are metaphors that challenge pre-existing configurations of the world. If the trope is reduced to a simplistic substitution, the text becomes a banal albeit fanciful description of the world and not an evocative predication that can be applied to other persons or situations.

This discussion depends upon the identification of the Olivet discourse as a metaphor. In response to Wright's description of Jesus' apocalyptic sayings (including Mark 13) as metaphors, Allison asks how the sayings would be different if they were meant to be read literally.[20] Ricoeur explains that to identify metaphor in narrative, we must begin by considering the referent of the text and not its sense, that is, its linguistic structure. If the referent of the narrative transgresses the accepted world configuration, the narrative functions as a metaphor. Because the narrative is to be considered as a whole and not piecemeal, the referent of the text is the plot. Therefore, when the plot of the narrative transgresses our understanding of how the world operates and challenges us to a reorientation of our world perspective, it may be the case that the narrative is a metaphor. In the case of a parable, its metaphoric import is recognized when the plot moves in a surprising way at the point of crisis. As Ricoeur puts it, metaphor (and religious metaphor in particular) can be discerned by "the element of extravagance which makes the 'oddness' of the narrative, by mixing the 'extraordinary' with the 'ordinary.'"[21]

To assess Mark 13 in this manner, I answer Allison's question by noting the surprising extravagance and the challenge to previously accepted configurations of the world which the narrative offers. When viewed in this way, that is, with Ricoeur's understanding of what makes a narrative a metaphor, this narrative qualifies as metaphor. The discourse is able to confound the reader's understanding of the world by re-categorizing the powers of the world and offering a new way to evaluate them. Forces which appeared to be in contrast with each other (e.g. the Roman empire, the Jewish religious establishment, and the Zealot revolutionaries) belong to the same category: destructive human forces which hamper and oppose the work of God. The temple and its attendant rituals and hierarchy, which appear to be allied with God's work in the world, actually oppose it. Those institutions which appear to be in control and permanent will be indicted and destroyed. Situations in which believers appear to be isolated and under the control of their adversaries are actually moments in which God's presence is particularly real and his opponents are challenged. The eschaton, which many people associate with dread and destruction, will be a time for being gathered together and glorified. These are a few examples of "paraphrases" of the metaphoric impertinence of the narrative. The plot of the discourse as a whole can therefore be considered to be metaphor.[22] However, this consideration does not mean that Wright is correct in claiming a metaphoric meaning for the Mark 13 discourse. Doing so would require equivocation regarding the definition of metaphor. As the next section explains, Wright's idea of a metaphor is very different from Ricoeur's.

CONTRASTING PERSPECTIVES

Other interpreters have also argued for figurative readings of Mark 13, as Chapter 1 outlines. Reading this text as a Ricoeurian metaphor is different from each of these other accounts. This section evaluates the proposals of Bultmann, Perrin, and Wright in light of the option for which I argue. The distinction between a Ricoeur-oriented reading of Mark 13 and these other readings is complicated by Perrin's use of Ricoeur's work to argue for a different conclusion, and Wright's claim to offer a metaphorical reading as well.

Bultmann considers the early Christian's belief in the imminent and radical disruption of the world order by God to be untenable today because our reliance upon scientific principles does not allow for theories of causation to be overridden by supernatural intervention (cf. p. 11). He advocates a search for the "deeper meaning behind the mythological conceptions," in order to interpret Jesus' eschatology in a way that is significant for today's reader.[23] Bultmann argues that because the worldview of the Christian Bible presumes that spiritual forces control world events, it is irrelevant to people who reject the existence and efficacy of such powers in favor of "rational causes" and "scientific thinking."[24] But this offense against naturalistic causation is an aspect of apocalypticism's metaphorical function. These texts claim that there is more to the world than what can be explained through physical or psychological means. Mark 13 offers an alternate narrative for world events. Spiritual causative forces are at work within, under, and through observable dynamics of cause and effect. The offense which for Bultmann makes these texts inaccessible to modern minds is the very challenge which they are able to offer. Perrin disputes Bultmann's "demythologizing" program by pointing out that he uses the term "mythological" in a different way from others. For Bultmann, "mythological" implies "prescientific."

Perrin argues that Bultmann, in contrast to Weiss and Schweitzer, does not therefore declare Jesus' use of "the kingdom of God" to be an outdated and inaccessible symbol for modern audiences. Instead, he seeks to discern how the "inner core of meaning" could be released from its mythological expression so that modern readers could realize the existential crisis of decision which it offers.[25] Perrin argues that Bultmann treats mythology as allegory; when the real-world referents for the elements of the myth are identified, the project of "demythologization" is complete. Perrin claims instead that myth, like metaphor, offers multiple meanings; one-to-one identification between the symbol and the symbolized is impossible. He argues that Bultmann fails to recognize this feature of New Testament texts.[26] Bultmann challenges his own thesis when he explains that discourse about the action of God can be understood not as a supernatural disruption of "the natural, historical, or psychological course of events," but as God working "within them."[27] Apocalyptic thought need not be a denial of rational theories of causation, but an alternate way to view them. As Bultmann puts it, "The scientific world-view does not comprehend the whole reality of the world and of human life, but faith does not offer another world-view which corrects science in its statements on its own level. Rather faith acknowledges that the world-view given by science is a necessary means for doing our work in the world. . . . This is the paradox of faith, that faith 'nevertheless' understands as God's action here and now an event which is completely intelligible in the natural or historical connection of events."[28]

Despite his argument against Bultmann's program and his use of Ricoeur's approach in other ways, Perrin also rejects a reading of Mark 13 that views it as a Ricoeurian metaphor. Relying upon Ricoeur's distinction between sign and symbol (in which the sign is a "transparent" element with straightforward one-to-one correspondence to a real world entity, and the symbol is an "opaque" device that offers multiple and "deeper" meanings), Perrin asserts that Second Temple apocalyptic texts, including Mark 13, function as a sign and not as symbol. That is, these texts offer no meaning other than being stand-ins for singular historical figures and events.[29] In contrast to Perrin, I suggest that whereas certain apocalyptic themes (such as "the abomination of desolation" or "the Son of Man") may have originally had straightforward historical referents, the continued use of the theme in subsequent contexts raised the trope from sign to symbol. References to the abomination after Antiochus' demise were no longer references to him, but to a set of concepts for which he is an evocative example. LaCocque similarly argues against Perrin's description of apocalyptic as allegory: that is, that each feature of the apocalyptic vision functions as rhetorical substitute for a real-world person or situation and that interpretation consists of deciphering. Instead, LaCocque asserts that the apocalyptic vision evokes meanings that are far more dynamic.[30] J. Collins also disagrees with Perrin's attempt to understand apocalyptic symbols "unambiguously" and one-dimensionally. In contrast with this apocalypse-as-allegory approach, he commends Ricoeur's plea for interpretations that recognize meaning which cannot be "exhausted by single referents." Collins claims that the very nature of apocalypses evokes an "element of mystery and indeterminacy" which ought not to be overlooked.[31]

Wright, the most prominent proponent today for a metaphorical reading of Mark 13 and other New Testament apocalyptic texts, claims that reading the text metaphorically does not diminish the impact of its message. "Metaphors have teeth; the complex metaphors available to first-century Jews had particularly sharp ones."[32] No matter how vicious Wright claims that his metaphors are, they differ substantially from Ricoeur's use of the term. What Wright calls metaphor is actually allegory: a story featuring images and characters which stand figuratively for literal features, and which can be substituted into the narrative with no effect upon the meaning of the text. His description of the representative nature of apocalyptic writings characterizes them more as allegory than metaphor: the fantastic beasts of Daniel 7 "represent" kingdoms and kings, for example. These allegorical representations, Wright explains, include the use of heavenly beings to describe sociological situations which closely resemble them.[33] Wright claims that attempts to seek referents to Mark 13 beyond events of the first century fail to be "loyal" to the text, and that they are motivated by attempts to preserve theological convictions that certain predicted events which have not yet happened will eventually occur.[34] In doing so, however, he demonstrates the simplistic understanding of metaphor that he charged others with.[35] He also betrays his understanding of metaphor as allegory: Statement A refers discreetly to Referent X, rather than to a superabundance of references.[36]

Because Wright believes that star showers and the descent of the Son of Man are too fantastic to be literal, he considers them to be figures for some other real world description that the text offers. But it is the *plot* of the discourse, not the *features* of it, which function as metaphor. Mark 13 is metaphor not because the descriptions are supposedly too outlandish to be read literally (an argument I dispute in Chapter 3), but because it challenges the reader to a new configuration of the world. The discourse presents a world in which that which appears to be permanent is not. That which appears to be illusory will ultimately triumph. That which wields power in a destructive manner will be overthrown. Those who appear to be powerless and dispersed have divine support and protection, and will be gathered together. He who appears to be absent from the affairs of the world will emerge in glory. It is through the assignment of new predications and categorizations for the world that the discourse operates as a metaphoric narrative. It opens a plethora of possible world-understandings for the readers who engage in it. This has remarkably little in common with so-called metaphorical interpretations of the discourse which reduce it to an allegorical description of the restoration of Israel, the triumph of the church, the individual's moment of deciding for God, or any of the variety of other options. Each of these interpretations paraphrase the text's narrative with incomplete propositional expositions of the meaning of the metaphor. But none of them are or could be fully explanatory. Metaphor, as described by Ricoeur, opens abundant possibilities for meaning which no amount of description can capture.[37]

Wright also confuses metaphor with hyperbole. He equates apocalyptic descriptions with hyperbolic expressions of significant events to indicate how they affect the speaker. He points out examples of how an event such as the removal of the Berlin Wall could be described as "earth-shattering," or how the death of a loved one would be "the end of the world."[38] Wright's characterization of apocalyptic imagery in this way fails to account for three factors. First, apocalyptic texts provide an extended description of cosmic upheaval which suggests that more is at work here than a rhetorical device to express intense or significant activity. One may counter by pointing out that an extended or detailed expression does not negate its metaphorical aspect, but this assertion must be supported by a detailed consideration of why the metaphor was constructed in such a particular way (not merely that it alludes to Old Testament texts). Second, a metaphor is the relation of one thing to another. To say that "man is a wolf" requires the speaker to recognize the existence of both concepts. In the case of Mark 13:24–25, a prior sense of literally earth-shattering events is necessary for metaphorical meaning to extend from it. If we accept Wright's contention that these expressions were never understood literally, they are meaningless for both Mark's original readers or for today's reader. Third, both of Wright's examples are "dead" metaphors; they fail to evoke challenging new patterns of thought because they are so conventional. For Wright's contention to succeed, one would need to determine whether these expressions were also "dead" in first century Jewish discourse. He appears to assume that they were, but he offers no evidence to support his contention. Wright's proposal that Jesus' apocalyptic discourse should be read as a metaphorical means of expressing hope for the restoration of Israel fails to capture the full meaning of the discourse. While the restoration of Israel may indeed be one aspect of the meaning that the metaphor of Mark 13 presents, it is not a full description of it.

MARK 13 AS AN EXPRESSION OF METAPHORIC TRUTH

Consideration of how Mark 13 is able to express truth depends upon prior discussion in this project: how fictional texts present truth (cf. pp. 33–36) and how metaphor expresses truth (cf. pp. 129–131). Chapter 3 demonstrates that Mark 13 is not history, as it does not correspond to world happenings. It operates instead as metaphor, and as such, it does not present truth as adequation (demonstrably accurate world descriptions) but as manifestation (creating and revealing new ways to understand the world). An assessment of the truth of Mark 13 as a fictive text and as metaphor is a process of validation, not verification.[39] The work of explanation for such texts is not a project simply to determine whether the text's world description corresponds with history, but to establish the probability or improbability of the reader's initial guess about its meaning. Critical examination of such texts supports claims of the logical possibility, not the proof, that they are true.

To determine whether Mark 13 expresses truth as metaphor is to answer the question "Does Mark 13's world presentation describe a new and true dimension of reality?" The text is true if the reader discovers that its configuration of the world, once validated by explanation as possible, is accurate and meaningful. She can evaluate the world of the text only by living into the world configuration that it presents. The process of exploring the text's configuration reveals whether or not it is a reliable way to experience life. A determination about the truth of Mark 13 cannot be made prior to the reader's appropriation of it. It is only as she seeks to integrate its world description with her prior world understanding that she is able to discover whether it is true or not. The goal of this project is to show how today's reader is able to appropriate Mark 13 as a true description of the world. It is not possible to prove that it is true; only to show how it might be true. If it is true, the reader can only recognize that truth by entering into it. The following chapter proposes what sort of truth a reader might discern if she chooses to do so.

NOTES

1. See my argument for this in "Five Moments of Communication in Hegel's *Phenomenology of Spirit*," in *Similarity and Difference in Translation: Proceedings of the International Conference on Similarity and Translation*, ed. Stefano Arduini and Robert Hodgson (Rimini, Italy: Guaraldi, 2004): 45–61.

2. Ricoeur, *Rule of Metaphor*, 196.

3. Text critics may argue that these logia were not originally associated. However, the author of the discourse as we have it has brought them together. Arguments that they had previously existed separately only strengthen the implications of reading them together.

4. McCarthy, "Script to Scripture," 353.

5. Dale C. Allison Jr., *Resurrecting Jesus: The Earliest Christian Tradition and Its Interpreters* (Edinburgh: T & T Clark, 2005), 123.

6. Ricoeur, "Metaphor and the Main Problem," 138.

7. Dale C. Allison, Jr., "A Response," in *The Apocalyptic Jesus: A Debate*, ed. Robert J. Miller (Santa Rosa, CA: Polebridge Press, 2001), 100–01.

8. Allison, "Jesus and the Victory of Apocalyptic," 132–34; cf. Allison, *Resurrecting Jesus*, 147–48.

9. Allison, *Jesus of Nazareth*, 218–19.

10. Ricoeur, "Creativity in Language," 132; cf. Ricoeur, "Metaphor and the Main Problem," 138.

11. Ricoeur, *Rule of Metaphor*, 97.

12. Stiver, *Ricoeur and Theology*, 71.

13. Ricoeur, "Biblical Hermeneutics," 88–93.

14. Apocalyptic texts could be understood to be "dormant," as Max Black describes some metaphors ("More About Metaphor," 26). The original import of the expression is unrecognized but still accessible. However, I propose that the metaphorical function of Mark 13 extends beyond the arousal of a now-sleeping metaphor; a new metaphor rises from a previously-conventional discourse.

15. Lacoque and Ricoeur, *Thinking Biblically* 301–03, as discussed in p. 51.

16. Sandra Wackman Perpich, "A Hermeneutic Critique of Structuralist Exegesis, with Specific Reference to Lk 10:29–37." PhD diss., Marquette University, 1981, 146–47.

17. Diaz, "Creation," 62.

18. Beasley-Murray, *Jesus and the Kingdom of God*, 341.

19. Diaz, "Creation," 61–2.

20. Allison, "Jesus and the Victory of Apocalyptic," 130.

21. Ricoeur, "Biblical Hermeneutics," 96–9.

22. Wallace cites the entire gospel of Mark as an example of a metaphorical narrative in which the plain sense is meaningless and argues that a Ricoeurian reading is more appropriate (Wallace, *Second Naiveté*, 46–50; cf. Wallace, "Parsimony," 208–212).

23. Bultmann, *Jesus Christ*, 11–18.

24. Ibid., 36–8.

25. Perrin, *Jesus and the Language of the Kingdom*, 71–5.

26. Ibid., 78.

27. Bultmann, *Jesus Christ*, 61–2.

28. Ibid., 65.

29. Perrin, *Jesus and the Language of the Kingdom*, 30–2.

30. Lacocque, *Daniel in His Time*, 127–28; cf. Lacocque, "Apocalyptic Symbolism," 6–7.

31. J. Collins, *Apocalyptic Imagination*, 16.

32. Wright, *Jesus and the Victory of God*, 321.

33. Wright, *New Testament and the People of God*, 289–92.

34. N.T. Wright, "In Grateful Dialogue: A Response," in *Jesus and the Restoration of Israel: A Critical Assessment of N. T. Wright's Jesus and the Victory of God*, ed. Carey C Newman (Downers Grove IL: InterVarsity Press, 1999), 265–66.

35. Ibid., 261–62.

36. Cf. Allison, "A Response," 100–01.

37. Ricoeur, *Rule of Metaphor*, 188.

38. Wright, *New Testament and the People of God*, 282–83; cf. Wright, *Jesus and the Victory of God*, 362.

39. Cf. Ricoeur, *Interpretation Theory*, 71–88.

Chapter 7

The Appropriation of Mark 13

Having demonstrated first that today's reader is able to identify meaning in Mark 13 that was not discernible when it was written, and having demonstrated that the reader can understand Mark 13 as a Ricoeurian metaphor, I conclude by proposing how she might appropriate the text in this way. This proposal is limited, however, by Ricoeur's failure to explain why the reader should accept this text, or the Bible more generally, as a true world configuration which informs, clarifies, or challenges her previous commitments, based solely on features of the text.

Scholars present many interpretations for Mark 13 as possible world-configurations that arise from the Olivet discourse, as Chapter 1 outlines. Even those that contradict each other can be instances of the breadth of meaning that the text presents as metaphor. This claim depends on rigorous explanatory efforts to justify proposals that each of these interpretations accord with what the text presents. We need not choose between Wright's restoration of Israel and Bultmann's existential choice, for example. If we follow Ricoeur's approach, we discover that multiple interpretations can exist amenably with each other. There is no need to prefer one interpretation over another; we only need to justify each of these through critical examination of the text. As long as each interpretation arises from and is validated by critical explanatory analysis of the text itself, it can serve as a possibility for self and world understanding by the reader. It goes beyond the scope of this project to detail such critical examination for each of these interpretive options. Instead, I provide explanatory justification for one possible metaphorical meaning that the text presents. Mark 13 describes a world in which oppressive and destructive forces that appear to dominate human affairs are not as total as they appear, and it claims that they will be disrupted. According to the text, the power of God which appears to be minimal will vindicate and unite the believers. This process occurs as an ongoing dynamic.

CUES FOR APPROPRIATION

As Chapter 2 explains, appropriation results from the reader's attempt to validate an initial understanding of a text by engaging in explanation: the critical analysis of the text. This validation as an exercise to recognize truth as manifestation rather than adequation, is not an exercise of correspondence, as would be the case for verification. Explanation is necessary to ensure that the text actually presents the meaning that the reader thinks it does. The initial understanding may be adapted, confirmed, or repudiated. Only then can the reader consider how the text's world configuration may affect her prior conceptualizations. In order to describe how today's reader is able to appropriate Mark 13, I first engage in explanatory work to discern cues from the text which show its meaning. These cues arise primarily from three sources: the genre of the text, the literary context of the text, and the structure of the chapter.

Genre

Mark 13 is an apocalyptic text, as I explain on pp. 45–46, This genre identification affects the way that the reader attends to the text, because it specifies that she reads the text according to the rules of that genre. Just as the identification of one text as a newspaper article and another as a love sonnet means that they are appropriated differently, the identification of Mark 13 as an apocalyptic text determines how it is read. I explain on pp. 36–40 that apocalyptic texts typically provide hope for people in oppressed circumstances by describing divine activity which will eliminate the persecutors. They often rely upon eschatological motifs in which God's victory is the culmination of history. The message of apocalyptic texts is typically so radical that they advocate a total rupture from the current state of worldly affairs.

The Olivet discourse, as apocalyptic, provides such a radical description of the culmination of history. But as it does so, it challenges the reader into new patterns of thought by confounding expectations that other apocalyptic texts offer. For example, Mark 13 describes the parousia primarily as a time of vindication for the elect rather than of punishment for the wicked. The Son of Man comes to earth instead of going into heaven. The Son of Man, a spiritual being, is equated with the Messiah, a human figure. The typical pattern for an apocalyptic experience is for a human figure to receive and report upon a vision or instruction from a heavenly being. Instead, Jesus is the heavenly being and the disciples are the human figures. Beasley-Murray points out that while apocalyptic writings typically provide timetables for the eschaton, Mark 13 does not. It describes events that will occur before the parousia, but it does not explain the sequence in which they will occur; nor does it provide a datable timeline for when they will happen. Mark merely describes the events of vv. 5–23 as things that will happen before the end; he does not tell us the order in which they will occur, how far into the future they lie, or how close to the parousia they will come. According to Beasley-Murray, this imprecise timing was meant to quell apocalyptic fervor while still affirming hope in the eschaton. He points out that the discourse warns against false teachers who will claim that these signs indicate an imminent return of Christ. Beasley-Murray argues that the signs to be interpreted indicate not the imminence of the parousia, but the activity of God in human affairs during the period between the Christ event and the eschaton.[1]

As an apocalyptic text, Mark 13 provides a vision of the world that is radically different from the one experienced by its readers, particularly with the predictions of vv. 24–27. But the text's significant departures from the norms of the genre indicate the meaning that emerges from this particular discourse does not conform to typical apocalyptic messages.

Literary Context

Inquiry into the meaning of Mark 13 includes consideration of the chapter's place within the larger structure of Mark's gospel. Scholars such as Pesch,[2] Grayston,[3] and Marcus[4] argue that Mark 13 is an insertion in the gospel that interrupts the narrative and should not be considered an integral part of the gospel. Marcus considers it to be an "interlude" in the logical progression from the story of a poor woman's sacrifice at the end of Chapter 12 to the narrative of Jesus' self-sacrifice that begins in Chapter 14. Grayston and Pesch both argue that by the end of Chapter 12 Jesus had already condemned the temple practices, and that Chapter 13 is an unnecessary insertion into what would otherwise be a smooth narrative transition into the final confrontation with the temple leadership in Chapter 14. Grayston suggests that the author added the apocalyptic discourse in order to relate eschatological hopes to Jesus' crucifixion. Without this connection, Grayston asserts, apocalyptic texts would compete with the gospel message as the source of hope for believers. The inclusion of the Olivet discourse unites potentially competing themes.[5]

Other exegetes, however, argue convincingly that Chapter 13 is consistent with the themes of Mark's gospel. Bolt advocates for an understanding Chapter 13 in its literary context and explains that it serves as a reflective pause in the narrative immediately before the gospel's climax. As such, it is "an integral part" of the overall work.[6] France considers the Olivet discourse to be a teaching interlude during the Jerusalem activities which echoes Chapter 4's interlude during the Galilee action.[7] C. Black points out that the persons involved with the rhetorical context of the discourse match those of other situations described in Mark's gospel: Jesus offers public teachings, followed by more detailed instruction with his personal entourage. On three other occasions, this private teaching is limited to an audience which even excludes the majority of the Twelve.[8] Interpreters focus particularly upon the affinity between Mark 8:27–9:1 and Mark 13. Beasley-Murray, drawing on the work of Lightfoot, Grayston, Busch, and Koch, sees a connection between the two pericopae. The first, which he considers to be a pivotal section for the entire work, consists of a proclamation of Jesus as Messiah, a prediction of Jesus' suffering, an explanation of how his followers would experience similar suffering of their own, and a description of the parousia. Both texts present the same lessons: Jesus' role as the Messiah, and proclamation of his messiahship, are connected with suffering. In order to receive a positive sentence at the final judgment, one must be faithful to him through one's own suffering.[9]

The Olivet discourse also stands as an integral part of the gospel's structure. Marcus is representative of interpreters who explain that the gospel consists of several relatively cohesive sections with no unified structure that draws them together.[10] This point undermines his argument that Mark 13 interrupts the gospel's narrative; if there is no comprehensive structure, it cannot be disrupted. Conversely, C. Black considers the Olivet discourse to be appropriately positioned within the greater context of Mark's gospel because of several factors. First, it overtly describes the termination of the temple cultus, to which Jesus alludes in the preceding chapters (and which he predicts in the logion that precipitates the discourse). Further, the destruction that the discourse describes prepares the reader for the narrative of Jesus' demise that immediately follows. Finally, the positioning of the discourse at this point in the narrative (i.e. right before the hero's death) qualifies it to be a farewell address to his followers.[11] Michaels also points out the harmonious relationship between Mark 13 and the rest of the book. It offers a description of events which will occur after 16:8, during a time when Jesus will no longer be present.[12]

Ricoeur's discussion of parables as narratives contained by larger narratives provides insight into the place of the Olivet discourse in the gospel. He describes parables as narratives given by the major character of a larger narrative. The overall narrative gives cues for understanding of the embedded narrative; the embedded narrative functions as a metaphor for the text as a whole. In the case of the parables, therefore, the narrative of the gospel as a whole suggests meaning for the parable. At the same time, the parable offers meaning for the gospel-narrative.[13] This description of parables informs our consideration of the Mark 13 discourse, which operates in the same manner. The "story" of the discourse is in dynamic interplay with the "story" of Mark's gospel. This interplay extends beyond the conflict between Jesus and the temple leadership and includes Jesus' challenge in Mark's gospel to the existing world-patterns and his call for disciples to "repent" or break from these patterns. Understanding of the overall narrative therefore guides understanding of the discourse, which in turn offers new insight into the gospel as a whole. Mark's gospel calls for its readers to resist opposition by entrenched powers and to testify to the kingdom of God, and these same themes are present in the Olivet discourse. As believers face opposition, God provides protection (v. 20) and guidance (v. 11). The forces of evil are not as potent as they appear. Resistance is not only possible, but effective. And while vv. 24–27 do not deal with the kingdom of God by name, their description of the parousia and its attendant events match the kingdom descriptions found elsewhere in the gospel.

Mark 13 relates smoothly with the immediately preceding and following material in the gospel. Deppe,[14] Focant,[15] and Malbon[16] identify the story of the widow in the temple (12:41–44) and that of the woman who anointed Jesus (14:1–9) as frames for the discourse. Both stories lift up women as role models who offer gifts at great personal expense, in contrast with men whom Jesus denounces. There is a progression, rather than a mere parallel, between the two stories that is possible only because of the content of the Olivet discourse. The widow's gift is directed to the temple, which Jesus subsequently condemns. The anointing woman gives her gift instead to Jesus. When seen together with the widow's gift, this action indicates that veneration which had previously been offered to the temple cultus ought now to be directed to Jesus, a point that Mark 13 makes. Duplicitous worship by temple leaders serves as the negative example in the widow's story; Judas' greed and rejection of Jesus fills the same role in the anointing narrative. While the negative examples share the qualities of greed and self-aggrandizement, the focus shifts from false temple leaders (i.e. those external to the community of Jesus' followers) to a wicked apostle (i.e. a leader within the community). This change directs the readers' attention from vigilance against external threats to those which arise within the Christian community, which the Olivet discourse describes (v. 12).

Pesch points out that the precipitating circumstances for the discourse flow organically from the events which immediately precede it.[17] They also reflect themes which are developed throughout the gospel. Following his cleansing of the temple (11:15–20), Jesus successfully faces the rhetorical challenges of the religious elite of Jerusalem (11:27–33, 12:13–17, 12:18–27, 12:28–34). After defending himself from each of these challenges, Jesus offers a challenge of his own that undercuts the scribes'

reputation for being Scriptural experts by demonstrating their error in referring to the Messiah as "son of David" (12:35–37). By removing this designation for the Messiah, Jesus sets the stage for his own designation of "Son
of Man" in 13:26. In Mark's narration, Jesus warns against being fooled
by the elaborate rituals, honors, and apparel of the temple elite (12:38–40).
Indeed, he pronounces judgment against them (12:40b), foreshadowing the
judgment to come in the discourse. He contrasts the apparent religiosity and
impressive nature of the elite with a poor and humble widow (12:41–44),
declaring that her unassuming and seemingly insignificant act of worship
is more pleasing to God than the ostentatious acts of the elite. That which
appears to be powerful and righteous will be condemned and destroyed,
while that which is weak and trivial will be exalted. The contrast between the
religious leaders and the faithful widow of Mark 12:38–44 introduces and
leads logically to the Olivet discourse. It is a contrast between the apparent
powers of the world that have an appearance of grandeur and strength while
actually subjugating God's people for their own purposes, and the faithful
elect who appear to be insignificant and weak while serving God faithfully
and receiving praise for it. Jesus' disciples, however, do not receive the message. Their thick-headedness is consistent with the way that Mark portrays
them throughout the entire gospel. Jesus' condemnation of the religious elite
is not a judgment against them personally, but against the *cultus* in which
they participate. As Mark describes it, he speaks against the entire temple
matrix: the building, the rituals, and the officials. But because the point is
lost on them, the disciples continue to be impressed by the apparent majesty
of the temple building (13:1). In response to an exclamation of admiration
for the temple, Jesus declares that it will be destroyed. This declaration flows
directly from the teaching that Jesus, as portrayed by Mark, has presented
since his entrance in Jerusalem. The temple, its officials, and the religious
practices that it represents are destined for destruction. Scribes with elaborate garments and arcane knowledge and the architectural wonders of the
temple building present an impressive appearance, but their apparent importance will be destroyed in the presence of God's actual power.

Deppe,[18] Lambrecht,[19] Allison,[20] and Malbon[21] also identify a relationship
between the Olivet discourse and the subsequent passion narrative. Deppe
describes their affinity in both subject matter and structure, and Lambrecht
recognizes a relationship between the summons for wakefulness in this parable and failure of Peter, James, and John to remain awake with Jesus in
Gethsemane. Allison outlines parallels between the discourse and the events
of the passion narrative "which cannot credibly be put down to chance,"
leading him to conclude that Mark presents the passion narrative as an
anticipation of the eschaton. Malbon asserts that the parallels mark a convergence between Jesus' experience and the future experience of his followers.

She points out several narrative and linguistic similarities which highlight this convergence. "Jesus speaks of the world's end just prior to his own end . . . [and] warns his followers that, before that time, his trials and sufferings will be echoed by their own." Beasley-Murray is less sure of this connection, but he agrees that the Olivet discourse can best be understood in relation with Jesus' suffering and death.[22] Dušek's semiotic analysis of Mark 13 identifies a series of contradictions which stand in tension with each other and leads to the conclusion that "the value 'death is life' is the value of truth of this text." Dušek equates this with the message of the passion and resurrection that follows the discourse.[23]

The strongest cue for the meaning of Mark 13 that we are able to discern from its literary context in the gospel is Jesus' rejection of the temple and its cultus.[24] Most notably Heil,[25] Pesch,[26] Beasley-Murray,[27] Dewar,[28] Bede,[29] and Gundry[30] identify affinity between the fig tree parable (v. 28) and the fig tree episode of 11:12–14, 20–21. The intercalation of narratives of the withered fig tree and of the cleansing of the temple strengthens the relationship of the two fig tree passages beyond their botanical link; they both allude to judgment against the temple cultus. Chapter 11 uses a fig tree to describe the temple cultus as withered, fruitless, and useless, while Chapter 13 refers to fig blossoms to describe the possibilities and hope of Jesus' parousia. Bolt[31] and Heil[32] explain that Jesus' words and actions in Chapters 11 and 12 demonstrate his condemnation of the people associated with the temple, and not of the edifice itself. Bolt points out that the clearing of the temple (11:15–19), the fig-tree incident (11:12–14, 20–24), and the parable of the tenants (12:1–12) are oriented toward the religious leaders, and he cites a number of pericopae prior to Jesus' entrance in Jerusalem that are also directed against Jewish religious leaders. Heil interprets the interactions between Jesus and the temple elite that precede the discourse as a progression in which Jesus asserts and describes his authority in contrast to the apparent but false authority of the temple and its associated practices. Heil explains that in 12:35–37 Jesus claims he has replaced the temple as the proper means for worship and that he is the supreme authority, lord even of the Davidic line. The temple leaders, in contrast, are parasites who rob from their charges instead of nurturing them. Heil asserts that the contributions of the wealthy to the temple associate the economic elite with the religious elite. The socially powerful people work together to advance their shared agenda, at the expense of vulnerable people, such as the widows of 12:40 and the expectant and new mothers of 13:17. Such influential societal forces are the sort of apparent powers whose downfall Jesus predicts.

France[33] and Marcus[34] point out that Jesus' indictment against the temple cultus is a condemnation not only of its pretentious and oppressive religious power, but also of its exclusionary and divisive practice. The apparent forces of the Olivet discourse are not only oppressive and abusive institutions, a relatively common target of apocalyptic discourse, but also patterns of thought which divide people against each other. This "us against them" mentality is a typical feature of apocalyptic that the discourse disrupts. It claims that hope lies not in the destruction of the outsiders and enemies, but in the removal of the concept that there is a group of outsiders at all. The gospel is preached to all peoples (v. 10), and response will come from across the world (v. 27).

Structure

The structure of the Olivet discourse also guides the reader's interpretation of this text, in addition to the genre and contextual cues discussed pp. 154–155 and 155–160 respectively. Analysis of the structure of the Olivet discourse is complicated by the fact that apocalyptic texts in general are notorious for being disorganized, with poor connections and transitions from one element to the next.[35] But this does not negate the importance of identifying an overall flow to the discourse. The disjointed character of the apocalyptic genre is an aspect of this evaluation; it is not incumbent upon the hermeneut to discern a smooth and coherent overall logic to the discourse if none exists.

As presented on pp. 67–68, I outline the structure of Mark 13 thus:

I.   Precipitating Logion (1–2)
II. Subsequent Questions by Disciples (3–4)
III. Extended Answer by Jesus (5b-37, introduced by 5a)
   A. Description of Life as a Disciple (5b-23)
      1. Warning against deceivers (5b-6)
      2. Destructive forces on earth (7–8)
      3. Persecution of believers by civil and religious authorities (9–10)
      4. The presence and guidance of the Holy Spirit (11)
      5. Persecution of believers within families (12–13)
      6. Time of calamity (14–20)
      7. Warning against deceivers (21–23)
   B. B. Parousia of the Son of Man (24–27)
      1. Destruction of World Powers (24–25)
      2. Appearance of the Son of Man (26)
      3. Ingathering of the Elect (27)
   C. Timeline of Events (28–37)
      1. Parable of Fig Tree: Imminence (28–30)
      2. Permanence of Words of Christ (31)
      3. Timeline unknown (32–33)
      4. Parable of householder: Watch (34–37)

The description of life as a disciple in the present age (vv. 5b-23) is arranged chiastically, with elements 1 and 7 (deception), 2 and 6 (calamity), and 3 and 5 (persecution) balancing each other respectively (cf. Chapter 3 for more on this point). This draws attention to the central and most significant element of the description: v. 11's assurance of the guiding presence of the Holy Spirit in the midst of distress.[36] This arrangement challenges the expectation that a description of the abomination of desolation would be central to a description of the age under his control.[37] The discourse's structure directs our attention instead to the work of God which may be overlooked in favor of a more visible contender. Despite appearances to the contrary, the text claims that God is in control even in present reality.

The meaning that the discourse presents may therefore be summarized as follows:

- False reports will threaten to deceive disciples.
- The world will suffer from warfare, earthquakes, and famine.
- Disciples will be handed over to civil and religious authorities, where they will suffer but where the Holy Spirit will also provide them the ability to bear witness.
- This witness will extend to the entire world.
- Intimate family relationships will become destructive.
- The desolating abomination will be revealed, prompting the need for hasty flight in the face of unprecedented suffering.
- False religious leaders will attempt to deceive the elect.
- The deceptive, destructive cosmic and societal powers of the world will be undone.
- The Son of Man will appear and will be glorified.
- Under the care of the Son of Man, the elect will be gathered together.
- It is necessary to recognize these circumstances and respond appropriately.

Some of these events had already begun to occur by the time of Mark's original readers.

POSSIBILITIES FOR APPROPRIATION

The insights gained from using the explanatory mode of Ricoeur's approach to interpret Mark 13 suggest a metaphorical meaning that today's reader is free to appropriate. Her engagement with the text enables her to recognize how it may be a true description of the world. As explained previously, this possibility for appropriating true meaning can be evaluated only in the process of interaction with the text; if it is a truth, it cannot be verified in advance.

The description of the Olivet discourse that follows is not a total explication of the text's meaning, because metaphor offers multiplicity of meaning. Nor is it intended to be the only possibility for true metaphorical meaning that the text creates.

An understanding of Mark 13 as metaphor read by today's reader may be paraphrased thus: negative forces continually and perpetually affect the world and the lives of believers. But their power is limited and is repudiated. God's positive power mitigates the influence of the negative forces and ultimately triumphs over them. This pattern repeats itself regularly. Worded differently, human experience is affected by powers which appear to be dominant, which are deceptive, and which cause calamity and persecution. Despite the apparent dominance of these forces, they are curtailed and undone on a regular basis, while forces of vindication and unification prevail. The following sections elucidate this description and suggest how the text's world configuration may affect the reader's prior conceptualizations.

Powers from the Limits of Human Experience

The recognition of the apparent and actual powers described by Mark 13 is an understanding of the influence of liminal forces on ordinary life. It is difficult for today's reader to accept texts which express such limit experiences (cf. pp. 48–50). As Perrin puts it, "One cannot live everyday on the boundary of human existence in the world, and yet it is to this boundary that one is constantly brought by the parables of Jesus."[38] Perrin's comment applies not only to the parables, but to all texts which have limit experience as a referent. For Ricoeur, this condition applies ultimately to all Biblical texts,[39] which testify to what exists beyond the limits of human experience. Commenting on Ricoeur, Wall explains the limit-experience of religious discourse is a violation of the attempt to view human existence as a coherent whole. The testimony of that which lies outside of human experience disrupts such projects and reveals them to be deception. Limit expressions claim that human life is not self-sufficient but is fallible and incomplete. These expressions do not necessarily present a coherent and holistic description of human experience; they demonstrate only that such descriptions are inadequate. Through the violation of the ordinary standards of self and world understanding, these texts disorient the reader by bearing witness to what lies beyond human experience, but upon which human experience depends.[40]

The Olivet discourse describes two sorts of the powers at work in the world. Those which are primarily negative and appear to be dominant are not as powerful and total as they seem. I refer to these as "apparent" powers: those that are observable and that present themselves to be in control but whose appearance is inaccurate. These powers include both societal forces such as the religious institution of the Jerusalem temple and the politico-military domination of Rome, as well as spiritual forces operating at the limit of human experience. These forces may be personified, such as the identi-fication of the abomination as the high priest (cf. p. 73) and of the celestial bodies which will collapse (cf. pp. 74–75). The threat which these powers present comes not merely from their sheer power but from the appearance that their power is total. When these apparent powers purport to be aligned with God, as is the case for the temple nexus, they are particularly dangerous. Ricoeur's descriptions of limit-experiences tend to focus upon the positive disruptive elements related to God, the Wholly Other from which a super-abundance of meaning and possibility flows. His considerations of radical evil tend not to be experiences or testimony of that which lies beyond human experience. On the contrary, he describes these considerations as limits or deficiencies in the human condition.[41] While it lies beyond the scope of this project to provide a consideration of Ricoeur's understanding of evil, I iden-tify encounters with radical evil as limit-experiences. Ricoeur himself opens the possibility for this when he raises the example of a Nazi death-camp as a limit experience.[42] Radical evil is not merely a deficiency in the human condition, but lies beyond the horizons of human experience and impinges upon it. Rather than offering overflowing possibilities for meaning, as is the case for more positively-oriented religious discourse, such radical evil (i.e. at and beyond human experience) stifles and obscures possibilities for existence. In the Olivet discourse, the abomination of desolation is an evoca-tive figure for such radical evil.

I refer to the second type of power that the discourse describes as the "actual" power of God that contrasts with and triumphs over the apparent powers. This actual power is surreptitious and subversive in the life described in vv. 5–23, but it is discernible with careful observation. As Marcus explains, the discourse's description of the tribulations experienced by the Christian communities indicates "not that the powers of evil have triumphed," but that it is time for God to conquer these forces and to vindicate the faithful.[43] The second section of the discourse, vv. 24–27, describes how the true nature of the apparent and actual powers will be revealed. The apparent powers will be disrupted and removed, as demonstrated by the downfall of the celestial bodies. This collapse of the apparent powers is not a condemnation that results in their punishment, as would typically be the case in other apocalyptic texts. Rather, they are removed from a false position that they presumed for themselves. Conversely, the actual power of God is revealed. It contrasts with the apparent powers not only in its scope (absolute rather than relative) but also in its nature (redemptive instead of destructive). The chief manifestation of the Son of Man's "great power and glory" in human experience is the vin-dication and ingathering of the elect.

The discourse's presentation of these two sorts of liminal forces centers on the double foci of the appearance of the abomination of desolation and the subsequent distress (vv. 14–23), and the appearance of the Son of Man and the subsequent vindication (v. 26–27). The predictions of deception, suffering, and persecution (vv. 5b-13) are precursors to the appearance of the abomination; the prediction of celestial turmoil (vv. 24–25) is a similar precursor to the arrival of the Son of Man. Each figure's appearance is preceded by the distress of his adversaries: Christians on the part of the abomination, and spiritual powers on the part of the Son of Man. The events which follow the appearance of each figure reveal their true nature: tribulation and calamity on the part of the abomination, and restoration and vindication on the part of the Son of Man. The discourse thus contrasts the believer's experience in the present age dominated by evil powers epitomized by the abomination with the coming age ruled by God's agent. The discourse provides significantly more description of human existence under the apparent control of destructive and deceptive forces, indicative of the text's emphasis on instruction for life in the present situation, rather than encouragement of eschatological fervor.

This explanation of the true nature of the spiritual and human forces at work in history also allows the reader to comprehend the significance of the account in Mark's gospel of Jesus' death and resurrection. The forces opposed to Jesus prevailed over him and the vindication of his resurrection was ambiguous at best. The Olivet discourse's message that the domination of malevolent powers is only apparent helps the readers recognize that their ultimate undoing and God's final triumph applies not only to the struggles which they experience but also to the passion and resurrection of Jesus.

The Apparent Powers

The first major section of the discourse, vv. 5–23, serves as a description both of the cosmos as it is under the supposed domination of forces and beings opposed to God and of the life that the disciples and believers will endure under that domination. I heuristically name this state "the age of the abomination," employing the temporal designation that the discourse offers. The chiastic structure of this section emphasizes the triple characteristics of this age: deception, destructive calamity, and persecution. However, the control of the abomination and associated beings and forces in this age is illusory. Throughout the distress and confusion which the disciples endure, the text presents the power of God as a mitigating factor and a source of hope and instruction. The chiasm of this section places the inspiring guidance of the Holy Spirit at the most prominent point (v. 11). The text presents a world configuration for the reader in which confusion, destruction, and opposition are not as profound as they appear to be. It claims that God intervenes even (or especially) in the worst circumstances.

The Olivet discourse comes in response to questions that arise from Jesus' prediction of the temple's destruction. This framing for the discourse, in conjunction with the preceding narratives of Chapters 11 and 12 in which Jesus physically assaults the temple, defeats its leadership in debate, and condemns the institution and its practices, indicates that the discourse is spoken against the Jerusalem temple cultus. But that which is spoken against in the discourse extends beyond the temple itself. As the text presents it, Jesus expresses himself with synecdoche: the destruction of the temple is an element of a larger whole. Its downfall is the epitome of God's action against the deceptive and oppressive forces in the world. The discourse associates the temple with other institutions that he also denounces but which had not typically been equated with the temple. Indeed, the institutions which are associated with each other were typically viewed in opposition with or unrelated to each other: the Jewish religious hierarchy, the Roman military, demonic powers, and natural disasters. The discourse challenges the reader by naming what is purportedly affiliated with God's positive authority as demonic and evil. The naming of the high priest, the quintessential holy person of God, as the abomination of desolation, the epitome of evil, demonstrates this shock most fully. The discourse challenges the reader to evaluate those people and institutions which are assumed to be godly and good, to perceive whether that is really the case. I leave it to the reader to consider elements of current society to which this designation may apply.

While discussions about the identity of the abomination of desolation (cf. pp. 71–74) are helpful, it is promising to consider this figure not only as a particular historical person or event but as the personification of the apparent powers which work in opposition to God. Such a meta-identification suits the apocalyptic nature of the discourse: a concealed influence which affects the world in such a way as to cause destruction generally and tribulation for the elect in particular. That which is a surprising association for today's reader of heretofore unrelated elements was the relationship of closely associated subjects for the original readers. For them, the triple association of (1) evil social forces and powers, (2) spiritual beings opposed to God, and (3) celestial objects meant that the destruction of one would mean the undoing of all three. Today's reader can understand the warning against an abomination of desolation as a reference to an individual or practice that appears to be aligned with God but is actually opposed to him. The abomination is particularly dangerous because of the close association with institutions which seem to be divinely oriented or beneficent. The abomination is the epitome of radical evil that influences the human condition. In his consideration of Ricoeur's ethics of hope in the face of radical evil in light of liberation theologians such as Gutiérrez, Wall notes that Ricoeur fails to consider "structured political oppressions" which hope confronts. He explains this omission as an aspect of Ricoeur's sense of innate human goodness: structured oppressions are not an inherent part of the human condition but are deceptions to be unmasked and done away with.[44] Mark 13's depiction of human institutions as demonic opposition to God's kingdom leads us to favor thinkers such as Gutiérrez over Ricoeur and recognize the apparent powers not merely as deceptions, but as that which stifles possible meaning and reconciliation in human experience.

Today's reader is able to associate the predictions of vv. 5–23 with events other than those of the Jewish War of the first century. Although Russell explains that the prediction of unparalleled θλῖψις, or suffering, in v. 19 is an apt description for the "ghastly" circumstances which the residents of Jerusalem endured during the Roman siege and sack,[45] it is difficult to consider these events to be unequaled in the course of human history. Calvin claims the suffering which precedes the parousia is not limited to the Roman sack of Jerusalem, but refers more broadly to the tribulations which Christians will endure in a hostile world until the eschaton.[46] A modern reader can easily identify terrible events which at least rival and most likely surpass the fall of Jerusalem: the Black Death of Europe, the Atlantic slave trade, the Holocaust of World War II, and the 2004 tsunami in the Indian Ocean, to name but a few. Each century between the first and the twenty-first offers candidates for consideration as the greatest tribulation ever to strike humanity. If we understand the descriptions of the discourse to apply not only to a generation of the first century but as explanations for the ongoing circumstances which believers face, that which appears to be a challenge to the text becomes a confirmation. As each generation endures the shock and suffering of unimaginable calamity, and as observers speculate that they have witnessed unparalleled suffering, the message of the discourse suggests how each generation can understand such events.

An ambiguous identification of the apparent powers described by the Olivet discourse is not a liability but an opportunity for appropriation. For example, Ricoeur argues that the Song of Songs is subversive in the sense that it challenges the conventions of erotic love and marriage. This subversion arises from the indeterminate text which allows multiple and even conflicting understandings.[47] This same subversion is present in the Olivet discourse, which challenges the presumed authority of the apparent powers of the world: the religious authority of the temple cult, the military and political power of the Roman Empire, and so forth. A simplistic reading of the discourse will lead us to understand it as a claim that these apparent powers are frauds and will be revealed as such with the coming of the Son of Man. The danger of such a reading, however, is to smash one set of idols only to establish another. It encourages the sort of deception which the discourse warns against: when the parousia is considered to be a singular and definitive "power" it can easily be hijacked by those who claim it for their own purposes. Indeed, this is precisely the indictment which Jesus levels against the temple leadership in Mark's gospel: they subvert the revelation of the law and prophets to suit their own purposes. This is the danger that the discourse's description of deception (vv. 6, 21–22) and persecution (v. 12, cf. pp. 70–71) within the Christian community identifies.

Mark 13 speaks to the limitations of the powers that seem to be in control of human life. It describes religious, political, and military social systems which are meaningless at best and destructive at worst. These systems fail on three levels. First, they do not provide the positive functions that they claim. The temple cultus is bankrupt because it no longer serves its purpose of connecting people to God.[48] The political systems (e.g. the councils, governors, and kings of v. 9) no longer order, protect, and nurture society but become that toward which testimony must be given. Military systems are revealed not to be the defenders of freedom and justice, but agents of destruction and injustice. The *pax Romana* is a terror from which people must flee (vv. 14–18). Second, the apparent powers do not exert the domination and authority that they claim. In each case, God's activity disrupts and threatens them. The apparent permanence and magnificence of the religious order, as embodied in the impressive temple complex, will collapse (v. 2). Political councils are invaded by the Holy Spirit, who counsels, instructs, and guides disciples even as they are in the very bowels of political power (v. 11). Military power is limited by God's control, who determines the extent of its destruction (v. 20). The text claims that God protects the elect from the deceptions of the apparent powers (22b). Third, the apparent powers will ultimately fail and be removed. That which appears to be as certain as the stars of the sky will be undone. Understanding their undoing as the "end of the world," in the sense that history comes to an end, misses the point of the discourse. Such an understanding would assume that the apparent powers are the actual powers; if they end, the entire universe ends. The text claims that the end of the apparent powers, which are limited, deceptive, and destructive, frees the world to experience the true power and authority of God. The claim of the Olivet discourse is similar to Frye's description of the "parody-demonic," or evil powers such as pagan nations which are temporarily successful. The demise of these powers leads to what he calls "manifest-demonic."[49]

The Actual Powers

The second section of the Olivet discourse (vv. 24–27) predicts the universal revealing of the actual powers that control the world, and the redemption and unity that they provide. The text's world configuration invites the reader to comprehend her world in a new way. She has the opportunity to hope for the triumph of goodness in a world that appears to be dominated by evil. As Allison explains, "Theodicy is at the heart of all apocalyptic, including Jesus' prophecies." We cannot speak of the total fulfillment of the expectations of God's perfect reign of peace and justice as we live in a world that is so obviously permeated with suffering, evil, and oppression. He explains that this disjuncture between hope and reality motivates Christian expectation for Jesus' return to complete what has been started.[50]

According to vv. 5–23, the influence of God's actual power is evident even before the parousia. Marcus comments on the significance of the phrase δεῖ γενέσθαι ("these things must happen") in v. 7 as an indication that the alarming events of warfare, earthquake, and famine are elements of God's unfolding plan. "Earthly rulers may appear to be in charge, but it is actually God who has the life and death of nations in his hand."[51] Calvin explains that v. 11 offers assurance to Christians that, even in the midst of severe challenges, God provides guidance and resources to deal with the situation.[52]

But the discourse describes the apparent powers more fully in its three predictions of vv. 24–27. First, it predicts that God's power will undo the apparent powers. The celestial objects are aspects of the forces that oppose God (cf. pp. 74–75). Nickelson asserts that vv. 24–25 explain that God can reverse normal expectations (such as the fact that the sun and moon produce light) and that God is able to disrupt seemingly inevitable and permanent forces which oppose him.[53] However, this defeat of the apparent powers is not the primary focus of the discourse's predictions. Beasley-Murray argues that dread of condemnation and judgment should not overshadow the predominantly hopeful promise of the parousia. While punishment of the wicked is an element of eschatological expectation, it is secondary to the primary message of restoration and mercy.[54] The downfall of the apparent powers does not primarily indicate judgment against them, but the permanence of the actual powers in relation to them. Second, the text predicts that the hidden influence of God will be exposed with the coming of the Son of Man. LaCocqueconsiders the glorification of the Son of Man in Daniel 7:13 to be the heavenly counterpart to the installation of the high priest in the Jerusalem temple.[55] The re-use of this motif here, with Jesus filling the role of the Son of Man, demonstrates in yet another way the claim by the text that Jesus supplants the Jerusalem temple and its human officers. Third, the ingathering of God's chosen ones (τός ἐκλεκτός) from the far reaches of the world indicates that what had been a national religion will become universal, presumably as a result of the worldwide dissemination of the gospel (v. 10). Such explains that in the aftermath of the destruction of the temple, Jerusalem and Judea cease to be the center of the Christian movement. It extends throughout the world and includes Gentiles as well as Jews. The person of Jesus has replaced the temple as the focal point of worship.[56]

The Dynamics of the Recurring Interaction Between Powers

The final section of the discourse, vv. 28–37, presents the temporal component of the revealing of God's actual authority over the apparent powers of the world. Admittedly, the Olivet discourse does not describe an ongoing situation or a repetition of events; it predicts a unique and ultimate course of events. This is consistent with the characteristics of the apocalyptic genre, which describes the singular and transformative activity of God in the future. The powers that appear to control the world will collapse, and the Son of Man will appear and vindicate the faithful. I argue that in addition to this prediction of a one-time transformative event, the text also suggests that the reader is able to understand ongoing circumstances in a new way that is informed by this prediction. There is present in the semantics of the text a further description of the dynamics of the world until these events occur. The presence and activity of God confounds the influence of evil upon world events in the interim. According to the text, although evil appears to dominate and control the world, the recurring activity of God mitigates its influence and provides hope until the eschatological events occur.

The contradiction between v. 30, in which Jesus presents a general prediction for when it will occur, and v. 32, in which he declares that he does not have this knowledge, creates an inherent tension in the text which directs the reader to recognize a metaphor, as described in Chapter 6. As metaphor, the collapse of the celestial bodies marks the overthrow of the apparent powers of the world, which are deceptive, destructive, and persecuting. And as metaphor, the coming of the Son of Man indicates the in-breaking of God into human experience. Read as metaphor, the text presents Jesus explaining that the world-description of vv. 5b-27 is a future situation which calls for vigilance. But as I discuss on pp. 42–44, events of the future are able to impinge upon the present. The future that the text describes interprets the present. That is, the reader is able to understand features of the present world because of her awareness of the future. Current conditions are contingent expressions of God's ultimately decisive actions in the future.

Some of the future occurrences which Mark 13 describes did not happen within the predicted time, but we do not know if they will ever take place. It is a challenge to the reader's preconceptions to consider if they could ever happen. One choice for our reader is to reject the prediction of these occurrences at any point in the future, because they do not conform to her preconceptions. As Chapter 2 notes, this is the approach of a Bultmann-oriented reader. For him, the text must conform to modern concepts of what is believable.

But the reader may also choose to consider these events as a future possibility. By doing so, she follows Ricoeur's suggestion to open herself to the way the text describes the world without requiring it to conform to her assumptions. This self-suspicion enables the reader to imagine that the events of vv. 24–27 could take place in the future. Considering this possibility does not require the reader to accept it as a certainty. But if it is possible for these singular, ultimate, and transformative events to take place in the future, the text's prediction of them informs the reader's understanding of the present. Traces of the future exist in the present, even if that future is hypothetical and not certain.

Mark 13's prediction is false insofar as it describes these singular and ultimate events to occur during the generation of Jesus' contemporaries. But the falsity of one element of a prediction does not make the entire prediction false. For example, a Pittsburgh football fan may predict that Coach Mike Tomlin will lead the Steelers to a Superbowl victory. This prediction contains two elements: (1) the Steelers will win the Superbowl, and (2) Mike Tomlin will be the coach to lead them to that victory. If Mike Tomlin is fired as the team's coach in the middle of the season, the second element of the prediction cannot be fulfilled; he will not be the coach that leads the Steelers to victory. However, the first element of the prediction can be fulfilled if the Steelers win the Superbowl under the leadership of a different coach. The failure of one part of the prediction does not mean that all parts of the prediction fail. The prediction of the Olivet discourse also contains two elements: (1) certain transformative and singular events will take place, and (2) they will take place during the generation of Jesus' contemporaries. Today's reader can recognize that the second element of the prediction is false, but the first element may be fulfilled. The collapse of the apparent powers, the appearance of the Son of Man, and the vindication of the elect may yet occur, even if they do not take place in the predicted time.

Today's reader does not need to consider the prediction of the Son of Man's appearance as an objective future event as Mark and the original readers of his gospel did in order for the prediction to inform present understanding. But today's reader does not need to share this understanding. She may consider it to be a future potentiality whose influence upon the present does not depend upon an event that will actually take place. The text's description of future events impinges upon the present, even if the future events never take place. The future can be an aspiration, even if it is never achieved, and still affect the present. In the example of the Steelers fans, they may sing "Pittsburgh's going to the Superbowl," even if the team does not end up doing so. Their aspiration for the future affects what they do in the present.

The reader must deal with the unfulfilled element of the prediction: that these events will take place within a generation. This is the "is not" of the metaphor of Mark 13: that which is false. The dialectic between the text's world description (these events will occur in a generation) and the reader's world understanding (these events did not take place) allows the reader to recognize elements of the text's description that were not discernible when this element of the prediction had the potential to be true. As today's reader encounters the parable of the fig tree (vv. 28–29) and the generational prediction (v. 30), the failure of their prediction of imminent occurrence allows her to recognize a different feature which unites these two logia. What had been latent is now brought to the foreground. They both employ images of naturally recurring events: the passing of the seasons and the turning from one generation to the next. V. 28's image of the budding fig tree functions not only as a description of signs of coming events, but also as a seasonal marker.[57] V. 30's use of a generation not only indicates a period of time, but for today's reader can also indicate recurring events and dynamics. Instead of predicting only that a singular event will happen soon, they also describe a continually imminent condition. Each season and each generation will experience the domination and collapse of the apparent powers and the subversive but victorious power of God. As the discourse is read in today's context, the time element of the prediction can be understood differently from how it was in the first century. It is not merely a false prediction of imminent occurrences but also describes how the future events are imminent in all seasons and generations. The power of God subverts the powers that appear to dominate the world, and it does so to all three characteristics of the apparent powers. First, their deception (vv. 5b-6, 21–23) does not lead the elect astray (v. 22b). Second, their destruction (vv. 7–8, 14–20) is part of God's predetermined history (v. 7b) and is shortened by God (v. 20b). And third, God's instructive Spirit (v. 11b) is present in times of persecution (vv. 9–13). As today's reader encounters it, the text describes the influence of the future transformative events that is evident in each generation and season.

Although they do not identify a description of the recurring events and continuing dynamics in vv. 28–30, several interpreters explain that the events predicted in the Olivet discourse are not limited to first century happenings. Von Dobschütz[58] and A. Collins[59] note that throughout history individuals recognize events of their own time in eschatological Bible texts. This recognition is not necessarily eisegesis, or the reading of one's own situation into the text. Rather, it reveals the evocative nature of the text; it provides insight which is not limited to a particular historical or even cultural context. Augustine also acknowledges that the predicted wars and distress are ubiquitous to the human condition, but he concludes from this that believers in the past may have erroneously believed that their tribulations were portents of the parousia.[60] Augustine's point can be taken to heart if we understand the "end" not only as a singular historical event, but as those ongoing and perpetual crises which challenge our worlds of existence. Calvin understands the text this way, claiming that the discourse's twin commands to avoid deception and not to be alarmed by tribulation are references to the perpetual conditions of opposition, distress, and deceit that believers encounter.[61] Vv. 24–27 are explicit descriptions of the state of affairs about which vv. 5–23 hint about: the apparent powers are powerless, and God controls the amount of deception, destruction, persecution that they cause.

Today's reader is able to discern that the ongoing pattern of events began almost immediately after the production of the discourse by considering the triple predictions of vv. 24–27. First, the apparent power of the temple and its associated cultus (including the high priest, if we recognize him to be the abomination of desolation) collapsed in 70. Second, God, or God's agent, became knowable to the entire world through the widespread proclamation of the Christian message (v. 10). Third, the believers were not physically brought together but associated with each other as the church. These three factors (repudiation of apparent powers, revealing of God's presence, and the collection of the elect) are continuing features of the world. We may also see the continuing presence of the actual powers in the predicted events of vv. 9–11. First, the apparent powers of councils, synagogues, governors and kings are challenged by the testimony of the disciples (v. 9). Second, God's presence in the world is to be made known to everyone as the good news in proclaimed (v. 10). And third, God is present with the disciples (i.e. they are "gathered" into his presence) even or particularly during times of crisis (v. 11).

Vv. 31–32, the pair of logia between the parables of the fig tree and of the householder, describe two additional traits of the ongoing dynamic. First it is permanent, in contrast to the transience of everything else in the created order (v. 31). Second, it is mysterious and cannot be controlled or predicted. Because even heavenly beings do not know when the events will occur, the reader is not able to predict the timing either. She is encouraged instead to recognize that they do happen, with a regularity akin to the turning of the seasons and the passing of the generations. Dictatorships collapse, economic injustice is corrected, warfare gives way to peace, and the persecution of believers comes to an end.

The Call for Vigilance

As a number of interpreters point out,[62] watchfulness is an organizing feature of the entire discourse, which begins, ends, and is punctuated with the command for watchfulness βλέπετε ("watch," or "be vigilant"). But the summons for awareness and responsiveness to the ongoing situation is particularly evident in the final element of the discourse: the parable of the householder

(vv. 33–37). As it can be read today, the call for vigilance is no longer a call for anticipation of an impending event in the near but indeterminate future. Rather, it is an exhortation for awareness and response to ongoing conditions related to apparent and actual powers at work. The discourse presents a challenge for a new ethical and epistemological perspective. The apparent powers of the world, which have been revealed to be deceptive, destructive, and limited, are able to be resisted and challenged.

The Olivet discourse's call for vigilance and watchfulness stands in contrast to the passivity and complacency normally associated with the apocalyptic genre, indicating yet another way in which the discourse violates or subverts its linguistic code. The summons for vigilance includes both an encouragement for discernment and an exhortation for action. The reader is urged to resist hopelessness in the face of powers which appear to be total. The shocking identification of the high priest as the abomination, particularly as it is framed with descriptions of religiously-oriented deception (vv. 5–6, 21–23), alerts the reader that deception and destruction are present and must be repudiated even in settings which appear to be benign or beneficial. The discourse assures the reader that even in the harshest of situations, the protective and equipping power of God is at work. According to the text, the reader who resists deception and destruction will receive divine assistance for that resistance. God's providential care limits the extent to which destruction will occur. The forces which appear to be limitless are restricted by the greater power of God, which works in hidden and mysterious ways that are rarely if ever revealed. The discourse claims that the time will come when the powers of deception and destruction which appear to be dominant will be shown to be limited and ultimately powerless, and God's power, glory and community will be revealed.

NOTES

1. Beasley-Murray, *Jesus and the Last Days*, 372–75.
2. Pesch, *Naherwartungen*, 71–2.
3. Grayston, "Study of Mark," 371–73.
4. Marcus, *Mark 8–16*, 864.
5. Grayston, "Study of Mark," 385–87.
6. Bolt, "Mark 13," 12–13.
7. France, *Gospel of Mark*, 166.
8. C. Black, "An Oration at Olivet," 68–9.
9. Beasley-Murray, *Jesus and the Last Days*, 370–71.
10. Joel Marcus, Mark 1–8 : A New Translation with Introduction and Commentary, The Anchor Bible, vol. 27 (New York: Doubleday, 2000), 62–4.

11. C. Black, "An Oration at Olivet," 69.

12. In Beasley-Murray, *Jesus and the Last Days*, 254–55.

13. Ricoeur, "Bible and Imagination," 149–51.

14. Deppe, "Charting the Future," 98.

15. Focant, *Gospel According to Mark*, 520.

16. Malbon, "Literary Contexts," 109–10.

17. Pesch, *Naherwartungen*, 83; cf. Gundry, *Mark*, 750–51; Murphy, *Apocalypticism*, 240; Shively, *Apocalyptic Imagination*, 191–93.

18. Deppe, "Charting the Future," 97.

19. Lambrecht, *Die Redaktion*, 253.

20. Allison, *Constructing Jesus*, 60–61.

21. Malbon, "Literary Contexts," 115–16.

22. Beasley-Murray, "Vision," 46–47.

23. Dušek, "Saying True," 97–99.

24. Such, *Abomination of Desolation*, 88–90; Malbon, "Literary Contexts," 113–14.

25. John Paul Heil, "The Narrative Strategy and Pragmatics of the Temple Theme in Mark," *Catholic Biblical Quarterly* 59 (1997): 92.

26. Pesch, *Naherwartungen*, 176.

27. Beasley-Murray, *Jesus and the Last Days*, 441.

28. 1Dewar, "Chapter 13 and the Passion," 05.

29. In Aquinas, *Gospel of Mark*, 268.

30. Gundry, *Mark*, 746.

31. Bolt, "Mark 13," 16–19.

32. Heil, " Narrative Strategy," 81–7.

33. France, *Gospel of Mark*, 165–66.

34. Marcus, "Jewish War," 449–51; Marcus, *Mark 1–8*, 34–35; Marcus, *Mark 8–16*, 890–91.

35. Beasley-Murray, *Jesus and the Last Days*, 153–54.

36. Cf. Pesch, *Naherwartungen*, 80; Focant, *Gospel According to Mark*, 530–35; Shively, *Apocalyptic Imagination*, 164, 170.

37. Such an arrangement of the discourse, as a contrast between the apparent authority of the abomination and the true authority of the Son of Man, could be characterized thus:

I. Description of the Present Age (5b-23)
   A. Events Preliminary to the Advent of the Authority of the Age (5b-13)
      Deception, Destruction, Persecution
   B. The Arrival of the Authority of the Age
      The Standing of the *Abomination of Desolation* (14a)
   C. Events Subsequent to the Arrival of the Authority
      Flight, Haste, Danger, Deception (14b-23)
II. Description of the Coming Age (24–27)
   A. Events Preliminary to the Advent of the Authority of the Age
      Collapse of Opposing Spiritual Forces (24–25)
   B. The Arrival of the Authority of the Age

The Coming of the Son of Man (26)
C. Events Subsequent to the Arrival of the Authority
Ingathering of the Scattered Elect (27)

Cf. Shively, Apocalyptic Imagination, 199–200 for a similar consideration. This outline highlights the contest between the authority of the present age and the authority of the age to come. While apocalyptic literature in general is congenial to such dualist perspectives, the Olivet discourse offers a different perspective: the authority of the Son of Man belongs to an entirely different category from that of the abomination to the extent that comparison between the two is meaningless. We may note a similar repudiation of dualism in early Christian literature such as Revelation 12:7–9, in which Satan is defeated not by God but by Michael. Because of the lopsidedness of the contest between God, the true power, and the apparent powers of the present age, God's spirit is present and active even at the heart of the oppression by the apparent powers (v. 11), and God is able to limit the calamities which the faithful must face (v. 20).

38. Perrin, *Jesus and the Language of the Kingdom*, 200.

39. Paul Ricoeur, "Freedom in the Light of Hope," in *Essays on Biblical Interpretation* (Philadelphia: Fortress Press, 1980), 170.

40. John Wall, "The Economy of the Gift: Paul Ricoeur's Significance for Theological Ethics," *Journal of Religious Ethics* 29.2 (2001): 239–40.

41. Ibid., 241–42.

42. Ricoeur, *Memory, History, Forgetting*, 175–76.

43. Marcus, *Mark 8–16*, 916–17.

44. Wall, "The Economy of the Gift," 255–56.

45. Russell, *Parousia*, 73–4.

46. Calvin, *Commentary*, 146.

47. LaCocqueand Ricoeur, *Thinking Biblically*, 266–69.

48. Cf. Dodd, *Parables of the Kingdom*, 51–2.

49. Frye, *Great Code*, 140, 145.

50. Allison, "Jesus and the Victory of Apocalyptic," 140–41; cf. Eddy, "The (W) Right Jesus," 59–60.

51. Marcus, *Mark 8–16*, 880; cf. Calvin, *Commentary*, 122–21.

52. Calvin, *Commentary*, 125.

53. Nickelson, "Meaning and Significance," 147.

54. Beasley-Murray, *Jesus and the Kingdom of God*, 342.

55. Lacocque, *Book of Daniel*, 125–26.

56. Such, *Abomination of Desolation*, 143–47.

57. Marcus reports that unlike most trees in the region, fig trees lose their leaves each year. The predictability of the growth of new leaves, and even the amount of time that passes from the emergence of the leaves to the ripening of the fruit (fifty days) lead him to assert that the fig tree is an appropriate symbol for the eschaton (Marcus, *Mark 8–16* 915; cf. Pesch, *Naherwartungen*, 177; Focant, Gospel According to Mark, 549). These features of the fig tree also make it suitable for descriptions of repetitive historical cycles. Beasley-Murray compares the fig tree parable with the three nature parables of Chapter 4, the only other extended discourse in Mark, which describe the

nature and development of the kingdom of God through Jesus' ministry. The parable of the sower (4:3–9; 13–20) describes the irresistible growth and ultimate triumph of the kingdom of God despite the inevitable opposition that it faces. The parable of the seed growing secretly (4:26–29) indicates that the process has been initiated and will conclude with a final judgment and "harvest," or ingathering of God's people. Similarly, the parable of the mustard seed (4:30–32) describes the kingdom of God as something that rises from an insignificant beginning and concludes with its triumph as the greatest of all shrubbery. All three parables of Chapter 4 describe the beginning and conclusion of the development of the kingdom of God, but they also indicate a gradual, silent, but inevitable process of growth or development between the two. Beasley-Murray argues that the fig tree parable of 13:28–29 operates in the same manner. The tender branch tips and leafing of the fig tree are the "signs" which the disciples request, and indicate the imminence of the parousia (Beasley-Murray, *Jesus and the Last Days*, 438–41).

58. Dobschütz, *The Eschatology of the Gospels*, 42–43.

59. A. Collins, "Apocalyptic Rhetoric," 19–20.

60. In Oden, *Mark*, 181–82.

61. Calvin, *Commentary*, 119–20.

62. Deppe, "Charting the Future," 90–5; Beasley-Murray, *Jesus and the Kingdom of God*, 389–90; Gundry, *Mark*, 747–48; Dupont in Beasley-Murray, *Jesus and the Last Days*, 216–19; Hahn, "Die Rede von der Parusie," 250-51; Lambrecht, *Die Redaktion*, 198, Marcus, *Mark 8-16*, 918.

Bibliography

Adams, Edward. "Historical Crisis and Cosmic Crisis in Mark 13 and Lucan's Civil War." *Tyndale Bulletin* 48.2 (1997): 329–44.

————. *The Stars Will Fall from Heaven: Cosmic Catastrophe in the New Testament and Its World*. London, New York: T&T Clark, 2007.

Allison, Dale C., Jr. *Constructing Jesus: Memory, Imagination, and History*. Grand Rapids : Baker Book House, 2013.

————. "Jesus and the Victory of Apocalyptic." *Jesus and the Restoration of Israel: A Critical Assessment of N. T. Wright's Jesus and the Victory of God*. Ed. Carey C Newman. Downers Grove IL: InterVarsity Press, 1999. 126–41.

————. *Jesus of Nazareth: Millenarian Prophet*. Minneapolis: Fortress, 1998.

————. *Resurrecting Jesus: The Earliest Christian Tradition and Its Interpreters*. Edinburgh: T & T Clark, 2005.

————. "A Response." *The Apocalyptic Jesus: A Debate*. Ed. Robert J. Miller. Santa Rosa, CA: Polebridge Press, 2001. 83–105.

Allison, Dale C., Jr., and W. D. Davies. *A Critical and Exegetical Commentary on the Gospel According to Saint Matthew. Vol. 3, Commentary on Matthew 19–28. International Critical Commentary*. Edinburgh: T & T Clark, 1997.

Amherdt, François-Xavier. *L'herméneutique Philosophique de Paul Ricoeur et Son Importance pour L'exégèse Biblique: en Débat avec la New Yale Theology School*. Paris: Cerf; Saint-Maurice: Saint-Augustin, 2004.

Aquinas, Thomas. *Gospel of Mark*. Trans. William Whiston. Catena Aurea. London: J.G.F. and J. Rivington, 1842.

Beasley-Murray, George Raymond. Jesus and the Last Days: The Interpretation of the Olivet Discourse. Peabody, Mass: Hendrickson, 1993.

————. Jesus and the Kingdom of God. Exeter, England & Grand Rapids: Eerdmans, 1986.

————. "The Vision on the Mount: The Eschatological Discourse of Mark 13." Ex Auditu 6 (1990): 39–52.

Black, C. Clifton. "An Oration at Olivet: Some Rhetorical Dimensions of Mark 13." *Persuasive Artistry: Studies in New Testament Rhetoric in Honor of George A. Kennedy*. Ed. Duane F. Watson. Sheffield, England: JSOT Press, 1991. 66–92.

Black, Max. "More About Metaphor." *Metaphor and Thought*. Ed. Andrew Ortony. Cambridge: Cambridge University Press, 1979. 19–43.

Blomberg, Craig. "The Wright Stuff: A Critical Overview of Jesus and the Victory of God." *Jesus and the Restoration of Israel: A Critical Assessment of N. T. Wright's Jesus and the Victory of God*. Ed. Carey C Newman. Downers Grove IL: InterVarsity Press, 1999. 19–39.

Bolt, Peter. "Mark 13: An Apocalyptic Precursor to the Passion Narrative." *Reformed Theological Review* 54 (1995): 10–32.

Bosco, Francesca M., Monica Bucciarelli, and Bruno G. Bara. "The Fundamental Context Categories in Understanding Communicative Intention." *Journal of Pragmatics* 36.3 (2004): 467–88.

Brabant, Christophe. "Ricoeur's Hermeneutical Ontology." *Paul Ricoeur: Poetics and Religion*. Eds J. Verheyden, T.L. Hettema, P. Vandecasteele. Leuven : Uitgeverij Peeters, 2011.

Brandenburger, Egon. *Markus 13 und die Apokalyptik*. Göttingen: Vandenhoeck & Ruprecht, 1984.

Brandom, Robert B. "Pretexts." *Tales of the Mighty Dead: Historical Essays in the Metaphysics of Intentionality*. Cambridge MA & London: Harvard University Press, 2002. 90–118.

Bruns, Gerald. "Against Poetry: Heidegger, Ricoeur, and the Originary Scene of Hermeneutics." *Meanings in Texts and Actions: Questioning Paul Ricoeur*. Eds. David E. Klemm and William Schweiker. Studies in Religion and Culture. Charlottesville, Va: Univ Press of Virginia, 1993. 26–46.

Bultmann, Rudolf. *Jesus Christ and Mythology*. New York: Scribner's, 1958.

———. "New Testament and Mythology." Trans. Schubert Miles Ogden. New Testament and Mythology and Other Writings. 1941. Ed. Schubert Miles Ogden. Philadelphia: Fortress, 1984. 1–43.

Busch, Austin. "Questioning and Conviction: Double-Voiced Discourse in Mark 3:22–30." *Journal of Biblical Literature* 125.3 (2006): 477–505.

Byrd, Joseph. "Paul Ricoeur's Hermeneutical Theory and Pentecostal Proclamation." *Pneuma* 15 (1993): 203–14.

Caird, G.B. *The Language and Imagery of the Bible*. London: Duckworth, 1980.

Calvin, John. *Commentary of a Harmony of the Evangelists, Matthew, Mark, and Luke*. Edinburgh: Calvin Translation Society, 1843. Trans. William Pringle. Vol. 3. 3 vols. Grand Rapids: Baker, 1989.

Chmielewski, Philip J. "Toward an Ethics of Production: Vico and Analogy, Ricoeur and Imagination." *Philosophy & Theology* 9.3–4 (1996): 389–418.

Chronis, Harry L. "To Reveal and to Conceal: A Literary-Critical Perspective on 'the Son of Man' in Mark." *New Testament Studies* 51.4 (2005): 459–81.

Chrystostom, John. "Homilies on the Gospel of St. Matthew." In *A Select Library of the Nicene and Post-Nicene Fathers of the Christian Church*. Ed. Philip Schaff. Edinburgh & Grand Rapids: T & T Clark & Eerdmans, 1998.

Collins, Adela Yarbro. "The Apocalyptic Rhetoric of Mark 13 in Historical Context." *Biblical Research* 41 (1996): 5–36.

———. "The Eschatological Discourse of Mark 13." *The Four Gospels 1992: Festschrift Frans Neirynck*. Eds. Frans van Segbroeck and Christopher M. Tuckett. Louvain: Peeters, 1992. 1125–40.

Collins, John J. *The Apocalyptic Imagination: An Introduction to Jewish Apocalyptic Literature*. 2nd ed. Grand Rapids: Eerdmans, 1998.

Cranfield, Charles E. B. *The Gospel According to Saint Mark: An Introduction and Commentary*. Ed. C. F. D. Moule. Cambridge: Cambridge University Press, 1959.

———. "St Mark 13." *Scottish Journal of Theology* 6 (1953): 189–96, 287–303.

———. "St Mark 13." *Scottish Journal of Theology* 7 (1954): 284–303.

Crossley, James G. *The Date of Mark's Gospel: Insight from the Law in Earliest Christianity*. London & New York: T & T Clark International, 2004.

Davidson, Donald. "Metaphor and Religion: The Test Case of Christian Texts." *On Metaphor*. Ed. Sheldon Sacks. Chicago: University of Chicago Press, 1979. 29–45.

Deppe, Dean B. "Charting the Future or a Perspective on the Present? The Paraenetic Purpose of Mark 13." *Calvin Theological Journal* 41.1 (2006): 89–101.

Dewar, Francis. "Chapter 13 and the Passion Narrative in St Mark." *Theology 64* (1961): 99–107.

Diaz, Marian Kay. "Creation, Prophecy and Fulfillment: A Ricoeurian Study of Revelation 22:1–5." *Master's Thesis, Catholic Theological Union*, 1996.

DiCenso, James J. *Hermeneutics and the Disclosure of Truth: A Study in the Work of Heidegger, Gadamer, and Ricoeur*. Charlottesville: University of Virginia, 1990.

Dickinson, Colby. "The Absent Notion of 'Canonicity' in Paul Ricoeur's Memory, History, Forgetting." *Paul Ricoeur: Poetics and Religion*. Eds J. Verheyden, T.L. Hettema, P. Vandecasteele. Leuven: Uitgeverij Peeters, 2011.

Dobschütz, Ernst von. *The Eschatology of the Gospels*. London: Hodder and Stoughton, 1910.

Dodd, C. H. *The Parables of the Kingdom*. New York: Scribner, 1961.

D'Souza, Keith. "Ricoeur's Narrative Development of Gadamer's Hermeneutics: Continuity and Discontinuity." PhD diss., Marquette University, 2003.

Dunn, James D. G. "Jesus and the Kingdom: How Would His Message Have Been Heard?" *Neotestamentica Et Philonica: Studies in Honor of Peder Borgen*. Eds. David A. Aune, Torrey Seland and Jarl Henning Ulrichsen. Leiden & Boston: Brill, 2003. 3–36.

Dušek, Jan. "Saying 'True' According to A.J. Greimas." *Philosophical Hermeneutics and Biblical Exegesis*. Eds. Petr Pokorný and Jan Roskovec. Wissenschaftliche Untersuchungen zum Neuen Testament. Tübingen: Mohr Siebeck, 2002. 94–100.

Eddy, Paul R. "The (W)Right Jesus: Eschatological Prophet, Israel's Messiah, Yahweh Embodied." *Jesus and the Restoration of Israel: A Critical Assessment of N. T. Wright's Jesus and the Victory of God*. Ed. Carey C Newman. Downers Grove IL: InterVarsity Press, 1999. 40–60.

Elkins, William Wesley. "Learning to Say Jesus: Narrative, Identity, and Community: A Study of the Hermeneutics of Josiah Royce, Hans Frei, George Lindbeck, Paul Ricoeur and the Gospel of Mark." Drew University, 1993.

Evans, Jeanne. *Paul Ricoeur's Hermeneutics of the Imagination*. American University Studies: Series VII, Theology and Religion. Vol. 143. New York: Peter Lang, 1995.

Fast, Lesley D. "Rhetorical Dimensions of Speech Representation: A Study of the Speeches of Jesus in the Gospel of Mark." McGill University (Canada), 2002.

Fish, Stanley Eugene. *Doing What Comes Naturally: Change, Rhetoric, and the Practice of Theory in Literary and Legal Studies.* Durham, NC: Duke University Press, 1989.

———. "Intention Is All There Is: A Critical Analysis of Aharon Barak's Purposive Interpretation in Law." *Cardozo Law Review* 29.3 (2007–2008): 1109–146.

———. *Is There a Text in This Class?: The Authority of Interpretive Communities.* Cambridge, MA: Harvard University Press, 1980.

Fletcher-Louis, Crispin H. T. "Jesus, the Temple and the Dissolution of Heaven and Earth." *Apocalyptic in History and Tradition.* Eds. Christopher Rowland and John M. T. Barton. London: Sheffield Academic Press, 2002. 117–41.

Focant, Camille. *The Gospel According to Mark: A Commentary.* Translated by Leslie Robert Keylock. Eugene, OR : Pickwick, 2012

Fodor, James. *Christian Hermeneutics: Paul Ricoeur and the Refiguring of Theology.* Oxford: Oxford University Press, 1995.

France, R. T. *The Gospel of Mark.* New York Doubleday, 1998.

Frei, Hans W. *The Identity of Jesus Christ: The Hermeneutical Bases of Dogmatic Theology.* Philadelphia: Fortress Press, 1975.

———. "The 'Literal Reading' of Biblical Narrative in the Christian Tradition: Does It Stretch or Will It Break?" *Bible and the Narrative Tradition.* Ed. Frank McConnell. New York: Oxford University Press, 1986. 36–77.

Frye, Northrop. *The Great Code: The Bible And Literature.* New York: Harcourt Brace Jovanovich, 1982.

Glasson, Thomas Francis. *The Second Advent: the Origin of the New Testament Doctrine.* London: The Epworth Press, 1963.

Gorospe, Athena Evelyn O. "The Ethical Possibilities of Exodus 4:18–26 in Light of Paul Ricoeur's Narrative Theory: A Filipino Reading." Th.D diss., Fuller Theological Seminary, 2006.

Grayston, K. "The Study of Mark 13." *Bulletin of the John Rylands Library* 56 (1974): 371–87.

Grech, Prosper. "Inner-Biblical Reinterpretation and Modern Hermeneutics." *Philosophical Hermeneutics and Biblical Exegesis.* Eds. Petr Pokorný and Jan Roskovec. Wissenschaftliche Untersuchungen zum Neuen Testament. Tübingen: Mohr Siebeck, 2002. 221–37.

Grice, H. Paul. "Meaning." *Studies in the Way of Words.* Cambridge, MA: Harvard University Press, 1989. 213–223.

Gundry, Robert H. *Mark: A Commentary on His Apology for the Cross.* Grand Rapids: Eerdmans, 1993.

Hahn, Ferdinand. "Die Rede von der Parusie des Menschensohnes Markus 13." *Jesus und der Menschensohn: für Anton Vögtle* Eds. Rudolf Pesch and Rudolf Schnackenburg. Freiburg: Herder, 1975. 240–66.

Hall, W. David. *Paul Ricoeur and the Poetic Imperative: The Creative Tension between Love and Justice.* Albany: SUNY, 2007.

Hartman, Lars. *Prophecy Interpreted: The Formation of Some Jewish Apocalyptic Texts and of the Eschatological Discourse Mark 13.* Trans. N Tomkinson. Coniectanea Biblica. Lund: Gleerup, 1966.

Heiden, Gerrit Jan van der. *The Truth (and Untruth) of Language: Heidegger, Ricoeur, and Derrida on Disclosure and Displacement.* Pittsburgh: Duquesne University Press, 2010.

Heil, John Paul. "The Narrative Strategy and Pragmatics of the Temple Theme in Mark." *Catholic Biblical Quarterly* 59 (1997): 76–100.

Hettema, Theo L. *Reading for Good: Narrative Theology and Ethics in the Joseph Story from the Perspective of Ricoeur's Hermeneutics.* Studies in Philosophical Theology. Kampen, Netherlands: Kok Pharos, 1996.

Hirsch, E. D. "Meaning and Significance Reinterpreted." *Critical Inquiry* 11 (1984): 202–25.

———. *Validity in Interpretation.* New Haven: Yale University Press, 1967.

Holland, Norman N. "Re-Covering 'the Purloined Letter': Reading as a Personal Transaction." *The Reader in the Text: Essays on Audience and Interpretation.* Ed. Susan R. Suleiman and Inge Crosman. Princeton: Princeton UP, 1980. 350–70.

Humphrey, Hugh M. *From Q to "Secret" Mark: A Composition History of the Earliest Narrative Theology.* London: T&T Clark, 2006.

Iersel, Bastiaan Martinus Franciscus van. "Failed Followers in Mark: Mark 13:12 as a Key for the Identification of the Intended Readers." *Catholic Biblical Quarterly* 58 (1996): 244–63.

———. "The Sun, Moon, and Stars of Mark 13, 24–25 in a Greco-Roman Reading." *Biblica* 77.1 (1996): 84–92.

Iser, Wolfgang. *The Act of Reading: A Theory of Aesthetic Response.* Baltimore: Johns Hopkins University Press, 1978.

Johnson, Luke Timothy. "A Historiographical Response to Wright's Jesus." *Jesus and the Restoration of Israel: A Critical Assessment of N. T. Wright's Jesus and the Victory of God.* Ed. Carey C Newman. Downers Grove IL: InterVarsity Press, 1999. 206–26.

Kelsey, David H. *The Uses Of Scripture In Recent Theology.* Philadelphia: Fortress, 1975.

Kenny, Peter. "Conviction, Critique and Christian Theology: Some Reflections on Reading Ricoeur." *Memory, Narrativity, Self and the Challenge to Think God: The Reception within Theology of the Recent Work of Paul Ricoeur.* Ed. Maureen Junker-Kenny and Peter Kenny. Münster: Lit Verlag, 2002. 92–116.

Kermode, Frank. *The Genesis of Secrecy: On the Interpretation of Narrative.* Cambridge, MA: Harvard University Press, 1979.

Klemm, David E. *The Hermeneutical Theory of Paul Ricoeur: A Constructive Analysis.* Lewisburg PA & London: Bucknell University Press & Associated University Presses, 1983.

———. "Philosophy and Kerygma: Ricoeur as Reader of the Bible." *Reading Ricoeur.* Ed. David M. Kaplan. Albany: SUNY, 2008. 47–69.

Kloppenborg, John S. "Evocatio Deorum and the Date of Mark." *Journal of Biblical Literature* 124.3 (2005): 419–50.

Knapp, Steven, and Walter Benn Michaels. "The Impossibility of Intentionless Meaning." *Intention and Interpretation.* Ed. Gary Iseminger. Arts and Their Philosophies. Philadelphia: Temple Univ Press, 1992. 51–64.

Kümmel, Werner Georg. *Promise and Fulfilment: The Eschatological Message of Jesus.* Trans. Dorothea M. Barton. Naperville, IL: A. R. Allenson, 1957.

Lacocque, André. "Apocalyptic Symbolism: A Ricoeurian Hermeneutical Approach." *Biblical Research* 26 (1981): 6–15.

———. *The Book of Daniel*. Trans. David Pellauer. Atlanta: John Knox, 1979.

———. *Daniel in His Time*. Studies on Personalities of the Old Testament. Columbia: Univ of South Carolina Press, 1988.

Lacocque, Andrè, and Paul Ricoeur. *Thinking Biblically: Exegetical and Hermeneutical Studies*. Trans. David Pellauer. Chicago & London: University of Chicago Press, 1998.

Lakoff, George, and Mark Johnson. *Metaphors We Live By*. Chicago: University of Chicago Press, 1980.

Lakoff, George, and Mark Turner. *More Than Cool Reason: A Field Guide to Poetic Metaphor*. Chicago: University of Chicago Press, 1989.

Lambrecht, Jan. *Die Redaktion der Markus-Apokalypse: Literarische Analyse und Strukturuntersuchung*. Analecta Biblica. Vol. 28. Rome: Pontifical Bible Institute, 1967.

Leavitt, Robert F. "Raymond Brown and Paul Ricoeur on the Surplus of Meaning." *Life in Abundance: Studies of John's Gospel in Tribute to Raymond E. Brown*. Eds. Raymond Edward Brown and John R. Donahue. Collegeville: Liturgical Press, 2005. 207–30.

Leeuwen, Theodoor Marius van. "Texts, Canon, and Revelation in Paul Ricoeur's Hermeneutics." *Canonization and Decanonization: Papers Presented to the International Conference of the Leiden Institute for the Study of Religions (Lisor), Held at Leiden 9–10 January 1997*. Eds. Arie van der Kooij, Karel van der Toorn and Joannes Augustinus Maria Snoek. Leiden: E J Brill, 1998. 399–409.

Leim, Joshua E. "In the Glory of His Father: Intertextuality and the Apocalyptic Son of Man in the Gospel of Mark." *Journal of Theological Interpretation* 7.2 (2013) 213–232.

Levinson, Stephen C. *Pragmatics*. Cambridge & New York: Cambridge University Press, 1983.

Madigan, Kevin. "Christus Nesciens? Was Christ Ignorant of the Day of Judgment? Arian and Orthodox Interpretation of Mark 13:32 in the Ancient Latin West." *Harvard Theological Review* 96.3 (2003): 255–78.

Malbon, Elizabeth Struthers. "Literary Contexts of Mark 13." *Biblical and Humane: A Festschrift for John F. Priest*. Eds. Linda Bennett Elder, David L. Barr and Elizabeth Struthers Malbon. Atlanta: Scholars Pr, 1996. 105–24.

Marcus, Joel. "The Jewish War and the Sitz Im Leben of Mark." *Journal of Biblical Literature* 111.3 (1992): 441–62.

———. *Mark 1–8 : A New Translation with Introduction and Commentary*. The Anchor Bible. Vol. 27. New York: Doubleday, 2000.

———. *Mark 8–16: A New Translation with Introduction and Commentary*. The Anchor Bible. Vol. 27A. New Haven and London: Yale University Press, 2009.

McCarthy, John. "Script to Scripture: Multivalent Textuality." *Annali di Storia dell'Esegesi* 30.2 (2013): 347–367.

McDowell, John Henry. "Wittgenstein on Following a Rule." *Mind, Value, and Reality*. Cambridge, MA: Harvard University Press, 1998. 223–62.

McLean, B. H. *Biblical Interpretation and Philosophical Hermeneutics.* Cambridge, New York: Cambridge University Press, 2012.

Miller, Robert J. "Introduction." *The Apocalyptic Jesus: A Debate.* Ed. Robert J. Miller. Santa Rosa, CA: Polebridge Press, 2001. 1–13.

Murphy, Frederick J. *Apocalypticism in the Bible and Its World: A Comprehensive Introduction.* Grand Rapids: Baker Academic, 2012.

Nickelson, Ronald Lee. "The Meaning and Significance of Astronomical Disturbances as Depicted in Mark 13:24–27 and Synoptic Parallels." Trinity Evangelical Divinity School, 1997.

Oden, Thomas C. and Christopher A. Hall, ed. *Mark. Ancient Christian Commentary on Scripture, New Testament.* Ed. Thomas C. Oden. Vol. 2. Chicago, London: Fitzroy Dearborn, 1998.

Pellauer, David. "Reading Ricoeur Reading Job." *Semeia.*19 (1981): 73–83.

Perpich, Sandra Wackman. "A Hermeneutic Critique of Structuralist Exegesis, with Specific Reference to Lk 10:29–37." Marquette University, 1981.

Perrin, Norman. *Jesus and the Language of the Kingdom: Symbol and Metaphor in New Testament Interpretation.* Philadelphia: Fortress Press, 1976.

Pesch, Rudolf. *Naherwartungen: Tradition und Redaktion in Mark 13.* Düsseldorf: Patmos-Verlag, 1968.

Prince, Gerald. "Notes on the Text as Reader." *The Reader in the Text: Essays on Audience and Interpretation.* Eds. Susan R. Suleiman and Inge Crosman. Princeton: Princeton UP, 1980. 225–40.

Reinsdorf, Walter. "How Is the Gospel True?" *Scottish Journal of Theology* 56.3 (2003): 328–44.

Reynolds, Bennie H. *Between Symbolism and Realism: The Use of Symbolic and Non-Symbolic Language in Ancient Jewish Apocalypses 333–63 B.C.E.* Göttingen: Vandenhoeck & Ruprecht, 2011.

Ricoeur, Paul. "Appropriation." Trans. John B. Thompson. *Hermeneutics and the Human Sciences: Essays on Language, Action, and Interpretation.* Ed. John B. Thompson. Cambridge & New York: Cambridge University Press, 1981. 182–193.

———. "The Bible and Imagination." Trans. David Pellauer. *Figuring the Sacred: Religion, Narrative, and Imagination.* Ed. Mark I. Wallace. Minneapolis: Augsburg Fortress, 1995. 144–166.

———. "Biblical Hermeneutics." *Semeia* 4 (1975): 29–145.

———. "Biblical Readings and Meditations." Trans. Kathleen Blamey. *Critique and Conviction: Conversations with François Azouvi and Marc De Launay, 1995.* Cambridge & New York: Polity Press & Columbia University Press, 1998. 139–170.

———. "The Canon between the Text and the Community." *Philosophical Hermeneutics and Biblical Exegesis.* Eds. Petr Pokorný and Jan Roskovec. Wissenschaftliche Untersuchungen zum Neuen Testament. Tübingen: Mohr Siebeck, 2002. 7–26.

———. "Creativity in Language: Word, Polysemy, Metaphor." The Philosophy of *Paul Ricoeur: An Anthology of His Work.* Eds. Charles E. Reagan and David Stewart. Boston: Beacon Press, 1978. 120–33.

———. "Experience and Language in Religious Discourse." Phenomenology and The "Theological Turn": The French Debate. Ed. Dominique Janicaud, Jean-François

Courtine, Jean-Louis Chrétien, Michel Henry, Jean-Luc Marion, and Paul Ricoeur. New York: Fordham University Press, 2000. 127–46.

———. "Explanation and Understanding: On Some Remarkable Connections between the Theory of Texts, Action Theory, and the Theory of History." Trans. Kathleen Blamey and John B. Thompson. *From Text to Action: Essays in Hermeneutics, II*. Evanston, IL: Northwestern University Press, 1991. 125–143.

———. "Foreword." Trans. David Pellauer. *The Book of Daniel*. Ed. Andre Lacocque. Atlanta: John Knox, 1979. xvii–xxvi.

———. "Freedom in the Light of Hope." *Essays on Biblical Interpretation*. Philadelphia: Fortress Press, 1980. 155–182.

———. *Freud and Philosophy: An Essay on Interpretation*. Trans. David Savage. New Haven: Yale University Press, 1970.

———. "The Hermeneutical Function of Distanciation." Trans. Kathleen Blamey and John B. Thompson. *From Text to Action: Essays in Hermeneutics, II*. Evanston, IL: Northwestern University Press, 1991. 75–88.

———. "The Hermeneutics of Testimony." *Essays on Biblical Interpretation*. Philadelphia: Fortress Press, 1980. 119–154.

———. *Interpretation Theory: Discourse and the Surplus of Meaning*. Fort Worth: Texas Christian University Press, 1976.

———. "The Language of Faith." *The Philosophy of Paul Ricoeur: An Anthology of His Work*. Eds. Charles E. Reagan and David Stewart. Boston: Beacon Press, 1978. 223–238.

———. "Manifestation and Proclamation." Trans. David Pellauer. *Figuring the Sacred: Religion, Narrative, and Imagination*. Ed. Mark I. Wallace. Minneapolis: Augsburg Fortress, 1995. 48–67.

———. *Memory, History, Forgetting*. Trans. Kathleen Blamey and David Pellauer. Chicago, IL: University of Chicago Press, 2004.

———. "Metaphor and the Main Problem of Hermeneutics." *The Philosophy of Paul Ricoeur: An Anthology of His Work*. Eds. Charles E. Reagan and David Stewart. Boston: Beacon Press, 1978. 134–48.

———. "The Metaphorical Process as Cognition, Imagination, and Feeling." *On Metaphor*. Ed. Sheldon Sacks. Chicago: University of Chicago Press, 1979. 141–57.

———. "The Model of the Text: Meaningful Action Considered as a Text." Trans. Kathleen Blamey and John B. Thompson. *From Text to Action: Essays in Hermeneutics, II*. Evanston, IL: Northwestern University Press, 1991. 144–167.

———. "Naming God." Trans. David Pellauer. *Figuring the Sacred: Religion, Narrative, and Imagination*. Ed. Mark I. Wallace. Minneapolis: Augsburg Fortress, 1995. 217–235.

———. "Philosophical Hermeneutics and Biblical Hermeneutics." Trans. Kathleen Blamey and John B. Thompson. *From Text to Action: Essays in Hermeneutics, II*. Evanston, IL: Northwestern University Press, 1991. 89–101.

———. "Philosophy and Religious Language." Trans. David Pellauer. *Figuring the Sacred: Religion, Narrative, and Imagination*. Ed. Mark I. Wallace. Minneapolis: Augsburg Fortress, 1995. 35–47.

———. *The Rule of Metaphor: Multi-Disciplinary Studies of the Creation of Meaning in Language*. Trans. Robert Czerny. Toronto: University of Toronto Press, 1977.

———. "The Self in the Mirror of the Scriptures." Trans. David Pellauer. *The Whole and Divided Self.* Eds. David E. Aune and John McCarthy. New York: Crossroad, 1997. 201–20.

———. *The Symbolism of Evil.* Trans. Emerson Buchanan. New York: Harper & Row, 1967.

———. "The Task of Hermeneutics." Trans. Kathleen Blamey and John B. Thompson. *From Text to Action: Essays in Hermeneutics, II.* Evanston, IL: Northwestern University Press, 1991. 53–74.

———. *Time and Narrative.* Trans. Kathleen McLaughlin. Vol. 1. 3 vols. Chicago: University of Chicago Press, 1984.

———. *Time and Narrative.* Trans. Kathleen McLaughlin. Vol. 3. 3 vols. Chicago: University of Chicago Press, 1988.

———. "Toward a Hermeneutic of the Idea of Revelation." *Essays on Biblical Interpretation.* Philadelphia: Fortress Press, 1980. 73–118.

———. "What Is a Text? Explanation and Understanding." Trans. Kathleen Blamey and John B. Thompson. *From Text to Action: Essays in Hermeneutics, II.* Evanston, IL: Northwestern University Press, 1991. 105–124.

Robinson, John A.T. *In the End, God.* London: Harper & Row, 1968.

———. *Jesus and His Coming: The Emergence of a Doctrine.* London: Abingdon Press, 1957.

Rogers, William E. "Ricoeur and the Privileging of Texts: Scripture and Literature." *Religion & Literature* 18.1 (1986): 1–25.

Rorty, Richard. "Is There a Problem About Fictional Discourse?" *Consequences of Pragamatism (Essays: 1972–1980).* Minneapolis: University of Minnesota Press, 1982. 110–138.

Roskam, Hendrika Nicoline. *The Purpose of the Gospel of Mark in Its Historical and Social Context.* Leiden: Brill, 2004.

Russell, James Stuart. *The Parousia: A Critical Inquiry into the New Testament Doctrine of Our Lord's Second Coming.* London: T. Fisher Unwin, 1878. Grand Rapids: Baker Book House, 1983.

Schweiker, William. *Mimetic Reflections: A Study in Hermeneutics, Theology, and Ethics.* New York: Fordham University Press, 1990.

Schweitzer, Albert. *The Quest of the Historical Jesus: A Critical Study of Its Progress from Reimarus to Wrede.* 1910. Trans. W. Montgomery. New York: Macmillan, 1968.

Searle, John R. *Intentionality: An Essay in the Philosophy of Mind.* Cambridge: Cambridge UP, 1983.

———. *Speech Acts: An Essay in the Philosophy of Language.* Cambridge: Cambridge UP, 1969.

Shepherd, Michael B. "Daniel 7:13 and the New Testament Son of Man." *Westminster Theological Journal* 68.1 (2006): 99–111.

Shively, Elizabeth E. *Apocalyptic Imagination in the Gospel Of Mark: The Literary and Theological Role of Mark 3:22–30.* Berlin, New York: De Gruyter, 2012.

Slater, Thomas B. "Apocalypticism and Eschatology: a Study of Mark 13:3–37." *Perspectives in Religious Studies,* 40.1 (2013): 7–18.

Smith, Harold. *Ante-Nicene Exegesis of the Gospels.* Translation of Christian Literature, Series V. London: Society for Promoting Christian Knowledge, 1928.

Stiver, Dan R. *Life Together in the Way of Jesus Christ: An Introduction to Christian Theology.* Waco: Baylor University Press, 2009.

———. *The Philosophy of Religious Language: Sign, Symbol, and Story.* Oxford, Cambridge MA: Blackwell, 1996.

———. *Ricoeur and Theology.* London, New York: Bloomsbury, 2012.

———. *Theology after Ricoeur: New Directions in Hermeneutical Theology.* Louisville: Westminster John Knox, 2001.

Such, William A. *The Abomination of Desolation in the Gospel of Mark: Its Historical Reference in Mark 13:14 and Its Impact in the Gospel.* Lanham, Md: University Press of America, 1999.

Sutcliffe, Peter A. *Is There an Author in This Text? Discovering the Otherness of the Text.* Eugene, Oregon: Wipf & Stock, 2014.

Taylor, George H. "Derrick Bell's Narratives as Parables." *New York University Review of Law and Social Change* 31 (2007): 225–271.

———. "Editor's Introduction." *Lectures on Ideology and Utopia.* Ed. George H. Taylor. New York: Columbia University Press, 1986. ix-xxxvi.

Theophilos, Michael P. *The Abomination of Desolation in Matthew 24.15.* London: Continuum, 2012.

Tracy, David. *The Analogical Imagination: Christian Theology and the Culture of Pluralism.* New York: Crossroad, 1981.

———. *Plurality and Ambiguity: Hermeneutics, Religion, Hope.* San Francisco: Harper & Row, 1987.

———. "Religious Classics and the Classics of Art." *Art, Creativity, and the Sacred: An Anthology in Religion and Art.* Ed. Diane Apostolos-Cappadona. New York: Crossroad, 1984. 236–249.

Townsend, Dabney. "Metaphor, Hermeneutics, and Situations." *The Philosophy of Paul Ricoeur.* Ed. Lewis E. Hahn. The Library of Living Philosophers. Chicago: Open Court Press, 1995. 191–209.

Vanhoozer, Kevin J. *Biblical Narrative in the Philosophy of Paul Ricoeur: A Study in Hermeneutics and Theology.* Cambridge: Cambridge University Press, 1990.

Verheyden, Jozef. "Describing the Parousia: The Cosmic Phenomena in Mk 13, 24–25." *The Scriptures in the Gospels.* Ed. Christopher M. Tuckett. Louvain: Peeters, 1997. 525–50.

Wall, John. "The Economy of the Gift: Paul Ricoeur's Significance for Theological Ethics." *Journal of Religious Ethics* 29.2 (2001): 235–60.

Wallace, Mark I. *The Second Naiveté: Barth, Ricoeur, and the New Yale Theology.* Macon, GA: Mercer University Press, 1990.

———. "Parsimony of Presence in Mark: Narratology, the Reader and Genre Analysis in Paul Ricoeur." *Studies in Religion/Sciences Religieuses: A Canadian Journal: Revue Canadienne* 18.2 (1989): 201–12.

Wenham, David. *The Rediscovery of Jesus' Eschatological Discourse.* Gospel Perspectives. Sheffield: JSOT Press, 1984.

White, C. Jason. "Is it Possible to Discover 'the One' Intended Meaning of the Biblical Authors?" *Scottish Journal of Theology* 67.2 (2014): 178–94.

White, Hayden V. *Metahistory: The Historical Imagination in Nineteenth-Century Europe.* Baltimore: Johns Hopkins University Press, 1973.

Wright, N.T. "In Grateful Dialogue: A Response." *Jesus and the Restoration of Israel: A Critical Assessment of N. T. Wright's Jesus and the Victory of God.* Ed. Carey C Newman. Downers Grove IL: InterVarsity Press, 1999. 244–277.

———. *Jesus and the Victory of God. Christian Origins and the Question of God.* Vol. 2. Minneapolis: Fortress Press, 1996.

———. *The New Testament and the People of God. Christian Origins and the Question of God.* Vol. 1. Minneapolis: Fortress Press, 1992.

Yilpet, Yoilah K. "Knowing the Biblical Author's Intention: The Problem of Distanciation." *Africa Journal of Evangelical Theology* 19.2 (2000): 165–85.

Zimmerman, Joyce Ann. *Liturgy as Language of Faith: A Liturgical Methodology in the Mode of Paul Ricoeur's Textual Hermeneutics.* Lanham, MD: University Press of America, 1988.

Index

About the Author

Peter C. de Vries received his B.A. at the Pennsylvania State University (history, with world literature minor) in 1985, his M.Div. at Princeton Theological Seminary (New Testament focus) in 1988, and his Ph.D. at the University of Pittsburgh (religious studies) in 2010. His doctoral studies addressed issues of hermeneutics, textual interpretation, and philosophy of language, with a focus upon New Testament apocalyptic texts. He has taught New Testament and philosophy of religion courses at Carlow University of Pittsburgh, the University of Pittsburgh, and Pittsburgh Theological Seminary. He teaches regularly as a visiting lecturer at Peki Seminary (Ghana). Dr. de Vries is a Presbyterian minister and has served as a church pastor since 1988. His previous academic publications include "Five Moments of Communication in Hegel's Phenomenology of Spirit," in *Similarity and Difference in Translation: Proceedings of the International Conference on Similarity and Translation*, ed. Stefano Arduini and Robert Hodgson (Rimini, Italy: Guaraldi, 2004; New York: American Bible Society, 2007).

CPSIA information can be obtained
at www.ICGtesting.com
Printed in the USA
BVOW04*0356251116

468843BV00002B/5/P